B L A C

LA\

QUESTIONS
& ANSWERS

LAND LAW

Questions and Answer Series

Series Editors   Margaret Wilkie and Rosalind Malcolm

Titles in the Series

Other titles in preparation

LAND
LAW

SECOND EDITION

MARGARET WILKIE
Solicitor
Visiting Lecturer in Law, University of Surrey

ROSALIND MALCOLM
Barrister
Senior Lecturer in Law, University of Surrey

PETER LUXTON
Solicitor
Senior Lecturer in Law, University of Sheffield

BLACKSTONE
PRESS LIMITED

First published in Great Britain 1995 by Blackstone Press Limited, Aldine Place, London W12 8AA. Telephone: 0181 740 2277

© M. Wilkie, R. N. Malcolm, P. Luxton, 1995

First edition 1995
Second edition 1998

ISBN: 1 85431 808 X

British Library Cataloguing in Publication Data
A CIP catalogue record for this book is available from the British Library

Typeset by Montage Studios Limited, Tonbridge, Kent
Printed by Bell & Bain Limited, Glasgow

Contents

Preface

Examination technique is an important skill for the law student to learn. After months of hard work studying the law, to be let down in the examination, not by lack of knowledge or understanding of the law, but by technique in answering the questions set, is indeed a sad thing. It is not, however, at all uncommon. As tutors and examiners, we have seen many students fail to achieve their potential in examinations because they have not mastered the method of answering questions.

Law students necessarily spend much of their time reading cases in the reports, articles in law journals, and text books; but the style in which these are written is rarely the same style that is needed for an answer to an examination question. Much valuable guidance on examination technique, of course, will be given to the student in the form of tutorial discussion, and comments on essays written during the course. In our experience, however, only a minority of law teachers meet the issue head-on by providing students with suggested answers designed to show the student how a question might be tackled.

In our view, one of the best ways of learning is by example, and it is examples that this book provides. It is to be treated as a learning tool or aid. The answers are 'suggested' rather than 'model', to indicate that they are not the only way in which a question can be answered. Together, they are designed to help the student see how questions in general, rather than any particular question, can be tackled. We would advise readers that the rote learning of model answers will prove quite unprofitable.

The student can use the book in several ways. First, as another means of learning the law itself, through seeing the law applied to specific questions or problems. The relevant chapter could be studied in tutorial preparation. Many of the commentaries provide additional comments to help with this. Secondly, through the study of the answers to the questions, the student can learn how answers (whether to an examination question or a piece of assessed work) should be structured. In this regard, it can be useful for one student, or for a small group, to look at a question on an area studied, and then attempt an outline structure of an answer before comparing it with that suggested in this book. Thirdly, the book can be used to help the student prepare for the examination itself; there are suggestions on a variety of matters, including e.g., time management and the use of diagrams.

Finally, we thank everyone at Blackstone Press Ltd for their excellent work on the publishing side, and for the speed with which they have been able to produce the finished volume which you are now holding. We hope you enjoy reading it as much as we enjoyed writing it.

The law is stated as on New Year's Day, 1998.

Margaret Wilkie
Rosalind Malcolm
Peter Luxton

Table of Cases

Table of Statutes

1 Introduction

One of the difficulties that all three authors of this book have encountered is that students new to the study of land law often approach it with trepidation. Horror tales about its complexity abound and are frequently promoted by former students. Yet the subject must be covered at least by those undertaking a qualifying law degree and by all those who must pass the 'core subjects' for professional purposes. Land law is also the gateway to other subjects such as conveyancing and the law of landlord and tenant. Students on professional property courses such as surveying and estate management will find that land law is unavoidable. These are perhaps not the best reasons for embarking on the study of any subject and there are better reasons than these for tackling land law.

These reasons lie in the very nature of the subject itself. Although it is undoubtedly the case that land law is complex, it is a subject which is stimulating and challenging. Sometimes it is like following a detective story with different clues emerging until a composite picture of 'whodunit' eventually emerges. This analogy is important, for just as it is critical not to miss one episode in the detective story, so is it important not to miss one chapter in the study of land law. Land law does not consist of a number of discrete subjects. The subjects interlock and the earliest topics form the basis of an understanding of the whole area of land law. For example, initial lectures usually deal with such concepts as the distinction between real and personal property, proprietary and personal rights, legal and equitable interests. An understanding of these concepts is essential for an understanding of the transfer of title, the differences between registered and unregistered land and incumbrances.

This imperative of having to deal at the outset with concepts which seem to have no footing in 'the real world' causes many of the difficulties in the study of land law. Many students can get lost in the wilderness in their first few weeks and, once lost, it is very hard to find the way again. The moral is to get in there at the outset and stay there until the end! Here also lies the way to a true appreciation of the joys of the subject. If you can give yourself up to study at the beginning of a purely intellectual subject, then you will acquire a familiarity with the concepts which will make further study a pleasure. The concepts are like building blocks which form the foundation and like all foundations they must be carefully laid.

Answering examination questions requires the same rigorous approach. A question which is exclusively on easements may depend on an understanding of the distinction between legal and equitable easements, the equitable doctrine of notice, the difference between a registered and an unregistered title — all topics which will have been dealt with in the first part of the course. Of course, such information will not have to be spelt out in every question. In fact, it is unlikely that you will ever come across an exam question which requires you simply to state the difference between a legal and an equitable interest. The question will assume this knowledge and will require you to apply it in specified circumstances. When you have laid all the building blocks to make the wall you are not expected to dismantle it to explain its construction. At the end of the course you will be expected to be able to handle the concepts with ease. Herein lies the fascination of the subject. Once you have grasped the essentials, then it suddenly comes down to earth and is applicable in all the circumstances of daily life. We all have to live somewhere so we buy a freehold property or rent a flat. We may acquire rights over someone else's land in the process. We may give someone else rights over our land (very often a mortgagee!). We might buy property jointly with a spouse, partner or friend. Relationships sometimes break up and the property rights need to be disentangled. Families may come to blows over ownership of property. All these situations which make up our social activities require a knowledge and application of land law. It is an essential element of the organisation of our lives. Very often, exam questions will read like problems out of a soap opera and then you can perceive how that early understanding of airy concepts has a firm practical application.

Success in the examination requires a disciplined approach and attention to exactitude. Land law is the last subject in which vagueness will do. Answers must be clear and organised like a military encounter. Precision in language is essential. As with all subjects, a thorough knowledge of the cases is vital. In addition, you must be conversant with the Law of Property Act 1925 and its attendant legislation. Look at the original statutory material from day one. With a little perseverance, it is often easier to understand the meaning of a section directly than to understand someone else's explanation. At least, look at the section as well as reading the text book. It is particularly important to know your way around your statute book if you are allowed to take it into the exam. Find this out at the outset. Do not leave it until the examination itself to look at the original statutes. In the exam you should know exactly where to look up a particular section rather than waste time hunting for it. Familiarity with the statute book will also give you confidence (like taking a comfort blanket with you).

Land law does require commitment but if you give it that you will be repaid with success in your exam performance.

2 Definition of Land

INTRODUCTION

One of the earlier parts of most land law courses deals with the definition of land. Immediately, the unsuspecting student is confronted with the mysteries of law in the form of unfamiliar and seldom used words. Land does not simply mean something physical. The word 'hereditament', to which the student will be introduced, implies the nature of the right involved in the ownership of land. It is a clue as to what the study of land law is all about — not the land (the soil, the grass, the trees, the buildings), but the rights that people may have in land. Thus, land is to be reclassified as including corporeal and incorporeal hereditaments. Ownership of land may equally include ownership of a house and ownership of a right of way over someone else's house.

This classification has given rise to some jurisprudential debate as to the nature of corporeal and incorporeal rights and some courses may address this topic from that perspective (see, for example, Austin, *Jurisprudence*, 5th edn, London: Murray, 1885, vol. 1, p. 362). Other courses may, however, concentrate on the distinction between fixtures and fittings since this develops and applies the distinction between real and personal property which will have formed a part of an early lecture. The difficulty with the distinction between fixtures and fittings is that it rests on a factual basis and, although basic principles have been established and can be applied, there are numerous cases which have been decided on their own individual facts. Thus, in one case, seats can be a fixture, in another, a fitting.

There are also some Latin maxims on the loose here. *Cuius est solum eius est usque ad coelum et ad inferos* (the owner of the land owns everything up to the sky and down to the centre of the earth) and *quicquid plantatur solo, solo cedit* (whatever is attached to the land becomes part of the land) are regulars. Some discussion of these maxims and their application to practical problems may be anticipated. A good starting point is the Law of Property Act 1925, s. 205(1)(ix) which gives the statutory definition of land.

Apart from the Treasure Act 1996, there is nothing very novel in this topic. The cases are not on the move, so, from that point of view, the topic is a safe one to prepare. In addition, it does bring down to earth some of the airy concepts which usually (and inevitably) dog the beginning of most courses on land law.

QUESTION 1

Cuius est solum, eius est usque ad coelum et ad inferos (the owner of the land owns everything up to the sky and down to the centre of the earth).

Discuss.

Commentary

This question is either a dream or a nightmare. There is a vast amount of material to be covered and it is unlikely that you can deal with it all. You may be guided by what you have covered in lectures. Treasure trove, for example, has been topical (with the growth in the use of metal detectors) and this ancient law has been the subject of recent reform.

The usual advice not to regurgitate all you know holds good. Discuss the maxim critically: what are its limitations? Don't just dismiss it — consider to what extent it holds true.

Suggested Answer

This maxim, which was coined by Accursius in the thirteenth century, relates to the extent of the ownership enjoyed by the fee simple owner. There are, in fact, a number of limitations on the ownership of the fee simple owner. Some are statutory, others are founded in the common law.

The first aspect to be considered is the extent of the fee simple owner's rights in the airspace above the property. The owner's rights extend to such a height as is reasonably necessary for the ordinary use and enjoyment of the land. In *Baron Bernstein of Leigh* v *Skyviews and General Ltd* [1978] QB 479, Griffith J stated that it was necessary to balance the rights of an owner to enjoy the land against the rights of the general public to take advantage of all that 'science now offers in the use of airspace'. Thus, the rights of the owner were limited to such a height as is necessary for the ordinary use and enjoyment of the land and above that height the fee simple owner has no greater rights than any other member of the public.

Where there is an interference with the legitimate rights of the fee simple owner then these rights may be maintained by an action for nuisance or trespass. In *Kelsen* v *Imperial Tobacco Co. (of Great Britain and Ireland) Ltd* [1957] 2 QB 334, the action of the defendant in allowing an advertisement to overhang the plaintiff's premises amounted to a trespass as was the action of the defendant in *Woollerton and Wilson Ltd* v *Richard Costain Ltd* [1970] 1 WLR 411, in allowing the jib of a crane to swing over the plaintiff's property.

Under the Civil Aviation Act 1982, it is a defence for aircraft to fly at such a height which is reasonable under the circumstances.

The rights of the fee simple owner in water on the land are, in part, derived from statute. The right to abstract water is controlled by the Water Resources Act 1991 and depends on the grant of a licence from the Environment Agency.

Where water flows in a defined channel across the land, then there is a distinction between water which is tidal and that which is non-tidal. The water itself is not capable of ownership, but there are rights in the bed and the right to take the fish to be considered. Where the water is tidal, the bed belongs to the Crown and the public have a right of navigation and a right to fish up to the point where the water ceases to be subject to the ebb and flow of tides. In many rivers this point is determined by the presence of a lock-gate. Where the water is non-tidal, then the bed belongs to the riparian owner. If the water forms the boundary between two plots of land, then subject to any contrary agreement or evidence, the riparian owners own up to the midway point in the river. They are also entitled to take the fish, a valuable property right on many country estates.

Water percolating underneath the land and not contained in a defined channel, is not capable of ownership until such moment as it is appropriated, when it becomes the property of the person appropriating it (*Ballard* v *Tomlinson* (1885) 29 ChD 115).

Where water, such as lakes and ponds, lies on the land, it is the property of the landowner.

If the land verges on the seashore, then the fee simple owner owns that part of the land down to a point reached by an ordinary high tide.

The maxim also states that the landowner owns everything down to the centre of the earth. While it is true that at common law all minerals are owned by the landowner, ownership is in fact vested by various statutes in the Crown or other public bodies.

The fee simple owner is, *prima facie*, entitled to all chattels found on the land, in the absence of a legitimate claim from the owner of the chattel. Treasure is an exception to this. Under the Treasure Act 1996, treasure vests, subject to prior interests and rights, in the Crown. Treasure is defined by the Act to include any object at least 300 years old when found which:

(a)   is not a coin but has metallic content of which at least 10 per cent by weight is precious metal;

(b)   when found, is one of at least two coins in the same find which are at least 300 years old with the same percentage of previous metal as above; or

(c)   when found, is one of at least ten coins in the same find which are at least 300 years old.

In addition, further classes of objects at least 200 years old and of outstanding historical, archaeological or cultural importance are to be designated by the Secretary of State. Items which would have been treasure trove if found before the commencement of the Act, are also within the definition.

Wild animals are not subject to ownership but may be hunted by the fee simple owner on whose land they run. There are, however, a number of limitations to this right in respect of protected species (Wildlife and Countryside Act 1981 (as amended) and the Protection of Badgers Act 1992, for example).

Land is defined in the Law of Property Act 1925, s. 205(1)(ix) as including 'the surface, buildings or parts of buildings' and whatever is attached to the land becomes part of the land under another Latin maxim, *quicquid plantatur solo, solo cedit*. This raises, in practice, an important problem relating to ownership of those items which, but for the fact that they are attached to the land, would constitute chattels. The distinction needs to be drawn between those items which are fixtures, and therefore part of the realty, and those which are not, and therefore remain personalty.

There are two tests for determining whether an object is a fixture or a chattel. The first test relates to the degree of annexation. If the object is annexed to the land then it is, *prima facie*, a fixture. So, in *Holland* v *Hodgson* [1872] LR 7 CP 328, spinning looms bolted to the floor of a factory were attached other than by their own weight and were fixtures. In *Hulme* v *Brigham* [1943] KB 152, however, heavy printing presses which stood on the floor without any attachment other than the force of gravity, were chattels.

The paramount test, however, was foreshadowed by Blackburn J in *Holland* v *Hodgson* and relates to the purpose of annexation. Under this test, the question to be asked is whether the chattel has been affixed to the land for the better enjoyment of the object as a chattel, or for the more convenient use of the land. This leads to the result that the same object may constitute a fixture in one case, but a chattel in another. For example, in *Leigh* v *Taylor* [1902] AC 157, tapestries nailed to a wall were held not to be fixtures, but in *Re Whaley* [1908] 1 Ch 615, similar objects were held to be fixtures because the object of their annexation was to enhance the room. Lord Halsbury LC in *Leigh* v *Taylor* confirmed that the key test was the purpose of annexation, and this was confirmed in *Hamp* v *Bygrave* (1982) 266 EG 720 where garden ornaments that formed part of a landscape display were held to be fixtures despite the fact they rested on the ground simply by their own weight.

In *Elitestone Ltd* v *Morris* [1997] 1 WLR 687, the House of Lords held that what is of primary importance is the intention involved. It was indicated that this is an objective test to determine whether the object was intended for the use or enjoyment of the land, or for the more convenient use of the object itself. Clearly, the courts are prepared to apply a common-sense approach to this issue (*TSB* v *Botham* [1995] EGCS 3).

There are some exceptional cases where there is a right to remove fixtures. A tenant may remove trade fixtures that have been attached to the land for the purpose of carrying out the trade; ornamental and domestic fixtures provided their removal will cause no substantial damage to the property; agricultural fixtures in accordance with the procedure set out in the Agricultural Holdings Act 1986.

There are also a number of limitations on the right of the fee simple owner to enjoy the land in the form of the Town and Country Planning Act 1991 and related legislation, which controls developments on land, and the Housing Acts and Rent Acts, which control the standard for houses for human habitation and the security of tenure of tenants for years.

QUESTION 2

Abel has entered into a contract to sell his house to Baal. He consults you as to whether the following items (which were not mentioned in the contract of sale) are to be included in the sale:

(a) a replica of the 'Three Graces' which is standing in the garden;

(b) a stained glass lampshade, attached to the ceiling by a chain, which was given to him by friends when he got married;

(c) the fitted kitchen which Abel installed himself (he wants to dismantle it and adapt it for his new house);

(d) adjustable bookshelves which slot into strips of metal screwed into the wall; and

(e) an ornamental fireplace which is on hire-purchase from Quickfire Ltd.

Commentary

Unusual in a land law examination, this question concentrates on one aspect of a subject — that of the distinction between fixtures and chattels. There is an abundance of well-known case law in this area and the principles are well established. The judgment of Scarman LJ in *Berkley* v *Poulet* (1976) 242 EG 39 lays out the principles clearly and concisely, and the area was considered by the House of Lords in *Elitestone Ltd* v *Morris* [1997] 1 WLR 687. For the effect of hire-purchase agreements see Guest and Lever (1963) *Conv* (NS) 30; McCormack [1990] *Conv* 275.

Land and chattels are treated differently at law; land is real property and chattels are personal property. A contract to sell real estate will not include items of personal property unless they are expressly included. Sometimes an item that was once a chattel may become part of the land and there are, on occasions, difficulties in naming the distinction between fixtures (which form part of the land) and chattels (which remain items of personal property). Under the Law of Property Act 1925, s. 62, fixtures are included in a conveyance of land. This question deals with this fundamental distinction.

Suggested Answer

(a) There are two tests to determine whether an item has become part of the freehold:

(i)   the method and degree of annexation;

(ii) the object and purpose of the annexation.

The earlier law emphasised the first test, while later cases introduced the second test to alleviate the injustice where limited owners had affixed items of value to the land. The second test is now dominant, so if the item is physically annexed to the land this does not necessarily resolve the matter any more. Nevertheless the degree of annexation remains a relevant question. According to Scarman LJ in *Berkley* v *Poulet* (1976) 242 EG 39, if there is such a degree of physical annexation that an object cannot be removed without serious damage to, or some destruction of, the realty, then there is a strong case for the item to be classified as a fixture.

Thus, the determination of the question whether the 'Three Graces' is a fixture will depend on an application of the two tests. It is not clear whether the statue is physically fixed to the land, although it would seem from the question that it is merely 'standing' on the land. If that is the case, then, *prima facie*, the statue is not a fixture. In the case of *Berkley* v *Poulet* itself, a white marble statue of a Greek athlete weighing half a ton and standing on a plinth, was considered not to be a fixture. Similarly, a printing machine secured by its own weight and weighing several tons was held not to be a fixture (*Hulme* v *Brigham* [1943] KB 152). However, the general rule can be displaced where the object of annexation can be shown to be that it was intended that the item should become part of the land. Thus, a drystone wall which was constructed of blocks of stone placed one on top of another was held to have been intended to become part of the realty (*Holland* v *Hodgson* (1872) LR 7 CP 328). Intention refers to the purpose which the object serves, not to the purpose of the person who put the object in place: *Elitestone Ltd* v *Morris* [1997] 1 WLR 687 (HL).

The fact that the 'Three Graces' is an ornamental object may not be a conclusive indication that it is not intended to become part of the land. In *Lord Chesterfield's Settled Estates* [1911] 1 Ch 237, Grinling Gibbons carvings were held to be fixtures; and in *Re Whaley* [1908] 1 Ch 615, chattels, which were placed in the room in order to create a beautiful room as a whole, were held to be capable of being fixtures. In *D'Eyncourt* v *Gregory* (1866) LR 3 Eq 382, statues which were part of the architectural design of a property were held to be fixtures.

However, in this problem, regardless of the question whether the 'Three Graces' are in fact physically affixed to the ground, it would seem probable that the statue remains a chattel unless, as in *Hamp* v *Bygrave* (1982) 266 EG 720, it can be objectively viewed as a feature of, and part and parcel of, the garden, or, as in *D'Eyncourt* v *Gregory*, as a part of the architectural design of the house.

(b) The stained glass lampshade would not seem to pose the same difficulties. It is an object that is essentially a chattel and it is unlikely that any evidence could be adduced to change its character into a fixture. If the first test were to be applied alone, then there is a degree of physical annexation which might suggest that the lampshade was a fixture. This test is no longer decisive. In *Leigh* v *Taylor* [1902] AC 157, tapestries were fixed to the wall. The House of Lords held that the purpose of their annexation to the realty was for their better enjoyment as tapestries. Annexation on its own was not enough to make them fixtures. This decision was followed in the case of *Spyer* v *Phillipson* [1931] 2 Ch 183, where oak and pine panelling and a chimney-piece had been erected, and, in *Berkley* v *Poulet* (1976) 242 EG 39, in relation to pictures which were hung in recesses in a panelled room. Thus, it is likely that the lampshade will be a chattel.

(c) The fitted kitchen poses a different problem. In the first place it is clearly annexed so it raises the general rule that it constitutes a fixture. Secondly, it would seem to be unarguable that the object of its annexation was for any other purpose than to create a room which could be used as a kitchen. While the fitted furniture may have been aesthetically pleasing, its primary purpose was for use as a kitchen. In *Re Whaley* [1908] 1 Ch 615 the design of a beautiful room, 'an Elizabethan Room', by the installation of chattels of beauty, meant that those chattels became part of the room — they were fixtures. The unity of design of the room meant that the objects were part of the realty. The result in *Lord Chesterfield's Settled Estates* (above) was similar. This view is supported by the decision in *TSB Ltd* v *Botham* [1995] EGCS 3.

(d) Similar arguments might prevail in respect of the bookshelves. They are annexed although they could be easily removed with little damage. The object of their annexation is to make the room useful as a library (*Re Whaley*). In fact, there would seem to be no question as to their intrinsic merit as chattels. The bookshelves have been installed for the more convenient use of the property, not for their use as chattels. In *Vaudeville Electric Cinema Ltd* v *Muriset* [1923] 2 Ch 74, seats secured to the floor of a cinema hall were fixtures. Normally, free-standing seats would be considered chattels. Here, however, they were affixed to make the room more convenient as a cinema and were held to be fixtures. On these grounds, therefore, it is arguable that the shelves become fixtures.

(e) Here the fireplace is annexed to the room. It is described as ornamental and might, therefore, fall into the category of the tapestries in *Leigh* v *Taylor* which, although affixed, were deemed to be chattels because the object of their annexation was for their better enjoyment as such.

However, there is a further complication in that the fireplace is being purchased as part of a hire-purchase scheme. If the fireplace has been annexed to the land of the hirer, then it becomes annexed to the realty and the original owner (Quickfire Ltd) loses its title. It will be necessary to consider the contract of hire-purchase to see whether Quickfire Ltd has reserved to itself the right to remove the fireplace in the event of default in the payment of the hire-purchase instalments. If there is such a right of removal, then this confers on Quickfire Ltd an equitable interest in the land which is a right of entry (*Re Morrison, Jones & Taylor* [1914] 1 Ch 50).

Whether this right of entry is binding on Baal will depend on whether the land is registered or unregistered. If unregistered, then the equitable doctrine of notice prevails and Baal will be bound unless he is a *bona fide* purchaser of a legal estate for value without notice (*Poster* v *Slough Estates Ltd* [1969] 1 Ch 495). If the land is registered, then strangely enough, the right of entry will not bind a purchaser since it is not an overriding interest and may not be registrable as a minor interest.

3 Finders' Titles

INTRODUCTION

The law of finders' titles is often dealt with near the beginning of property law courses. One of the main advantages of studying this topic is that it illustrates the basic nature of property rights. Although the principles contained in the finders' titles cases are modified in land law (e.g., by the law of adverse possession), a study of finders' titles brings home to a student, perhaps more than any other topic, the realisation that titles are not absolute things but may vary in quality. The cases, indeed, reveal four significant points.

First, that ultimately all titles depend upon possession. For this reason, the finder of a chattel on someone else's land may acquire a title to the chattel if he takes it into his possession.

Secondly, that title is itself a relative concept: the finder of a chattel acquires a title weaker than that of its true owner, but (depending on the circumstances), perhaps stronger than that of anyone else.

Thirdly, that the relative strength of property rights depends largely upon the time at which they are acquired — titles acquired earlier in time generally have priority over those acquired later. Thus, if the owner of the land is found to have a better title to the object found than the person who discovered it, this will be on the basis that the owner of the land had a prior title to it — even though the landowner did not previously know that the object was there. This third principle is qualified by the word 'generally', because it appears that a trespasser or a dishonest finder will have their priority postponed: *Hibbert* v *McKiernan* [1948] 2 KB 142 (the case of the lost golf balls).

Fourthly, that the plaintiff wins merely by showing that he has a title better than that of the defendant. Thus the defendant cannot plead that someone else has a better right to the chattel than the plaintiff. The chimney sweep's boy in *Armory* v *Delamirie* (1722) 5 Stra. 505 succeeded in his claim against the jeweller; but he could not have resisted a claim brought by the true owner, and the case did not decide whether the boy could have resisted a claim brought by his master, or by the owner of the house in which the jewel was found. (A puzzle about the case is how a poor chimney-sweep's boy managed to finance an action in the courts at all — but that does not concern us here!)

A question on finders' titles will, therefore, inevitably be a test of the student's understanding of these fundamental principles. These are not, however, difficult to grasp, and the case law is itself interesting, involving matters as diverse as the finding of prehistoric boats, Roman coins, and bracelets in airport lounges.

QUESTION 1

Lord Blandish, the freehold owner of Brandy Towers, decided two years ago to open his home and its grounds to the public. In order to make the premises ready, he hired the firm of Dogget & Co. to construct a Visitors' Centre. One morning, Noggs, an employee of the firm, had just entered the main driveway of Brandy Towers while on his way to work, when he found a bag containing £500 in notes lying next to the driveway. All attempts to trace the owner of the bag and contents failed.

Shortly after this, Brandy Towers threw its gates open to the public. Victor, a member of the public, while visiting the grounds with his dog, Columbus, found Columbus digging in one of the flower beds. When Victor went to investigate, he found that Columbus had unearthed a bronze bracelet. Victor handed the bracelet to the receptionist at the Brandy Hall Visitors' Centre; but, despite the efforts of the staff, the owner of the bracelet (which was discovered to have been made in 1932) could not be found.

Lord Blandish had purchased Brandy Towers from Viscount Willow in 1980, who had himself purchased it in 1930. Expert evidence suggests that the bracelet had lain in the ground for at least 30 years.

Consider the relative strengths of the claims that may be made to the bag of notes and to the bracelet.

Commentary

The student should note carefully what is asked: to consider the relative strengths of the claims to the bag of notes and to the bracelet. This means that the student needs to identify who may have a claim to these items, and then to discuss the strengths of the claims relative to each other. It is not meaningful to attempt to state definitely who will be entitled to the items found, since this will depend upon who puts in a claim.

As in every problem question, the student should apply the law to the facts from the outset. The suggested answer, it will be seen, begins merely by setting out the basic principle in one short sentence, and then immediately seeks to apply such principle to the given facts. There then follows a discussion of the relative position of possible claimants to the bag: Lord Blandish, Noggs and Dogget & Co. Lord Blandish's claim is discussed first: this is logical, because his claim depends upon his having a title to the bag and its contents before they were found, in which case his title, being prior in time, would be better than those of the other potential claimants (with the exception, of course, of the true owner).

Suggested Answer

Possible claimants to the bag of notes are Noggs, as the finder; Dogget & Co., as his employer; and Lord Blandish, as the owner of land upon which it was found.

In English law, the person who can establish a prior possession has a better claim than another whose possession is later in time: *Armory* v *Delamirie* (1722) 5 Stra. 505. In this problem, the issue is whether Lord Blandish, the owner of the land on which the bag was found, can be considered to have possession of it before it was found. If he can, he has a right to it better than everyone other than the true owner. It is possible for Lord Blandish to have possession of a chattel lying upon his land, even without his knowing it is there, but only if he can show that he manifested an intention to exercise control over the land and the things upon it, i.e., an *animus possidendi*. This may be difficult to establish if the land upon which the chattel is found is open to the public. Thus in *Bridges* v *Hawkesworth* (1851) 21 LJQB 75 a travelling salesman who found a bag of money lying on the customer side of a shop was held to have a better title to it than the owner of the shop. More recently, in *Parker* v *British Airways Board* [1982] 1 QB 1004, the Court of Appeal held that an air passenger who found a gold bracelet in the international executive lounge of an airport had a better claim to it than the occupiers, the British Airways Board, because it was found that the Board did not have a policy of searching for lost articles.

If the bag had been found inside Brandy Towers itself, the requisite intention to possess would have been readily inferred: see Donaldson LJ in *Parker* v *British Airways Board* at p. 1020. Such intention might, however, be more difficult to establish in respect of the grounds. On the other hand, at the time the bag was found, the grounds were not open to the public. The answer will depend, therefore, upon an analysis of all the facts, including evidence as to the range of persons who commonly used the driveway, the frequency of its use, and whether it was barred by a gate.

If Lord Blandish is found not to have been in possession of the bag of money when it was found, it is necessary to consider the relative rights of Noggs and Dogget & Co. Where an item is found by an employee in the course of his employment, it appears that his employer has a better right to it than the employee: see *dicta* in *City of London Corporation* v *Appleyard* [1963] 2 All ER 834 at p. 839; and *South Water Co.* v *Sharman* [1896] 2 QB 44, as explained by D.R. Harris, 'Concept of Possession in English Law', in *Oxford Essays in Jurisprudence* (A.G. Guest, ed.), 1961. In the problem, however, it is uncertain whether Noggs found the bag in the course of his employment. Although he was travelling to work, it is arguable that his employment did not start until he reached that part of the grounds where the Visitors' Centre was being built. Against this, it might be contended that he was lawfully in the grounds only as an employee of Dogget & Co. He would therefore probably be treated as finding the bag in the name of his employers. Thus, only if Dogget & Co. did not claim, could Noggs assert a claim as finder.

As the bracelet is modern and made of bronze, it cannot be treasure within the Treasure Act 1996, so ownership would not vest in the Crown. Possible claimants to the bracelet might therefore include Victor, as the finder; Lord Blandish, as the present owner of the grounds; and, possibly, Viscount Willow, as the owner of the land at the time when the bracelet was deposited in it.

Where, as here, the chattel is attached to the land, the freehold owner of the land can generally establish a possession to it prior to that of the finder. Where the chattel is affixed to or buried in the land, the freehold owner's *animus possidendi* is presumed, so he will have rights to the chattel superior to those of the finder: *Parker* v *British Airways Board* at pp. 1017–1018. Thus in *Elwes* v *Brigg Gas Co.* (1886) 33 ChD 562, the life tenant was held to have a better title to the prehistoric boat contained in the soil than the finder, who was also a lessee. Lord Blandish's claim is even stronger in the present case because, unlike the finder of the prehistoric boat, Victor has no interest in the land.

Furthermore, although Victor is a lawful visitor to the grounds, his licence will almost certainly not extend to digging in the land: *Waverley Borough Council* v *Fletcher* [1995] 4 All ER 756 (CA). Since he finds the bracelet only by the excavations of his dog, he finds it as a trespasser. Whilst a trespasser may have some limited rights of possession, the court is even more likely in such circumstances to hold that Lord Blandish has a prior claim to possession (*Hibbert* v *McKiernan* [1948] 2 KB 142).

The final issue is therefore the relative strengths of the claims of Lord Blandish and his predecessor in title to the land, Viscount Willow. If Willow (or his estate) could establish that he was the true owner of the bracelet, and that he had lost (and not abandoned) it, he (or his estate) would have the prior claim

(*Moffatt* v *Kazana* [1968] 3 All ER 271). Apart from this, his claim to it would be merely as predecessor in title to the land. Fixtures, being part of the freehold, would have passed to Lord Blandish when Brandy Towers was conveyed to him; but the bracelet, even though it was apparently buried in the earth before the conveyance, is unlikely to be treated as a fixture (*Elwes* v *Brigg Gas Co.* (1886) 33 ChD 562). Furthermore, it seems that the Law of Property Act 1925, s. 62, will not operate to pass title to the bracelet on the conveyance (*Moffatt* v *Kazana* at p. 275).

None of the reported cases has decided the rights of a previous freehold owner. The Viscount's claim might, however, be based upon two lines of argument. First, an analogy might be drawn with the law relating to items concealed in goods after they have been sold. In *Merry* v *Green* (1841) 7 M & W 623, a sum of money was found in a secret compartment of a bureau after it had been sold at auction. It was held that the seller of the bureau, even though not the true owner of the money, had a better title to it than the current owner of the bureau who had discovered the money. Secondly, it might be contended that the rights of a previous freehold owner were akin to the rights of the life tenant in *Elwes* v *Brigg Gas Co.*. In that case, the life tenant was held to have a prior claim to the boat, even though it was discovered by lessees in possession under a 99-year lease.

However, whilst the lessor ceases to occupy the land upon the commencement of the term, he retains a reversionary interest in the land, unlike a vendor who conveys the freehold. The second argument is therefore a weaker one. Furthermore, it has been pointed out that there could be, in theory at least, 'an indefinite chain of claims from previous occupiers or their personal representatives' (Hoath, [1990] *Conv* 348, at p. 352). There is no fear of this in the problem, since the bracelet was deposited in the ground no earlier than 1932. Nevertheless, the courts might prefer to adopt the principle that the rights to the bracelet would have passed to Lord Blandish 'as an ordinary common law incident of land ownership' (Hoath, [1990] *Conv* 348, at p. 350).

In the case of both the bag of money and the bracelet, the true owner of the item in question will have six years from the time of the find before his rights are barred (Limitation Act 1980, ss. 2, 4 and 32). Time does not, however, run against a dishonest finder, i.e., one who does not attempt to trace the true owner. It has also been argued that time does not in any event run against a true owner until he makes a demand (Marshall, (1949) 2 *CLP* 68, referring to *Spackman* v *Foster* (1883) 11 QBD 99).

QUESTION 2

Julian and Julia were joint tenants both at law and in equity of a plot of land in Sevenoaks in Kent, which comprises a dwelling-house and an area of woodland. In 1985 they leased the plot to Noel for a term of 99 years. Julian died in 1987, leaving all his personal property to charity. Julia died in 1988, leaving her entire estate to their daughter, Dorothy, who is now the owner of the freehold reversion on the lease.

A number of trees in the wood fell in the Great Storm of 1987; but Noel, a keen environmentalist, decided to leave them as they were, and he began using the trunk of one of them, an ancient oak, as a seat. In 1998, however, while Noel was attempting to sit on the trunk, it gave way. Noel discovered inside it a clay pot, which contained a solid gold locket, and some coins. Noel contacted his local museum, which identified the locket and coins as dating from the early sixteenth century. The latter were found to be made of an alloy of silver and base metal. The silver content of some of the coins was 20 per cent; of others, only 5 per cent.

Crafty read about the find in a report in the local newspaper, and entered the wood at the dead of night with a metal detector. By this means, he uncovered, beneath the roots of a birch tree, a silver ashtray that had been made in 1900. Crafty took the ashtray home and hid it in a cupboard. His nocturnal activities have now come to light.

Last week, Noel found an old deed box under the floorboards of the attic. It contained £20,000 in bank notes. Evidence has revealed that the deed-box and its contents belonged either to Julian or to Julia, or to both of them; but more precise evidence of ownership is lacking.

Consider who is entitled to the items found.

Commentary

The mere length of a question deters many candidates from answering it. The length of a question on the examination paper, however, is no guide to its difficulty. This problem, though relatively long, is not particularly difficult; indeed, some of the information given is used to create an atmosphere rather than to convey facts of legal significance.

Although not divided into sections by letters or numbers, the question naturally divides into several parts. The question-setter has been fairly kind, because each part is broadly contained in a separate paragraph. The candidate should take care, however, because one possibly vital piece of information relating to the money in the deed box is contained in the opening paragraph.

Suggested Answer

Since the items found by Noel and Crafty were found in 1998, they may belong to the Crown as treasure under the Treasure Act 1996, subject to prior interests and rights: s. 4(1). Prior interests and rights include any (or those which derive from any) which were held when the treasure was left where it was found: s. 4(2). The successor in title to the owner of the property at the time it was left or deposited in the ground would have a prior interest and right, but if the clay pot and its contents have been in the earth for hundreds of years it is highly unlikely that there will be any person able to make such a claim to them. There may be a slightly better chance of a claim by the successor in title to the true owner of the ashtray.

Subject to this, the Crown's claim depends upon the items comprising treasure, which is defined in s. 1. An object which is at least 300 years old when found and which is not a coin ranks as treasure if it has a metallic content of at least 10 per cent by weight of precious metal (which means gold or silver: s. 3(3)). The solid gold locket therefore qualifies as treasure. Since the coins are at least 300 years old, they will all rank as treasure, whatever their metal content, if there are at least ten of them in the same find; if there are fewer than ten, each will rank as treasure only if it has a precious metal content of at least 10 per cent by weight. If, therefore, there are only four coins, the two at 20 per cent qualify under this criterion, but not those of merely 5 per cent. Each of the latter may still qualify as treasure, however, as being an object which, when found, was part of the same find as an object which was treasure (i.e., the locket and the 20 per cent silver coins). Objects which are found together are part of the same find: s. 3(4)(a). The clay pot may also qualify on this basis. It may also qualify as treasure if (being an object at least 200 years old when found) it belongs to a class designated by the Secretary of State as being of outstanding historical, archaeological or cultural importance: s. 2(1).

A person who finds an object which he believes or has reasonable grounds for believing is treasure must notify the coroner for the district in which the object was found within 14 days from the day after the find (or, if later, within 14 days beginning with the day on which the finder first believes or has reason to believe the object is treasure): s. 8. Failure to comply with this requirement is a criminal offence punishable by imprisonment or a fine, or both.

If treasure has vested in the Crown and is to be transferred to a museum, the Secretary of State must determine whether a reward is to be paid by the museum before the transfer and (if it is) the amount of the reward (which must not exceed the treasure's market value) and to whom it should be paid. If it is payable to more than one person, he must also determine how much each is to receive. The reward may be payable to the finder, to the occupier of the land at the time of the find and to any person who had an interest in the land at that time, or who has had such an interest at any time since: s. 10. The determination of the Secretary of State must be in accordance with a code of practice which he is required to prepare: s. 11. Any reward is therefore likely to be divided between Noel (assuming that he has reported the find in time), as both finder and leaseholder, and Dorothy, as owner of the freehold reversion.

Assuming that the ashtray found by Crafty is not itself part of the same find as an object which is treasure, it is unlikely to be treasure. Whatever its silver content, it was made too recently to satisfy any of the above mentioned criteria. The Treasure Act does, however, provide that any object which would have been treasure trove had it been found before the Act came into force is treasure within the meaning of the Act. Under the law of treasure trove, even a relatively modern object can comprise treasure trove provided it is substantially of gold or silver (which appears to mean at least 50 per cent: *A-G for the Duchy of Lancaster* v *G. E. Overton (Farms) Ltd* [1982] Ch 277). It must also be impossible to identify the true owner, and the object must not have been lost or abandoned; rather it must have been hidden by the true owner with the intention of retrieving it at some later date. The court may draw an inference from surrounding circumstances: *Overton (Farms)* case. The unusual location of the ashtray may suggest that it was hidden with a view to being retrieved. The Crown's title to treasure may, however, be disclaimed at any time, in which case the treasure may be delivered to any person in accordance with a code to be prepared by the Secretary of State: s. 6. In practice, even if the ashtray ranks as treasure trove at common law, and therefore as treasure under the new Act, as it is a modern object the Crown's title to it is likely to be disclaimed. Since Crafty was both a trespasser and a dishonest finder, it is unlikely that the ashtray, following a disclaimer, would be delivered to him.

Assuming that the ashtray is not treasure, the next issue is to identify who has the best title to it. Crafty was a trespasser on the land and, since he took no steps to trace the true owner, was also dishonest. He will not therefore be able to assert a prior title: *Hibbert* v *McKiernan* [1948] 2 KB 142. Indeed, he may be subject to a criminal prosecution for theft. Noel will have a claim to the ashtray as lessee and occupier of the land on which it was found.

Dorothy may argue that she has a prior title as freehold owner. In *Elwes* v *Brigg Gas Co.* (1886) 33 ChD 562, the tenant for life was held to have a prior title to the prehistoric boat found by his lessees. The boat had been in the land before the lease had been granted; the property granted by the lease did not extend to the boat; and the lease itself was for a particular purpose only, namely, for the exploration and extraction of gas.

By contrast, in *City of London Corporation* v *Appleyard* [1963] 2 All ER 834, contractors, hired by lessees in possession to demolish a building, found a wall safe containing a large sum of money in bank notes. The court held that the lessors were not in possession of the notes before they were found; however, on the facts, they were able to assert, as against the lessees, at least a (superior) equitable title because of an express clause in the lease which reserved articles of value to the lessors. But for this clause, the lessees, as the persons in possession of the premises, and so in *de facto* possession of the notes, would have had the better claim. In regard to the general principle, *Appleyard* might be distinguished from *Elwes* either on the timing of the deposition (which, in *Appleyard*, must have occurred during the lease) or on the degree of annexation (on the principle that an object buried in the ground is more deeply embedded than one merely lodged in a safe).

Noel's lease will need to be scrutinised for restrictions or reservations such as were contained in the leases in *Elwes* or *Appleyard*. In the absence of any clear term or of any evidence as to the date of the ashtray's deposition, it will be difficult to ascertain which of Noel or Dorothy has the better right to it.

In the absence of any further evidence as to the ownership of the deed-box and its contents, the court will apply the presumption that the ownership of land carries with it ownership of the chattels it contains. This principle was applied (to somewhat similar facts) in *Re Cohen* [1953] Ch 88, where Vaisey J said (at p. 94) that the principle was 'a straw to be grasped at by the swimmer in this sea of ambiguity'. Since, by virtue of the right of survivorship, Julia acquired the sole legal title to the reversion on Julian's death, she will also be treated as the sole owner of the deed-box and its contents. Therefore, upon her death, the box and the money it contains will pass under her will to Dorothy. The charity will receive nothing.

4 Adverse Possession

INTRODUCTION

The principle of relativity of titles applies not merely to titles to chattels (as exemplified in the law relating to finders' titles), but also to titles to land. The application of the principle to land emerges very strongly in the law of adverse possession; and it is this which makes this topic a particularly useful one to study.

A person who takes adverse possession of land thereby acquires a title to it, i.e., an estate in fee simple. Until his title is barred by statute, however, the dispossessed owner retains an estate in the land. This means that, where the person dispossessed has an estate in fee simple, there are two fee simple estates in the land: that of the dispossessed owner and that of the adverse possessor. Since a fee simple estate can exist at law only if it is in possession (Law of Property Act 1925, s. 1), it would appear that, from the moment the adverse possession begins, the dispossessed owner loses his legal estate and retains merely an equivalent estate in equity. Whether this is indeed the case, however, appears never to have been decided in a reported case.

Until 12 years' adverse possession have expired, the dispossessed owner has the better title, so that he can obtain possession against the squatter. After 12 years' adverse possession, his title (in unregistered land) is barred; in registered land, it is held in trust for the adverse possessor.

You should note that the concept of adverse possession works negatively, i.e., by barring a title; whereas the concept of prescription (which applies in the law of easements and profits) works positively, by conferring a right which did not exist before.

QUESTION 1

In 1978, Len leased a plot of land called Greenacre, the title to which is unregistered, to Tim for a term of 99 years at a premium of £50,000. The lease contains (*inter alia*) covenants by Tim as follows:

(a)   to pay an annual ground rent of £20;

(b)   not to part with possession of Greenacre; and

(c)   not to build any dwelling-house on Greenacre.

In 1981 Adrian entered into adverse possession of Greenacre. He was, however, dispossessed in 1990 by Sue, who has remained in possession of Greenacre since that date. Tim continued to pay the ground rent under the lease until last year, but the rent is presently £20 in arrears. Sue intends to build a house on Greenacre, and has already obtained planning permission for this purpose.

Len wishes, if possible, to regain possession of Greenacre in order to grant a fresh lease of it to Tim. If he cannot achieve that, he wishes at least to prevent Sue from building the dwelling-house. Adrian cannot at present be traced.

(a)   Advise Len.

and

(b)   How (if at all) would your advice differ if the title to Greenacre were registered?

Commentary

This question involves an analysis of the legal position where an adverse possessor is squatting upon land subject to a lease, both where the title is unregistered and where it is registered. Whilst this may appear to be a somewhat narrow point, it does in fact involve a discussion of fundamental principles of property law. The two central cases to be discussed are *Fairweather* v *St Marylebone Property Co. Ltd* [1963] AC 510 and *Spectrum Investment Co.* v *Holmes* [1981] 1 WLR 221. The student who merely states what the cases decided will not achieve the higher marks: these will be reserved for the candidate who reveals an understanding of the underlying principles, and who indicates the problems to which the decisions may give rise.

It is to be noted that, although the question is one on adverse possession, it also demands some knowledge of other areas: a basic knowledge of leases, some particular knowledge of restrictive covenants, and an understanding of the application of the principles of registered land. All these topics throw additional light on the problem. It will therefore be clear that, if you miss out a topic which you have been taught, you reduce your basic understanding of land law as a whole, and this could reduce (even if only slightly) your ability to produce a good answer to a question on a topic which you have revised.

It should be remembered that a restrictive covenant in a lease is not registrable as a land charge under the Land Charges Act 1972. The doctrine of the *bona fide* purchaser therefore applies; and a squatter (such as Sue) will be bound by such a covenant since a squatter acquires title not by purchase (in the technical legal sense) but by operation of law. Similarly, an adverse possessor of freehold land, not being a 'purchaser' within the Land Charges Act 1972, s. 4(6), will take subject to a restrictive covenant even if it is not protected by registration.

Part **(b)** calls for a comparison with the position in registered land. It is quite clear that the system of land registration was not intended to change the substantive law relating to land. Nevertheless, the impact of the 12 years' adverse possession is necessarily different in the case of registered land because the person whose title would, in unregistered land, have been barred, instead retains his legal estate until his title is closed. In the meantime, he holds that estate upon trust for the adverse possessor. The decision in *Spectrum Investment Co.* v *Holmes* appears to suggest a substantive difference between unregistered and registered titles; but this may not be so (see the valuable article by Cooke, (1994) 14 *Legal Studies* 1).

Suggested Answer

(a)   Where, as in this problem, land which is adversely possessed is subject to a lease, the Limitation Act 1980, s. 15(1), operates, at the end of 12 years, to bar the title of the tenant. It would appear that Greenacre has been adversely possessed for such a period, because an adverse possessor is permitted to add the period of adverse possession of the person whom he dispossesses (*Willis* v *Earl Howe* [1893] 2 Ch 545). Thus, the period of adverse possession, which was begun by Adrian in 1981, was continued by Sue, so that Tim's title was barred in 1993. If Adrian were to be traced, he would be able to bring an action for possession against Sue, since, although his period of adverse possession was merely ten years, his possession was prior in time to hers (*Asher* v *Whitlock* (1865) LR 1 QB 1). This would not, however, avail Tim, since his title, once barred in 1993, cannot be subsequently revived. Any action by Adrian would itself be barred 12 years after his dispossession by Sue, i.e., in 2002.

The title of the landlord, Len, is not barred, however, unless the adverse possession continues for 12 years after the expiration of the lease (Limitation Act 1980, sch. 1, para. 4), which has not yet occurred. By the same token, however, until Tim's lease comes to an end, Len is not entitled to bring an action for possession against Sue. This is because the statute bars the tenant's title only as regards the adverse possessor; *vis-à-vis* the landlord, the tenant's lease continues.

Thus it would seem that Sue has acquired, through 12 years' adverse posssession, a legal estate in fee simple in Greenacre, despite the possibility of its being brought to an end by Len's exercise of his right of re-entry (Law of Property Act 1925, s. 7). If, therefore, Len is to gain possession of Greenacre immediately, he must seek to terminate the lease. If (as will usually be the case) the lease contains a right of re-entry for breach of covenant, Len may be able to forfeit the lease for existing breaches. He will not, however, be able to effect a forfeiture for the breach of the covenant against parting with possession for two reasons: first, by accepting rent from Tim after Adrian went into adverse possession, he has waived the right to forfeit for that breach; secondly, since the breach occurred more than 12 years ago, the statute has itself barred any right of action based on that breach (Limitation Act 1980, s. 15(1), and sch. 1, Pt I, para. 7(1)).

Len may, however, bring an action for forfeiture against Tim for breach of the covenant to pay rent. Since Tim's title has already been barred by Sue, there is no reason for him to defend the action: on the contrary, the termination of the lease will be to his advantage in ending his own continuing liability under it. Although there seems to be no reason why the adverse possessor should not be entitled to pay the rent on the tenant's behalf (see Wade, (1962) 78 *LQR* 541), the rent in the problem is already in arrears. Len may therefore be able to forfeit on this ground. It has been held, moreover, that an adverse possessor of a leasehold title, lacking privity of estate with the landlord, is not entitled to claim relief from forfeiture (*Tickner* v *Buzzacott* [1965] Ch 426). Thus, relief is not available to a squatter under the Common Law Procedure Act 1852, ss. 210–212, since the squatter cannot claim under the lease.

If, however, the lease in the question contains no such proviso for re-entry, Len may still be able to terminate the lease by accepting a surrender from Tim. The House of Lords has held that a surrender by the tenant gives the landlord the right to immediate possession, thereby accelerating his right of action against the adverse possessor (*Fairweather* v *St Marylebone Property Co. Ltd* [1963] AC 510 (criticised, however, by Wade, above, on the ground that it offends the maxim, *nemo dat quod non habet*)). An alternative possibility would be for Len to purchase Tim's lease, and thereby bring it to an end through the doctrine of merger.

If Len cannot use any of these methods to terminate the lease, he will be unable to gain possession of Greenacre from Sue. Furthermore, since the statute does not transfer Tim's title to Sue, who has her own independent title to Greenacre, there is no privity of estate between Len and Sue. Therefore, Len cannot bring an action against Sue for the rent. Len can, however, sue Tim, who remains liable to pay the rent and observe and perform the leasehold covenants even after his title is barred in 1993.

Sue will, however, be subject to the leasehold covenant against building. Such a covenant, being restrictive in nature, is enforceable in equity against anyone coming to the land other than a *bona fide* purchaser of the legal estate without notice. Sue cannot establish this defence since an adverse possessor does not take by purchase (*Re Nisbet and Potts' Contract* [1905] 1 Ch 391). Len can, therefore, obtain injunctive relief to restrain Sue from building.

(**b**)   If the title to the land were registered, there could be no surrender by Tim if Sue had already obtained a registered title at HM Land Registry. In *Spectrum Investment Co.* v *Holmes* [1981] 1 WLR 221, following 12 years' adverse possession, the tenant's title had been closed and the squatter registered as proprietor of a leasehold interest. It was held that the tenant did not have any title to surrender. In that case, therefore, the registration of the squatter as proprietor of the lease would appear to have effected just that parliamentary conveyance which had been rejected (in *Tichbourne* v *Weir* (1892) 67 LT 735) in the system of unregistered land. If this were so, it would also follow that the registration would then make the squatter the tenant under the lease, and therefore subject him to its rights and obligations. Thus, if Sue were registered in the same way as the squatter in *Spectrum*, she could, as tenant, apply for relief from forfeiture.

The registration of the squatter in *Spectrum* with the leasehold title was, however, somewhat unusual. Normal Land Registry practice is to register a squatter who has barred the title of the tenant with a qualified freehold title, which thereby excepts from it the claims of the landlord when the lease determines (see Cooke, (1994) 14 *Legal Studies* 1, at p. 9). If Sue were so registered, her rights upon registration would correspond with the rights she would have were the title to the land unregistered.

More difficulty arises if Sue has not yet obtained a registered title. In contrast to the position in registered land, Tim's estate is not extinguished at the end of 12 years' adverse possession; instead, it is held in trust for Sue (Land Registration Act 1925, s. 75(1)). Until his title is closed, Tim retains the legal term created by the lease (s. 69(1)) and therefore the capacity to surrender it to Len. The imposition of the trust, however, means that any surrender of his estate to Len would comprise a breach of trust. Whether the trust would be binding on Len is uncertain. The doctrine of notice is generally considered to have no place in registered land (Land Registration Act 1925, ss. 20(1)(4), and 59(6)). Yet equity will not allow a statute to be used as an instrument of fraud, and a constructive trust was imposed on the holder of a registered title (albeit in different circumstances) in both *Peffer* v *Rigg* [1977] 1 WLR 285 and *Lyus* v *Prowsa Developments Ltd* [1982] 1 WLR 1044. It is, however, no fraud for a person to rely on his legal rights (*Midland Bank Trust Co.* v *Green* [1981] AC 513), and it is therefore doubtful if the equitable maxim could be invoked in the present circumstances.

Alternatively, it might be argued that Len would in any event take subject to Sue's rights as beneficiary under the trust because they are rights of a person in actual occupation (Land Registration Act 1925, s. 70(1)(g)). This argument may, however, be circular because Sue's rights are always subject to Len's (cf. *Paddington Building Society* v *Mendelsohn* (1985) 50 P & CR 244), so that he is entitled to possession against her once the lease has come to an end. It is therefore probable that, until Sue is registered, she can (as in *Fairweather*) still be dispossessed following a surrender, although she would be able to claim damages for breach of trust against Tim.

QUESTION 2

In 1975 Squirrel, whose garden adjoined a plot of waste land, decided to make use of it for his own benefit. He levelled the plot, made a path across it, constructed flower-beds and made a lawn. He also put a child's swing on the plot. From that time, Squirrel and his family used the plot as part of their own garden.

The fee simple owner of the plot in 1975 was Little Oakhorn Ltd (Oakhorn). The company soon became aware of Squirrel's use of the plot, but took no steps to remove him, as it intended to develop the plot in due course as a housing estate when the requisite planning permission could be obtained, and it therefore had no use for the plot at the time.

In 1985 Oakhorn went into liquidation, and the plot was sold and conveyed by the liquidator to Nutkin Estates Ltd (Nutkin), which immediately wrote to Squirrel asking him by what right he claimed to be in occupation of the plot. Squirrel did not reply. In 1990 Squirrel fenced the plot off from the surrounding land on all sides except where it adjoined his garden. Last year, Nutkin, which had just obtained planning to permission to build, again wrote to Squirrel. This time he replied that he intended to use the land only until Nutkin needed it for development. Following receipt of this letter, Nutkin brought proceedings against Squirrel for possession of the plot.

Advise Squirrel.

Commentary

When the court is determining whether a title has been barred by adverse possession, it is generally engaged in an application of the legal principles to a complex set of facts. A range of different acts may have been performed on the land, and whether they amount to acts of adverse possession depends on their combined impact. Since law and fact are here intertwined, it is probable that your lectures on this topic will go through the facts of some of the cases in a fair amount of detail. The student must however appreciate that the cases turn on their own particular facts, and that a holding that a specified act in a given set of circumstances comprises an act of adverse possession does not mean that such an act will inevitably be held to have the same effect in a later case.

The structure of the answer to this particular problem is as follows:

    (a)   act of adverse possession:
       varies with nature of the land;
       rejection of the doctrine of *Leigh* v *Jack* (1879) 5 ExD 264, which links
into:

    (b)   *animus possidendi;*

    (c)   implied licence;

    (d)   conclusion.

At each stage of the answer, the law is related to the facts of the problem. There is a tentative conclusion based on an application of the law to the totality of the facts supplied. No definite answer is, however, possible, since too much turns on the interpretation of the facts and the inferences which may be drawn from them. The examiner will expect a clear statement of the relevant law and an application of the law to the facts given. It is, however, quite likely that the facts of an examination problem on adverse possession will be capable of more than one interpretation. If this is so, you should point this out, and not try to suggest that there is only one possible answer. To do so may indicate a failure to appreciate a basic principle — the difference between law and fact.

Suggested Answer

Squirrel will be unable to resist Nutkin's action for possession unless he can establish that he has been in adverse possession of the plot for at least 12 years after the right of Nutkin, or his predecessor in title, Oakhorn, first accrued (Limitation Act 1980, s. 15(1)). Nutkin's right of action to recover will have accrued only from the time (if any) that, being in possession of the plot, either Nutkin or Oakhorn was either dispossessed or discontinued possession (Limitation Act 1980, sch. 1, para. 1).

It is, nevertheless, not enough that the plot is merely left vacant; Nutkin (or his predecessor) must have ceased possession and Squirrel must have taken adverse possession of it. For possession to be adverse, two elements must be present. First, Squirrel must have taken exclusive possession of the plot without the consent of the person entitled to possession. Secondly, Squirrel must establish that he had the necessary *animus possidendi* (intention to possess).

What acts comprise sufficient acts of adverse possession varies with the circumstances of each case. Fencing off the land is generally considered the strongest act of adverse possession (*George Wimpey & Co. Ltd* v *Sohn* [1967] Ch 487; *Williams* v *Usherwood* (1983) 45 P & CR 235). However, although Squirrel did indeed fence the plot off, such act was performed only in 1990, i.e., less than 12 years ago. If, therefore, this was the first act of adverse possession, Nutkin's right to recover will not in any event have been statute-barred.

Thus, if Squirrel is to resist Nutkin's action, an earlier act of adverse possession must be found. This is possible since fencing is not the only act capable of amounting to adverse possession. Other acts may sometimes suffice, depending (*inter alia*) upon the character and value of the property, and the uses to which it can be put (*Lord Advocate* v *Lord Lovat* (1880) 5 App Cas 273). Thus, in *Red*

House Farms (Thorndon) Ltd v *Catchpole* (1976) 244 EG 295, the mere act of shooting rabbits on marshy land (which could be used for little else) was enough. By contrast, in *Tecbild Ltd* v *Chamberlain* (1969) 20 P & CR 633, the playing of children and the tethering of ponies were held, in the circumstances, too trivial to amount to acts of adverse possession. Similarly, in *Boosey* v *Davis* (1987) 55 P & CR 83, the grazing of goats on land which could (subject to planning permission) be developed, was insufficient: the quality and quantity of such acts was minimal. Again, the growing of vegetables on the land, and the erection of s ɔds for breeding greyhounds were held to be inadequate in *Williams* v *Raftery* [1958] 1 QB 159. Acts that change the nature or potential use of the land, however, are likely to suffice (*Treloar* v *Nv* [1976] 1 WLR 1295 (infilling of a gully)).

Since the land in the problem is capable of being developed, it is therefore unlikely that the placing of the swing (which can presumably be easily removed), the planting of flowers or the making of a lawn, can be considered anything more than trivial acts. The levelling of the plot, however, indicates some change in the nature of the land, and this act may be more significant, depending upon how extensive such alterations were.

It used to be thought that, in order to defeat a title by dispossessing the true owner, the acts done had to be inconsistent with his enjoyment of the soil for the purposes for which he intended to use it: *Leigh* v *Jack* (1879) 5 ExD 264. This doctrine meant that, if the owner had no present use for the land, but intended to use it only in the future (e.g., when planning permission could be obtained), it was very difficult for acts done in relation to the land to comprise acts of adverse possession. The existence of such doctrine was, however, rejected by the Court of Appeal in *Buckinghamshire County Council* v *Moran* [1990] Ch 623. In that case, Nourse LJ stated that the intentions of the true owner in regard to future use were relevant only to the extent that, if they were known to the person claiming to be in adverse possession, they might affect the quality of his own intention, and reduce it below that required to constitute adverse possession. *Moran's* case was recently affirmed by the Court of Appeal in *Hounslow LBC* v *Minchinton* (1997) 74 P & CR 221. Thus the mere fact that Squirrel's acts in relation to the plot may not be adverse to the future intended use of, first Oakhorn, and then Nutkin, will not prevent his being in adverse possession, unless he lacks the requisite *animus possidendi*.

The *animus* required of an adverse possessor is an intention to possess to the exclusion of all others including the true owner (*Littledale* v *Liverpool College* [1900] 1 Ch 19). The court will require clear and affirmative evidence on the part of the trespasser, not merely that he had such intention, but that he made such intention clear to the whole world (*Powell* v *McFarlane* (1977) 38 P & CR 452). In most instances, the intention of the trespasser will need to be inferred from his acts. In the problem, the act of fencing is probably sufficient to indicate the requisite *animus*. It is evidence of such intention, however, only from the date the fence was constructed, i.e., from 1990; whereas for Nutkin's title to be barred, it is necessary to show that the intention to dispossess continued for at least 12 years.

Squirrel's admission last year that he intended to use the land only until Nutkin needed it for redevelopment is a clear indication that his intention was not to dispossess the true owner. If this is treated as evidence of his intention from the moment he started using the plot, it will preclude Squirrel from establishing any period of adverse possession, and Nutkin's action will succeed. It is, however, possible that Squirrel's statement will be treated as indicating only his intention at the time of making it, in which case, he may still be able to resist Nutkin's action if he can show that, before such admission was made, Nutkin's title was already statute-barred.

Squirrel's possession will not be adverse if it was with the consent of the owner. In *Wallis's Cayton Bay Holiday Camp Ltd* v *Shell-Mex and BP Ltd* [1975] QB 94, Lord Denning MR stated that, where the acts alleged to comprise adverse possession do not interfere with the true owner's future intended use of the land, the occupier is to be treated as being under an implied licence, which will prevent the acts from amounting to possession. The Limitation Act 1980, sch. 1, para. 8(4), however, provides, in effect, that an implied licence is not to be inferred from such circumstances alone, but may be inferred from additional facts. The evidence of Oakhorn is therefore crucial: its reasons for failing to take steps to remove Squirrel may justify a finding of an implied licence.

In conclusion, it must be conceded that it is unlikely that Squirrel will be able to show a period of adverse possession for 12 years. First, the acts upon which he must rely (which therefore exclude the act of fencing, which was effected too late in the day) are, given the nature of the land, relatively trivial. Secondly, his admission last year may be taken to be evidence of an intention from the start not to dispossess the true owner. Thirdly, the circumstances may in any event suggest that, at least until 1990, he was there with the implied permission of the true owner. Nutkin's action will therefore probably succeed.

5 The 1925 Legislation and Transfer of Title

INTRODUCTION

The 1925 legislation is the statutory basis of our present-day system of land law. It comprised six statutes. The four most concerned with land law are the Law of Property Act, the Settled Land Act, the Land Charges Act and the Land Registration Act. The Land Charges Act 1925 has been replaced by the Land Charges Act 1972; and after the Trusts of Land and Appointment of Trustees Act 1996 (TLATA) came into effect on 1 January 1997, no new settlements can be made under the Settled Land Act, although it will continue to apply to existing pre-1997 settlements.

The reforms effected by the legislation were sweeping, including the eventual introduction by the Land Registration Act 1925 of an entirely new system of conveyancing. Hardly surprisingly, there have been problems with this, and particularly with the overriding nature of the interests of persons in actual occupation of the land under the Land Registration Act 1925, s. 70(1)(g). Conveyancing practice has developed to cope with this however, and although the system has its critics, it works reasonably well for the majority of conveyances. It is not the fault of the legislature that it is able to simplify only one part of the conveyancing system (the title to land), so that the ideal of quick and cheap transfer of land still remains elusive.

Question 1 in this chapter takes an overall view of the main simplifications effected by the legislation. Question 2 considers the extent to which the old equitable doctrine of notice has, in practice, been eradicated in the new system. Although there can be little doubt that it was the intention of the legislature to expunge this equitable doctrine in the context of registered land (with one notable exception), the doctrine's influence can be detected in many difficult decisions, including some recent ones in the House of Lords. The attraction of the doctrine is its basic fairness, which a system based entirely on registration may lack.

Question 3 is on a particular problem concerning estates created by the Law of Property Act 1925, s. 1(1), which was dealt with by the Law of Property (Amendment) Act 1926. You should be guided by your lectures and tutorials in deciding how much time you need to devote to this topic.

Questions 4 and 5 show how, in practice, incumbrances may, or may not, bind a purchaser of land in the new system. Both questions deal with this in registered and unregistered title — a common form of examination instruction.

Question 6 considers the requirements for an enforceable contract to sell land under the Law of Property (Miscellaneous Provisions) Act 1989, and some of the cases in which the courts have had to interpret the statute.

The 1925 legislation is an important area which, if you are to understand and enjoy the intellectual challenges of land law, you must get to grips with at a fairly early stage of your studies. Together with basic common law concepts such as the doctrine of estates and possession, it is the foundation and structure upon which the whole edifice of land law is built. Once this has been conquered, however, the rest of the edifice will slot into place like pieces in a jigsaw puzzle, so you should have no further very serious problems with the subject. Failure to understand the basic structure of the legislation, though, could leave you with pieces of the puzzle fitting badly, or perhaps never at all.

QUESTION 1

'The main object of the 1925 legislation was the simplification of conveyancing, and the Committee that was appointed was instructed by its terms of reference "... to advise what action should be taken to *facilitate and cheapen the transfer of land*"' (*Cheshire & Burn's Modern Law of Real Property*, 15th edn, London: Butterworths, 1994).

How did the 1925 legislation set out to achieve this object, and how successful has it been?

Commentary

This question looks at the structure of our property and conveyancing system, which was established in its present form by the 1925 legislation. There have been statutory and judicial modifications, the most fundamental being the Trusts of Land and Appointment of Trustees Act 1996 (TLATA) but the structure remains basically the same. For a proper understanding of land law, you need to understand the underlying objectives of this legislation.

To answer the question well, you will need to have a very brief knowledge of certain aspects of property law before the legislation. However, most land law courses and text books will include some reference to these, which assist in understanding our present day system.

The question can be considered very much in conjunction with Question 2 in this chapter, as equitable notice was a central problem which the 1925 legislation had to address. Many of the social factors mentioned in the introduction to Question 2 are also relevant to the second part of this question — how successful has the legislation been? Its inadequacy in some of the areas is due to the very changed social background in which we now live.

The Land Charges Act 1925 was replaced by the Land Charges Act 1972, which is itself rapidly becoming otiose as land throughout the whole country is now subject to compulsory registration (speeded up by the Land Registration Act 1997). The TLATA 1996 provides that equitable beneficial interests in land shall in future take effect behind a trust of land. It has repealed and amended those sections of the Law of Property Act 1925 which deal with trusts for sale, and has repealed the Settled Land Act as regards all future settlements of land.

Suggested Answer

The main purpose of the legislation was to make land more freely alienable and to reduce the onerous task of a purchaser in investigating title, whilst at the same time affording protection to the owners of equitable interests in the land. The problem in land law is to achieve a balance between the interests of a purchaser (in the broad definition of the Law of Property Act 1925 and including a lessee and a mortgagee) on the one hand, and those of the owner of an equitable interest in the land on the other hand.

A purchaser of land was always bound by legal estates and interests in the land (rights '*in rem*'), but was not bound by equitable ones if he was a *bona fide* purchaser for value without notice of them (equity's darling).

Because of the reduction in the number of estates which *may* subsist at law to two (Law of Property Act 1925, s. 1(1)), and the number of interests which *may* subsist at law to five (s. 1(2)), there was a drastic reduction in the number of legal estates and interests by which a purchaser would be bound.

The effect of the Law of Property Act 1925, was inevitably to increase the number of estates and interests which became equitable. The reason for this was to remove these as far as possible from the title to the legal estate which the purchaser is buying. The legal estate is vested in an estate owner, who conveys it to a purchaser. Certain types of equitable interests which arose under a settlement or a trust for sale were overreached by a sale by two trustees. This meant that they attached to the proceeds of sale of the land instead of to the land itself. Where this was not possible because the equitable interests were of the type which attached to the land itself (generally commercial interests), they were made registrable and a purchaser can discover them by searching the register. After 1925, therefore, most equitable interests became either over-reachable or registrable.

Overreachable interests were the old estates which, because of the Law of Property Act 1925, s. 1(1), became necessarily equitable. These included life estates, fee tails and fee simples which were not absolute or in possession (although it should be noted that some fee simples subject to a right of re-entry were re-instated as legal interests by the Law of Property (Amendment) Act 1926, as to which see Question 3). They all have the common feature that they give a right, at some time, to beneficial ownership and occupation of the land. After 1925, such interests could only take effect behind either a trust for sale or a settlement. The Law of Property Act 1925, s. 2(1), provided that they were overreached on a sale of the land, which meant that they no longer attached to the land itself, but attached instead to the proceeds of sale of the land. They were protected by the overreaching machinery of the trust for sale and the settlement, namely, that a purchaser would not get a good title to the land unless he got a good receipt for the purchase moneys from two trustees. This same machinery protects the purchaser also, because if the purchaser complies with the requirement for a receipt from two trustees, he gets a good title to the legal estate, freed from the equitable interests.

The trust for sale and settlement allowed considerable flexibility of interests in land, but not at the expense of complicating the title to the legal estate. These two forms of trust were mutually exclusive, but wherever land was held on limited forms of ownership (for any estate less than a fee simple absolute in possession), then these had to take effect behind one or the other.

For the reasons set out in the suggested answer to Question 1 in **Chapter 8** on Trusts of Land, there were problems with both settlements and trusts for sale which led to the passing of the TLATA 1996, which came into force on 1 January 1997. This converted most existing trusts for sale into trusts of land and provides that all future trusts of land shall take effect not as trusts for sale or settlements but as trusts of land under the Act. The doctrine of conversion, which applied to a trust for sale, disappears and there is a more realistic recognition that a beneficiary's interests are in the land itself and not in the proceeds of sale. The basic protection of those interests and the protection given to a purchaser by the overreaching provisions of s. 2(1), Law of Property Act remain unchanged.

The simplification of title to land is illustrated also by the 1925 provisions for co-ownership. After 1925, only a joint tenancy may subsist at law (s. 34(2), Law of Property Act 1925); and as the right of survivorship applies to this, there can be no fragmentation of the legal title. A purchaser therefore knows that he can take a conveyance of the legal title from the remaining joint tenants. Wherever there is co-ownership of land there is a trust of land and the equitable interests of the co-owners may be either a joint tenancy or a tenancy in common, and so may either pass to the surviving joint tenants or to their estates. There were possible hazards for a purchaser in taking a conveyance from only one surviving joint tenant, however, as there could have been a hidden severance of the equitable joint tenancy before the death of the predeceasing joint tenant. The Law of Property (Joint Tenants) Act 1964 therefore provided that a purchaser would get a good title from a single surviving joint tenant if he conveyed as beneficial owner, or the conveyance specifically stated that the vendor was a beneficial owner, and there was no endorsement of a severance on the conveyance to the joint tenants. The Law of Property (Miscellaneous Provisions) Act 1994, dealing with the implied covenants for title, abolishes the technicality of conveying 'as beneficial owner', so the 1964 Act should now be complied with by stating in the conveyance that the surviving vendor is a beneficial owner.

The provision of a trust and the overreaching mechanism did not, however, cater for the types of equitable interests which attach to the land itself. Many of these had also been legal interests before 1926, but necessarily became equitable because of s. 1(2) of the Law of Property Act 1925. There were others which could only be equitable, and their binding effect on a purchaser depended upon the equitable doctrine of notice. The Land Charges Act 1925 (now Land Charges Act 1972) made these interests registrable. They include restrictive covenants, equitable easements, estate contracts, options to purchase and general equitable charges. They are protected, in unregistered title, by registration under the Land Charges Act, and a purchaser may search the register to discover these. Registration, where applicable, replaces the old doctrine of notice. Constructive notice was particularly hazardous for a purchaser, as he might find himself bound by an equitable interest which the court decided that he *should have* discovered, even though he had no actual knowledge of it at all. After 1925, the purchaser will be bound only by those registrable interests which are registered irrespective of notice (*Midland Bank Trust Co.* v *Green* [1981] AC 543).

Even in 1925, the legislation did not cater for all equitable interests, and there was a residual class of equitable interests to which the old doctrine of notice still applied. It was obviously felt to be too onerous a task to register all the old restrictive covenants affecting land, and so the Land Charges Act 1925 provided for registration of only those restrictive covenants and equitable easements created after the legislation came into force on 1 January 1926. Those interests created before that date still depend upon the old doctrine of notice for their validity against a purchaser.

Moreover, a bare trust (where there is a schism of the legal and equitable ownership in land, arising, for example, from a resulting trust) is not protected by the overreaching machinery, which requires two trustees, and its binding effect on a purchaser is again determined by notice.

Since 1926, the courts have evolved the equitable doctrine of estoppel, and now recognise proprietary interests created by estoppel. These interests are not registrable however (see Lord Denning MR in *E. R. Ives Investment Ltd* v *High* [1967] 2 QB 379), and so must depend for their validity against a purchaser of the land upon the doctrine of notice.

The main 'breach' of the 1925 scheme has arisen in hidden co-ownership. Due to changing social circumstances, working wives and cohabitees frequently contribute to the high price of a home. The courts have recognised that such persons may acquire a beneficial equitable interest in the home under a resulting or constructive trust, or both, even though their names do not appear on the legal title. The Law Commission's Report on the implications of *Williams & Glyn's Bank Ltd* v *Boland* (Law Com. No.115, (1982)) recommended that co-ownership interests should be made registrable, but this has not been implemented, and it is difficult to see how it could be when such interests are acquired informally, and may often be disputed by the owner of the legal title. However, the decision in *Williams & Glyn's Bank Ltd* v *Boland* [1981] AC 487 that such interests were overriding under s. 70(1)(g) of the Land Registration Act 1925 in the registered land system has caused conveyancers to enquire avidly about the 'occupiers' of property they are buying. The underlying rationale for s. 70(1)(g) is that occupation is usually notice of an interest in the land. The influence of this type of notice in registered land has influenced notice in the unregistered system and was a relevant factor in *Kingsnorth Finance Co.* v *Tizard* [1986] 1 WLR 783, so that the increased caution of conveyancers has reduced the potential hazards in this area for a purchaser.

It is important to realise, however, that if there is a sale (or mortgage or other dealing) by two co-owners of land, then any hidden beneficial interests in the land are overreached and attach instead to the proceeds of sale. They can then no longer be 'rights' in the land for the purposes of s. 70(1)(g), and so are not binding on the purchaser (*City of London Building Society* v *Flegg* [1988] AC 54).

One of the difficulties of the registration of land charges in unregistered title is that they are registrable against the name of the estate owner. For such a system to work however, it is necessary to have the full and correct name of the estate owner. In *Diligent Finance Ltd* v *Alleyne* (1972) 23 P & CR 346, a wife registered a Class F land charge against her husband in the name of Erskine Alleyne, whereas his full name on the conveyance of the property was Erskine Owen Alleyne. The wife's registration was held to be void against a mortgagee who obtained a clear search against his full name. In *Oak Co-operative*

Building Society v *Blackburn* [1968] Ch 730 an estate contract was registered against the name of an estate agent as Frank (not Francis) David Blackburn. A subsequent mortgagee obtained a clear search against the name of Francis Davis Blackburn. It was held that where there is an error in the search as well as in the name against which the charge is registered, the charge will be good against the subsequent purchaser.

In theory, a purchaser needs to search against all estate owners since 1 January 1926 when the statute came into force. A purchaser was given only 30 years' title however, and so, from 1956 onwards, could not know the names of persons against whom he had to search. The situation was further aggravated when the Law of Property Act 1969 reduced the period of title to 15 years (s. 23). The Act therefore made some allowances for this difficulty, and s. 24 provides that as regards a *purchaser* a land charge shall be binding only if he actually knows of it. It also provides for compensation to a purchaser adversely affected by not having a root of title sufficiently old to disclose registered land charges (s. 25). In practice, land charges searches are carefully kept by solicitors with the deeds, so that there is often a complete chain of them going back for many years, and very few claims for compensation have been made.

Another criticism which may be made of the Land Charges Act system is that, because registration is the sole criterion of whether an interest is binding or not, it may operate unfairly. Its provisions may be used to deliberately evade interests of which a purchaser has actual knowledge. In *Midland Bank Trust Co.* v *Green* [1981] AC 583, a collusive sale, not for value, was held to defeat an option to purchase which had not been registered. In *Hollington Bros* v *Rhodes* (1951) 2 TLR 691, a purchaser who bought the freehold reversion on an equitable lease was held not to be bound by it because it had not been registered, notwithstanding that he paid a discounted price because of the equitable lease.

It should of course be borne in mind that the Land Charges Act 1925 was only ever intended to be a stopgap measure. The Land Registration Act 1925 extended the system of registered title to land, and when the title to land becomes registrable, the Land Charges Act 1972 (formerly 1925) no longer applies. All those interests which, prior to registration of title, were registrable in the Land Charges Registry at Plymouth (under the Acts of 1925 or 1972) are then registrable in the local Land Registry. In 1925, it was envisaged that the title to all land in the country would be registered very much more quickly than in fact happened, so that the problems arising because of the length of title were not foreseen.

The Land Registration Act 1925 provides for the title to land to be registered at the local Land Registry. There are three registers — the property register, the proprietorship register and the charges register. The register is intended to be a 'mirror' of the title, and title is deduced by furnishing a purchaser's solicitor with office copy entries on the register. This avoids the necessity for a vendor to deduce 15 years' title to a purchaser each time the land is sold. The Land Certificate, issued by the Land Registry, contains a copy of the register entries and the date when it was last compared with the register, and this is the document of title to registered land. A purchaser takes subject to any minor interests which are noted on the register, and subject in any event to any overriding interests. Many of the overriding interests (although not all) are the same as the legal interests in unregistered title, and many of the minor interests are equitable interests in unregistered land.

Most conveyancers would probably agree that registered title is an easier system of conveyancing than unregistered, and it was finally introduced for the last area in the country in 1990. Even this system is not perfect, and J.T. Farrand has made scathing attacks on it (*Contract & Conveyance*, 4th edn, London: Oyez Longman, 1983). He has commented on the claim that the register is a 'mirror of the title' (Ruoff, *The Torrens System*), that 'The view may be taken by conveyancers that [overriding interests and rectification of the register] render the mirror image seriously and unacceptably incomplete ...'. (It is possible, in certain circumstances, to rectify the register against a registered proprietor). Although the system may be cheaper in some saving of solicitors' time, this is probably offset by the Land Registry's fees!

Given the enormous social changes of the past 70 years, which have undoubtedly caused problems for the scheme set up by the 1925 legislation, it is remarkable that the basic structure remains mostly intact, and that the courts have largely been able to adapt it to our modern requirements.

QUESTION 2

'In my opinion therefore, the law as to notice as it may affect purchasers of unregistered land, whether contained in decided cases, or in a statute ... has no application even by analogy to registered land.' (Lord Wilberforce in *Williams & Glyn's Bank Ltd* v *Boland* [1981] AC 487.)

Explain and discuss this statement.

Commentary

This question addresses the central issue of any system of land law and conveyancing, namely, the balance to be achieved between the desire of a purchaser for a clear title to land, and the protection of a possible third party's rights and interests in the land.

It is a problem dealt with differently in the unregistered and registered systems of conveyancing. However, the old principles of the unregistered system were not entirely abandoned in the Land Registration Act 1925, and recent cases suggest that the old doctrine of notice is gaining favour again with the judiciary as a fair and just way to solve this central problem (see the speech of Lord Browne-Wilkinson in *Barclays Bank plc* v *O'Brien* [1993] 3 WLR 786).

The problem has been further aggravated by the continually changing social patterns of the last 30 years or so. Although at one time unusual, it is now quite normal for a wife to contribute to the purchase price of a matrimonial home, and her resulting property rights have been recognised. Cohabitation, comparatively rare some 30 years ago, is recognised and accepted today. This includes lesbian (*Tinsley* v *Milligan* [1993] 3 WLR 126) and male homosexual (*Wayling* v *Jones* [1993] EGCS 153) relationships. It is recognised that partners in such relationships may acquire property rights in a shared home. So the social background in which we now apply the 1925 legislation has changed drastically since its enactment.

Given these social changes, it is surprising that the courts have largely been able to adapt the legislation to the requirements of modern life, and that much of the basic structure still remains.

For a fuller discussion of this subject (although not up to date) see R.H. Maudsley 'Bona fide purchasers of registered land' (1973) 30 *MLR* 25.

Suggested Answer

The quotation expresses what may come to be seen as the high-water mark of the rejection of the doctrine of notice in registered land. As will be discussed in this answer, the trend more recently has been tacitly to recognise that the doctrine has a limited role to play. In any event, Lord Wilberforce's words are best considered in the context of the property reforms of 1925.

The main aim of the 1925 legislation was to simplify conveyancing (see Question 1). To this end, it provides that the legal fee simple estate shall be vested in an estate owner, who, on sale, deduces title and conveys it to a purchaser. Any equitable interests are 'off the title'. On sale, those which take effect behind a trust are overreached and attach to the proceeds of sale of the land; if not overreachable, they are registrable under the Land Charges Act 1972 (formerly the Land Charges Act 1925) and so are discoverable by a purchaser.

The overreaching provisions of the Law of Property Act apply also where the title to land is registered (*City of London Building Society* v *Flegg* [1988] AC 54). The trustee estate owners are the registered proprietors and a restriction in the proprietorship register alerts a purchaser to the existence of a trust and of the necessity to obtain a receipt for purchase moneys from two trustees. Those equitable interests registrable under the Land Charges Act 1972 become registrable as minor interests in the register of the local Land Registry (usually in the charges register).

One of the problems of pre-1926 conveyancing, which this system sought to solve, was the hazard to a purchaser of the doctrine of notice. In particular, it was recognised that constructive notice (the notice which a purchaser should have had if the proper enquiries had been made) was a haphazard affair which could expose a purchaser to considerable risks. To avoid this, those equitable interests which attach to the land itself, and are not capable of satisfaction out of the proceeds of sale of the land, were made registrable under the Land Charges Act 1925. Moreover, the Law of Property Act 1925, s. 199, provides that any registrable interest which is not registered is void against a purchaser of the land. This means that, where applicable, registration is the sole determinant of whether a registrable interest will bind a purchaser of the land or not.

The overall decisiveness of registration under the Land Charges Act 1972, even at the expense of justice, is demonstrated by the case of *Midland Bank Trust Co.* v *Green* [1981] AC 513. In that case, an unregistered option to purchase was void for want of registration even against someone who *actually* knew of it, had not given value, and was most certainly not *bona fide*. The case might be treated as an example of the adage that hard cases make good law. Lord Wilberforce recognised this, but said 'The Act is clear and definite . . . it should not be read down or glossed; to do so would destroy the usefulness of the Act'. The decision is nevertheless open to criticism in that it permitted the destruction of an equitable interest by a fraudulent conveyance. Lord Denning MR, in the

Court of Appeal in the same case, gave a dissenting judgment in which he said 'No court in this land will allow a person to keep an advantage which he has obtained by fraud. ... Fraud unravels everything'.

Even in 1925, however, it was conceded that the legislation could not cover all equitable interests. It was obviously too mammoth a task for the Land Charges Registrar to register all the old restrictive covenants on unregistered titles (many over a century old), and the binding effect of these, and equitable easements, was left dependent upon the old doctrine of notice. Since 1926 the doctrine has also been applied to beneficial interests arising under a bare trust and estoppel interests. Both these interests tend to arise from informal arrangements, and this in itself would present a difficulty in registering them. This difficulty with regard to registering co-ownership interests was recognised by the Law Commission in its report on the implications of the *Boland* case (Law Com. No.115, (1982)), in which it was said:

> Co-ownership can arise ... through a succession of informal and sometimes indistinct events. ... In such cases, the co-owner may be unaware even of the existence of a co-ownership interest, let alone the need to register it.

In registered title, interests are either overriding (binding in any event on the registered proprietor or a transferee from him) or minor and binding only if protected by an entry on the register. It is a curious paradox, therefore, that, at the same time as registration alone could make an interest binding in unregistered titles, the Land Registration Act 1925, s. 70(1)(g), introduced into registered titles what can only have been intended to be a limited and particular form of notice. This section makes overriding 'the rights of every person in actual occupation of the land ... save where enquiry is made of such person and the rights are not disclosed'.

Although, as Lord Wilberforce said in *Boland*, 'In the case of registered land, it is the fact of occupation that matters', the section is nevertheless a concession to the old doctrine of notice. It roughly corresponds with the old rule in *Hunt* v *Luck* [1901] 1 Ch 45, which was of general application to unregistered land before 1926, but which was largely superseded by the Land Charges Act 1925. The rule fixes a purchaser with notice of rights which he should have discovered by reason of persons in occupation of the land. The rule did not operate however to fix a person with notice of rights which were consistent with, and therefore not discoverable by reason of, the occupation (*Barnhart* v *Greenshields* (1853) 9 Moo PCC 18).

This rationale was applied in *Caunce* v *Caunce* [1969] 1 WLR 286, a case involving unregistered title, where it was held that a wife's occupation of the matrimonial home with her husband did not give a mortgagee notice of the fact that she had a beneficial interest in the home. Stamp J said 'She was there, ostensibly, because she was the wife, and her presence there was wholly consistent with the title offered by the husband to the bank'. This case was regarded as wrong in *Boland*, and in 1981 it would probably have been decided differently, as co-ownership by wives was by then much more common. It was, however, decided very much according to the application of the rule in *Hunt* v *Luck*.

The notice imposed by the rule in *Hunt* v *Luck* did not apply where an occupier had concealed his rights, and, in registered land, the saving in the Land Registration Act 1925, s. 70(1)(g), reflects this. Where a purchaser has enquired of *the person in actual occupation* (not merely of the vendor's solicitor or agent), he has a clean bill of health and takes free from any interests which *that person* has failed to disclose. In *Lloyds Bank plc* v *Rosset* [1989] Ch 350 (CA) (reversed on other grounds by the House of Lords, [1991] 1 AC 107), Mustill LJ said '[E]ven if constructive notice no longer applies in this field, the old law still gives a flavour to the new words of [s. 70(1)(g)]'. Otherwise, he said, s. 70(1)(g) would produce an unacceptable contrast with the workmanlike solution in *Caunce* v *Caunce*.

Regarding occupation as the sole determinant of whether a right is binding upon a purchaser or not has caused problems in the registered system of conveyancing, as it is not always apparent that an occupier has *rights*. The mortgagee in *Boland* did not expect the wife to have rights in the property, and the purchaser in *Hodgson* v *Marks* [1971] Ch 892 assumed that the lady who was walking up the garden path was the housekeeper and not the beneficial owner of the property. These cases, where the inference that occupiers had rights could not necessarily be drawn, therefore involved an extension of the rule in *Hunt* v *Luck*.

Happily, these problems have been largely overcome by improved conveyancing practice. The very whisper of an occupier, other than the vendor, sends shivers down the spine of any experienced conveyancer, and will produce a barrage of questions as to his status and rights. Such questions are now included in all forms of conveyancers' pre-contract enquiries. Mortgagees require applicants to sign declarations as to who will occupy the mortgaged property, thereby seeking to obtain an admission that only the mortgagor has rights in the property. There is much to be said for this improved practice which takes account of s. 70(1)(g).

Moreover, there has been some cross-fertilisation from the registered to the unregistered system. In *Kingsnorth Finance Co.* v *Tizard* [1986] 1 WLR 783, the standards of enquiry as to occupation in registered land were applied to unregistered title. A mortgagee was found to have constructive notice of the rights of a wife whose occupation, although intermittent, should have been apparent, and whose existence was evident from the mortgage application form.

There has, however, been an ominous trend in some cases to invoke a constructive trust in order to give effect to interests which were void for want of registration, but which would have been binding under the old equitable doctrine of notice. In *Lyus* v *Prowsa Developments Ltd* [1982] 1 WLR 1044, an estate contract which had not been registered as a minor interest in registered land, and was not overriding, was held to be binding on a subsequent purchaser who took expressly subject to it. The rationale for this was that 'equity will not allow a statute to be used as an instrument of fraud'. The case contrasts starkly however with the earlier decision in unregistered title of *Hollington Bros* v *Rhodes* [1951] 2 TLR 691. There, a purchaser who paid less than the market price for property because of an equitable lease affecting it, nevertheless took free from the lease as it was not registered. In *Peffer* v *Rigg* [1977] 1 WLR 285, Graham J was prepared to find a constructive trust to protect a beneficial minor interest in registered land which had not been registered (although he also reached the same conclusion by ascribing requirements of good faith to the Land Registration Act 1925, s. 59(6), and the decision has been strongly criticised).

More recently, in *Barclays Bank plc* v *O'Brien* [1993] 3 WLR 786, the House of Lords have applied notice as the criterion to determine whether a lender should be bound by any undue influence which a borrower might have over a surety or a co-borrower. It is not clear whether this case concerned registered or unregistered title, but presumably the principle is intended to apply to both. (This was queried by Professor Mark Thompson in his note on the case in (1994) *Conv* 140.)

In *Barclays Bank plc* v *Boulter* [1997] 2 All ER 1002, Mummery LJ said that in cases like *O'Brien* it was irrelevant whether the land was registered or unregistered title; but in *Woolwich Building Society* v *Dickman & Todd* (1996) 72 P & CR 470, signed consents by tenants to the legal owner mortgaging property in which they were living, although sufficient to supplant their rights of occupation, were not effective to extinguish their overriding interest under s. 70(1)(g) of the Land Registration Act 1925.

The reality, then, is that the courts appear to be ready, in some circumstances, to recognise the unjustness of a system depending entirely upon registration. They are prepared to resort to the old doctrine of notice as offering a fair and just solution to the problem of whether a purchaser should be bound or not by an interest in the land. Despite Lord Wilberforce's words in the quotation from *Boland*, notice was never entirely expunged from the (then) new system of conveyancing under the Land Registration Act 1925, and it still lurks in the muddy depths of our land law as a life-raft and saving for equitable rights in land.

QUESTION 3

Consider the effect of the following dispositions made in 1997:

(a) 'The Red House to Angela, founder of Ambridge Harassed Mothers Ltd in fee simple until such time, not exceeding 80 years, as it is no longer used as a day nursery for children under five years old resident in Ambridge.'

How (if at all) would your answer differ if the disposition had been to Ambridge Harassed Mothers Ltd instead of to Angela?

(b) 'The Golden Mansion to my son James in fee simple, but if he shall marry a person of the Fireworshippers' Faith, then to my daughter Rachel.'

Commentary

This question arises from the definition of a fee simple absolute in possession in the Law of Property Act 1925, s. 1(1), which states that such an estate is one of the two estates 'capable of subsisting or of being conveyed or created at law' after 1925. This meant that, after the Act came into force on 1 January 1926, conditional and determinable fees simple were necessarily only equitable with some unsatisfactory consequences which the Law of Property (Amendment) Act 1926 sought to correct.

This is an area which your lecturer may or may not consider important. You should therefore be guided by your lecture notes and tutorials as to how large it should feature in your studies.

Suggested Answer

(a) The disposition to Angela creates a determinable fee simple as there is an ultimate time specified for the existence of the estate. This prevents it from being a fee simple 'absolute', and so it is not capable of being a legal estate within the Law of Property Act 1925, s. 1(1). It must therefore take effect in equity behind a trust of land.

The limitation was one of those included in the Settled Land Act 1925, s. 1(1)(ii)(c), as a settlement. No new settlements under the Act can be located after 1996 however. It will therefore take under a trust of land of which the grantor (or his personal representatives if the disposition is contained in a will) will be the trustees.

At common law, the reversionary interest is vested from the date the disposition is made, and is not therefore subject to the rule against remoteness of vesting. Statute changes this however: the reversionary interest under a determinable fee is made subject to the rule against perpetuities because the prior interest is treated, for the purposes of the rule, as subject to a condition subsequent (Perpetuities and Accumulations Act 1964, s. 12(1)(a)). A perpetuity period not exceeding 80 years may be specified by the instrument creating the interest (s. 1(1)).

If a disposition may vest (if at all) outside the perpetuity period, and so would be void at common law, it is possible, under the Perpetuities and Accumulations Act 1964, s. 3, to wait and see if the interest does in fact vest within the perpetuity period. For this purpose, the perpetuity period will be the statutory life or lives in being plus 21 years, or in the absence of statutory lives, 21 years (s. 3(4)). Whereas under the common law rule in *Cadell* v *Palmer* (1833) 1 Cl & Fin 372, an interest was void *ab initio* if it was not bound to vest within the period, it is now treated as valid until such time as it becomes apparent that it cannot vest within the time.

Since the settlor has expressly provided that the event bringing about the limitation on the fee given to the Ambridge Borough Council must occur within a period of 80 years, the disposition is valid for the purposes of perpetuity at common law, as modified by the Perpetuities and Accumulations Act 1964, s. 1(1). There is, therefore, no need to wait and see. If the house ceases to be used as a day nursery within 80 years, the limitation will take effect: in this event, the fee will determine automatically, and will revert to the donor or to the donor's heirs. If, however, the limitation does not operate within the 80 years, the fee will become absolute so that the legal estate will then vest indefeasibly in Angela.

If the disposition had been to Ambridge Harassed Mothers Ltd, the position would be the same. Although the Law of Property Act 1925, s. 7(2), provides that a fee vested in a corporation may be regarded as a fee simple absolute and therefore a legal estate, this is the case only if it is liable to determine by reason of the dissolution of the corporation. This fee would still be liable to determine for other reasons.

(**b**)   The limitation in this disposition is a fee simple subject to a condition subsequent. The full fee simple has been granted, but it is liable to be prematurely cut short on the occurrence of a specified event.

It differs from a determinable fee only in its terminology, a difference which was said by Pennycuick V-C in *Re Sharp's Settlement Trusts* [1973] Ch 331 at p. 340 to be 'an extremely artificial distinction' and, referring to a dictum of Porter MR in an Irish case (*Re King's Trusts* (1892) 29 LR IR 401 at p. 410) 'little short of disgraceful to our jurisprudence'.

A conditional fee simple, which is subject to a right of re-entry, is again not an absolute one, and so necessarily became equitable after 1925. At that time, there were many freehold properties, in certain areas of the country, subject to a rentcharge (an annual charge on freehold property). The owner of the rentcharge would have a right of re-entry against the fee simple owner if the rentcharge was not paid, so that such fees simple were effectively conditional fees. The effect of the Law of Property Act 1925, s. 1(1), was to render all such fees simple equitable on 1 January 1926 when the legislation came into force, and so invoke the cumbersome machinery of the Settled Land Act 1925.

To deal with this problem, the Law of Property (Amendment) Act 1926 amended the Law of Property Act 1925, s. 7(1), by providing that 'a fee simple subject to a legal or equitable right of entry or re-entry is for the purposes of this Act a fee simple absolute'. Although the intention of the amendment was to deal primarily with the unhappy situation in which the owners of land subject to a rentcharge found themselves, the wording of the amendment is not confined to rights of re-entry on non-payment of a rentcharge, but extends to all fees simple subject to a right of re-entry. The amendment therefore appears to turn all fees simple which are subject to a condition subsequent into fees simple absolute, and thus legal estates within the Law of Property Act 1925, s. 1(1). James will therefore have a legal fee simple absolute in possession.

The determining event, if it occurs at all, must occur during James' lifetime, and so the disposition does not infringe the rule against perpetuities to which conditional fees are subject.

Although a total restraint against marriage would be a void condition as against public policy, a partial restraint such as this is acceptable and valid.

QUESTION 4

Peter is considering purchasing a freehold house from Vincent. The title is unregistered and Peter has discovered the following matters:

(a)   Two sets of restrictive covenants, one made in 1922 and one made in 1945.

(b)   The next door neighbour uses a track across the bottom of the garden as access to his garage, which he cannot reach in any other way. Vincent has told Peter that this is an informal arrangement which he made with the neighbour some years ago, before the garage was built.

(c)   Although Vincent appears to be living alone in the property, there is a Class F land charge registered against his name at the Land Charges Registry.

Advise Peter how these matters may affect his title to the property.

How would your answer differ if the title to the house were registered?

Commentary

This is a very common type of examination question. Even if the subject-matter is not addressed as directly as it is here, it may feature in a more disguised form in other questions!

You need to consider the nature of the interests created (unless, as with the restrictive covenants, you have actually been told about them) and then to decide whether or not they will bind a purchaser of the legal estate in the land.

It is usual to ask the question for both unregistered and registered titles, and the answers may be different! For an amusing and lightly written comparison of the binding effect of certain interests in the two systems, see the article by J. G. Ridall 'Unwin Avenue and Reginald Road' (1977) *Conv* 405.

Suggested Answer

(a)   Restrictive covenants entered into before 1926 are not registrable under the Land Charges Act 1972 (formerly the Land Charges Act 1925). Their binding validity against a purchaser of the land therefore depends upon the doctrine of notice. If Peter were a *bona fide* purchaser for value of the land without notice of the covenants, he would take free from them. His investigation of the title appears to have revealed the covenants however, so that he will take subject to them as he has actual notice of them.

The 1945 restrictive covenants were registrable under the Land Charges Act 1925 (now the Land Charges Act 1972), and if registered, will be binding on Peter. They will be registered against the name of the estate owner in 1945, which Peter is unlikely to have on his title as the period of title deduced to a purchaser was reduced to 15 years, starting with a good root, by the Law of Property Act 1969. However, there may well be an old search with the deeds showing the covenants. But if Peter enters into the contract without *actual* knowledge of the covenants, the Law of Property Act 1969, s. 24, provides that he may avoid the contract.

If the title to the land were registered, the restrictive covenants would be registered in the charges register as minor interests. They are binding if so registered, but not binding if not registered. In practice, many old pre-1926 restrictive covenants are registered in the charges register of a registered title. They are evident from the title as each subsequent conveyance of the land is made expressly subject to them.

(b)   The neighbour is enjoying a right of access which is similar to an easement, and Peter needs to investigate this situation.

If the neighbour has used the track for 20 years, then he may have a *prima facie* right to a claim for an easement under the Prescription Act 1832, or possibly under the doctrine of lost modern grant. The right may be negatived (in either case) by permission having been granted to him, as one of the essentials of all forms of prescription is that the user upon which they are based must be as of right. It is possible that the 'informal arrangement' may amount to an oral permission at the start of the 20-year period and it may be sufficient to defeat it if it refers to the continued user throughout the period. If the neighbour has acquired an easement by prescription, then it will be a legal one, which will be binding upon Peter.

If the right of access was informally granted before the garage was built, then it may be possible for the neighbour to claim a right of access supported by estoppel. In *E.R. Ives Investment Ltd* v *High* [1967] 2 QB 379, the facts were similar to this and a neighbour, relying upon an agreement for access, built a garage. The successor in title to the person who had agreed to the access was estopped from denying the right. There were, however, other considerations, as the doctrine of *Halsall* v *Brizell* [1957] Ch 169, also applied. Nevertheless, the court also recognised a right of access supported by an estoppel in *Crabb* v *Arun District Council* [1976] Ch 179.

If the neighbour is therefore able to say that he built the garage in reliance upon the agreement for access, and so acted to his detriment, then it may well be binding on Vincent. As an unregistrable equitable interest, it would be binding upon Peter unless he was a *bona fide* purchaser for value without notice of it. As he clearly has notice, he would not appear to fall into that category.

In registered title, a legal easement acquired by prescription is an overriding interest under the Land Registration Act, s. 70(1)(a), which specifically refers to 'rights of way'.

The binding effect of an equitable easement in registered title is less clear. In *Celsteel Ltd* v *Alton House Holdings Ltd* [1985] 1 WLR 204, Scott J at first instance noted that estoppel interests had been found by Lord Denning MR in *E.R. Ives Investment Ltd* not to be registrable under the Land Charges Act 1925. He felt however that the reference to 'equitable easements' in the Land Registration Act 1925, s. 70(1)(a), should not be so restrictively construed. By reference to the Land Registration Rules 1925, r. 258, he found that equitable easements could be capable of being overriding interests under the Land Registration Act 1925. If this is correct, then presumably the equitable easement created by estoppel in this case might also be an overriding interest.

(c)   A Class F land charge indicates that Vincent's wife is claiming a right of occupation of the matrimonial home under the Matrimonial Homes Act 1983. It is irrelevant that she has actually left the home. It was held in *Watts* v *Waller* [1973] QB 153 that a wife not in occupation of the matrimonial home still had a conditional right of occupation capable of registration as a land charge under the Matrimonial Homes Act 1967, s. 2(6), the forerunner of the 1983 Act. Peter will have to insist that this charge is cleared off the title before he completes the purchase of the property.

As he is aware of the existence of a wife, he should also make enquiries as to whether she has any beneficial interest in the matrimonial home. This is sufficiently usual nowadays for a purchaser to enquire if put on notice that there is a wife (*Kingsnorth Finance Co.* v *Tizard* [1986] 1 WLR 783). So although the Class F land charge will not protect any such beneficial interest and only protects a wife's right of occupation, it might well be held to give a purchaser notice that there is a wife who might have a beneficial interest.

In registered title, the statutory right of occupation of a spouse under the Matrimonial Homes Act 1983 is registrable as a minor interest, and would be binding on Peter if so registered. Section 2(8) of the Act provides that it will not become an overriding interest, even if the wife were in actual occupation within the meaning of the Land Registration Act 1925, s. 70(1)(g). Any beneficial interest, which would be a minor interest, would be binding on Peter if protected by a restriction on the register. It could not be an overriding interest under s. 70(1)(g) as the wife is not in actual occupation.

QUESTION 5

Petra has entered into a contract to purchase the freehold title in a bungalow, which was registered in 1960. The present registered proprietor, Vera, has told Petra that:

(a)   in 1940 Vera's predecessor in title granted to a neighbour, Nell, a right of way across the back garden; and

(b)   in 1980 Vera made a declaration of trust in relation to the property in favour of her son, Sid, on the occasion of his 21st birthday; and

(c)   in 1990 Vera leased a garage at the side of the bungalow to her friend, Freda.

Advise Petra whether she will take the land free from or subject to the interests of Nell, Sid, and Freda.

What difference would it make to your answer if the land were unregistered?

Commentary

There are really six parts to this question because each part has to be subdivided into registered and unregistered land. Keep the two apart at all costs. If you can keep registered conveyancing in a watertight compartment separate from unregistered conveyancing, then you should be able to keep your head while all around are losing theirs.

Note that in part **(b)** there is a perhaps unexpected point about the doctrine of overreaching. Very often exam questions deal with the classic overreaching situation demonstrated in *Williams & Glyn's Bank Ltd* v *Boland* [1981] AC 487. In that case, overreaching was not available because the preconditions of the Law of Property Act 1925, s. 2(1), were not satisfied — there was only one trustee. However, in this problem, the reason overreaching does not work is because it is not a situation to which the doctrine is applicable in the first place. Under the section (as amended by TLATA 1996), the doctrine applies where a trust of land, arises with two trustees. Here, a bare trust arises with only one trustee. It would be different if the beneficiary were a child. There is a Law Commission Report on this which recommends that the concept of overreaching should be extended to conveyances by bare trustees ('Report on Overreaching: Beneficiaries in Occupation' (Law Com. No. 158 (1989)) paras 2.17, 3.10, 4.27).

Suggested Answer

(a) *Registered land*

Nell has a right of way across Vera's garden. To be a legal easement this must comply with the definition contained in the Law of Property Act 1925, s. 1(2). Thus, it must be for a period equivalent to a fee simple or a term of years. The use of the word 'granted' implies that it was created with all the due formalities required by the Law of Property Act, s. 52. If it was created by deed, then it will be binding as a legal interest. If it was not created by deed then it may be possible to argue that provided the right of way has been exercised openly and without permission or the use of force and has been used without interruption since 1940, a legal easement has been created by prescription.

A legal easement will often be protected by entry in the property register in registered land. Even if it is not entered on the register it will be protected as an overriding interest under the Land Registration Act 1925, s. 70(1)(a). A purchaser of registered land takes the land subject to everything on the register together with overriding interests.

If the easement is not legal, it may still be enforceable in equity. It will be necessary to show that there is an enforceable contract in respect of which equity would grant specific performance. Since such a contract would have been entered into in 1940, it will be necessary to show that it complied with the rules in the Law of Property Act 1925, s. 40 (now repealed and replaced by the Law of Property (Miscellaneous Provisions) Act 1989, s. 2). This requires that there must be some written evidence of the contract signed by the party to be charged or an agent. If there is no such written evidence then it may be possible to rely on the equitable doctrine of part performance (Law of Property Act 1925, s. 40(2)). Thus if there is an oral agreement between Vera's predecessor in title and Nell as to the right of way and Nell has exercised the right in reliance on the agreement to the knowledge of the other party, this may be enforceable in equity (*Morritt* v *Wonham* (1994) NPC 2).

As an equitable easement, it can be protected in registered land either as a minor or an overriding interest. In *Celsteel Ltd* v *Alton House Holdings Ltd* [1985] 1 WLR 204, it was held that the intention of the Land Registration Act 1925 was that equitable interests should be protected either on the register or as overriding interests. Since an equitable interest was capable of being covered by the Land Registration Rules 1925, r. 258, as a right enjoyed with the land, it was, therefore, an overriding interest and, if not protected on the register as a minor interest, still bound the purchaser.

Alternatively, if Nell can be regarded as being 'in actual occupation' of the land, then it could be protected as an overriding interest under the Land Registration Act 1925, s. 70(1)(g). This seems somewhat unlikely however (see Question 4, **Chapter 12**).

Unregistered land

If the title to the bungalow is unregistered, then if the easement is legal, it binds Petra since legal interests bind the whole world. The issue as to whether it is legal or equitable depend on the same arguments as in the first part of the answer.

If the right of way is equitable, then, as it was created after 1925, it must be registered as a Class D(iii) land charge under the Land Charges Act 1972, s. 2(5). If it is not registered as such it is unenforceable against Petra as the *bona fide* purchaser for value of a legal estate (*Midland Bank Trust Co.* v *Green* [1981] AC 513). There is no equivalent category in unregistered land to the overriding interest, so, if the equitable interests is not registered it is unenforceable by Nell, regardless of the state of knowledge of the purchaser, Petra.

(b) The declaration of trust means that Vera is the estate owner as trustee and Sid is the equitable owner. Vera is a bare trustee since she has no active duties to perform as trustee and Sid is entitled to call for the legal estate to be transferred to him (*Saunders* v *Vautier* (1841) Cr & Ph 240). A purchaser can take free of an equitable interest where the doctrine of overreaching applies under the Law of Property Act 1925, s. 2(1). Section 2(1) applies to trusts of land, which now expressly includes bare trusts (TLATA 1996, s. 1(2)(a)). It does not, however, apply unless a purchaser gets a receipt for the purchase moneys from two trustees, so Petra cannot rely on the doctrine of overreaching (*Hodgson* v *Marks* [1971] Ch 892). This conclusion prevails whether the title is registered or unregistered.

Registered land

If the title were registered, Sid's interest would be a minor interest and as such could be noted on the register. If not so noted, then, if he is in actual occupation of the bungalow, his interest would constitute an overriding interest (*Williams & Glyn's Bank Ltd* v *Boland* [1981] AC 487). If an enquiry is made of Sid, and he does not reveal his interest, then he will not be able to rely on the protection of the overriding interest. The enquiry would have to be directed to him, not Vera. If he is not in actual occupation of the bungalow and his interest is not protected as a minor interest, then Petra is not bound by it.

Unregistered land

In unregistered land, Sid's interest would constitute a family equitable interest of the type which is not registrable and binds a purchaser of the legal estate with notice. Notice can be actual, imputed or constructive. In *Kingsnorth Finance Co.* v *Tizard* [1986] 2 All ER 54 the wife kept her possessions at the property and returned to look after the children and prepare herself for work. It was held that the surveyor who inspected the property had constructive notice of her presence which was imputed to the mortgagee. Thus Petra would be bound by Sid's interest where she has notice.

(c) *Registered land*

The lease, if a legal lease for more than 21 years, is a substantive interest which is capable of registration. Where the lease is for a period not exceeding 21 years it will be an overriding interest under the Land Registration Act 1925, s. 70(1)(k). It has been held that the interpretation of the words, 'leases granted ...', in this subsection excludes equitable leases (*City Permanent Building*

Society v *Miller* [1952] Ch 853). However, if Freda could be said to be in actual occupation of the garage, then it may be possible for her to bring her lease within the protection of the Law of Property Act, s. 70(1)(g). It has been held that the intermittent use of a garage can amount to actual occupation (*Kling* v *Keston Properties Ltd* (1983) 49 P & CR 212. Since the lease relates to a garage which can clearly be subject to physical occupation, it would seem that Freda's lease would be protected even where it is equitable as an overriding interest under s. 70(1)(g).

Unregistered land

Again, if the lease is legal, it will bind the whole world. To be legal, the lease must be for a term certain and must be created by deed in accordance with the Law of Property Act 1925, s. 52, except where s. 54(2) applies. This subsection provides that leases taking effect in possession for a term not exceeding three years at the best rent which can reasonably be obtained without taking a fine can be created by parol.

If the lease is equitable, then, provided a valid contract complying with the requirements of the Law of Property (Miscellaneous Provisions) Act 1989, s. 2 has been entered into, it is registrable as an estate contract under Class C(iv) of the Land Charges Act 1972, s. 2(4). For the same reasons that prevailed in respect of an equitable easement, if it is not registered, it is unenforceable against Petra.

QUESTION 6

Alan is the registered proprietor of a row of three cottages — Nos. 2, 4 and 6 Cowslip Lane. His friend, Betty, telephones him to ask if she can rent No. 2 while she is looking for somewhere to buy. Alan agrees and she moves in and starts paying rent on a monthly basis from 1 January.

Alan decides to put No. 4 on the market and he receives two offers from Carl and Damien. Carl makes the higher offer but wishes to defer completion of the contract until he returns from a six-month contract abroad. Carl suggests to Alan's estate agent that the property should not be sold to Damien, that Carl will better any offer from Damien by £5,000 and will exchange contracts within a month, but with completion to be deferred until his (Carl's) return from abroad. The estate agent telephones Alan, who agrees to this proposal. The next day, however, Alan receives a draft contract from Damien and Alan and Damien exchange contracts by the end of that week.

Alan is short of money and he approaches his bank for a loan. The bank agrees to lend him £10,000 but suggests that it should hold the deeds of No. 6 (which are held in a safety deposit box at the bank) as security for the loan. Alan agrees.

Alan has now decided to emigrate and he agrees to sell Nos. 2 and 6 to Edith. Edith moves into No. 2, but is surprised when Betty, who has been away on holiday, lets herself into the cottage. Edith then receives a letter from the bank threatening to foreclose on the mortgage on No. 6. Damien receives a letter from Carl, saying that he has an agreement with Alan which takes precedence over Damien's agreement.

Advise Edith and Damien whether Betty, the bank and Carl have contracts which are enforceable against them.

Commentary

This question concerns the judicial interpretation of the Law of Property (Miscellaneous Provisions) Act 1989, s. 2. In particular, it deals with the thorny issue of whether loans secured by the deposit of title deeds can now amount to equitable charges and the status of so-called lock-out agreements or collateral contracts. The case law in these areas is fairly lively and likely to remain dynamic for some time, so last minute updating prior to the examination could pay dividends. There are some casenotes in the *Conveyancer* covering these issues, for example, *Pitt* v *PHH Management*, Thompson, [1994] *Conv* 58 and *Record* v *Bell*, Harwood, [1991] *Conv* 471. By comparison, the part of the question dealing with leases is straightforward. As usual, the advice is to separate out the issues and deal with each in turn. If the precedents are conflicting, say so, but grasp the nettle and suggest what, in your view, is the likely outcome.

Suggested Answer

There are three issues to be addressed in this problem:

(a) whether Edith is bound by the agreement between Alan and Betty;

(b) whether Edith is bound by the agreement between Alan and the bank;

(c) the effect of the agreement between Alan and Carl on Damien.

(a) Betty

Betty is occupying No. 2 and is paying rent. Under the Law of Property (Miscellaneous Provisions) Act 1989, s. 2 a contract in writing is required for the sale or other disposition of an interest in land. There is no suggestion of writing in Betty's case; the agreement appears to have been concluded over the telephone. However, there is an exception in s. 2(5) in respect of contracts to grant a lease for a term not exceeding three years to which the Law of Property Act 1925, s. 54(2) applies. Section 54(2) applies to leases taking effect in possession for a term not exceeding three years at the best rent which can be reasonably obtained without taking a fine. If the lease is a monthly periodic tenancy (which from the agreement it would appear to be), then it falls within s. 54(2) and, therefore, within the exception to s. 2. This means that there would be a valid contract, and, once Betty has taken possession, a legal lease in existence.

(b) The bank

The bank is seeking to foreclose the mortgage. It is necessary to decide whether there is a contract for a mortgage. It has long been the rule that the deposit of title deeds as security for a loan is sufficient to create an equitable charge on the land to which the deeds relate. The principle was set out in *Thames Guaranty Ltd* v *Campbell* [1985] 1 QB 210 by the Court of Appeal where it was made clear that it is not the mere deposit which creates the charge; it is necessary to show that the deeds were deposited for the purpose of securing the loan. This is the first step that must be established and, although Alan had initially placed the deeds with the bank for safekeeping, it would seem that there was a new agreement between Alan and the bank which changed the reason for their retention by the bank.

The next issue relates to the question of whether the principle that the deposit of title deeds creates an equitable charge, first established in *Russell* v *Russell* (1783) Bro Ch 269, has survived the Law of Property (Miscellaneous Provisions) Act 1989, s. 2, which requires a written contract. One argument which has been used to justify this principle has been that it was an application of the equitable doctrine of part performance. This equitable doctrine was expressly preserved by the Law of Property Act 1925, s. 40(2), which was repealed by the 1989 Act. An alternative argument is that the principle is effective in creating an equitable charge independently of contract, a *sui generis* exception. This interpretation creates difficulties, in that it is arguable that it falls under the Law of Property Act, s. 53(1)(c) which requires the disposition of an equitable interest to be made by signed writing. A deposit on its own would not suffice to satisfy s. 53(1)(c). Nor is it likely that an implied trust arises as a consequence of the deposit which might have been saved by the Law of Property Act 1925, s. 53(2), which exempts such trusts from the operation of s. 53(1)(c). According to the Court of Appeal decision in *United Bank of Kuwait plc* v *Sahib* [1996] 3 WLR 372, the effect of s. 2 has been to render the deposit of title deeds as security for a loan ineffective in creating an equitable charge. This judgment is contrary to the accepted view expressed by academic writers. For instance, in *Emmet on Title* it is considered that the principle in *Russell* v *Russell* operates independently of contract in creating an equitable charge. However, the advice is also given that it would be unwise for lenders to continue to use this method as has been shown by the decision in *United Bank of Kuwait plc* v *Sahib*.

On the authority of this case, therefore, the loan by the bank has been ineffective in securing an equitable charge over No. 6 and Edith need not be concerned about the letter from the bank, which would need to pursue any personal remedies it may have against Alan.

(c)   Carl

The validity of Carl's agreement with Alan depends on whether it may be said to amount to a contract to exchange contracts or a 'lock-out' agreement. If it can be construed so as to impose an obligation on Alan to exchange contracts with Carl, then it needs to be in writing in accordance with the requirements of the Law of Property (Miscellaneous Provisions) Act 1989, s. 2. If it is a negative agreement simply preventing Alan from negotiating with anyone else, then it does not require formality.

In *Walford* v *Miles* [1992] 2 WLR 174, there was an agreement that, in consideration for the plaintiffs' agreeing not to withdraw from negotiations, the plaintiffs would terminate negotiations with any third party. This was held to be simply an agreement to negotiate and was not actionable (other than as a misrepresentation). Other types of agreement occurring at the point of exchange of contracts are sometimes classifiable as collateral contracts. In *Record* v *Bell* [1991] 1 WLR 853, an oral warranty as to the state of the title was given as an inducement to exchange contracts. Again, it was held that such a warranty was outside the requirements of s. 2. Similarly, in *Pitt* v *PHH Asset Management Ltd* [1994] 1 WLR 327, an agreement whereby the vendor's agent agreed not to consider any further offers for the property on the basis that the plaintiff would exchange contracts within two weeks of the receipt of the draft contract, constituted a lock-out agreement outside the ambit of s. 2. However, in *Dallia* v *Four Millbank Nominees* [1978] Ch 231, an agreement which required the vendor to exchange contracts if the purchaser attended a meeting with a draft contract and a banker's draft was held unenforceable as it did not comply with the Law of Property Act 1925, s. 40.

The agreement between Carl and Alan that Alan will not sell to Damien amounts to a lock-out agreement in that it prevents any further negotiations with Damien. In that respect, it is outside the ambit of s. 2 (*Pitt* v *PHH Management*). However, the agreement also commits Carl to exchanging contracts within a month. It is arguable that such an agreement concerns an interest in land and requires formalities for it to be valid (*Dallia* v *Four Millbank Nominees*). But, it may instead fall into the category of collateral contracts as in *Record* v *Bell*. Clearly, it is difficult to reconcile the authorities. However, on the basis of *Pitt* v *PHH Management*, where the agreement did include an obligation to exchange within a month, and *Record* v *Bell*, where the warranty related to the title of the property, it would seem more likely that the courts would construe Carl's agreement not to sell to Damien as not subject to the requirements of s. 2. In that event, the agreement not to sell to Damien would be enforceable as a separate agreement between Carl and Alan.

If, therefore, pursuant to his contract with Damien, Alan conveys No. 4 to Damien, Alan will be liable in damages to Carl for breach of the lock-out agreement. If, on the other hand, Alan were to convey No. 4 to Carl (with whom he has no valid contract of sale), he would be liable in damages to Damien for breach of contract; but Damien's contract will be binding upon Carl only if Damien had protected it by registration as a minor interest.

6 Acquisition of Title on Death

INTRODUCTION

Some land law courses consider the three basic ways in which an estate in land can be acquired: by a disposition *inter vivos*, by adverse possession, and by will. The last method will usually involve a study of the formal requirements for a valid will — a topic sometimes studied separately in a course on succession.

If your land law or property course does involve a study of the formal requirements for wills, do not imagine that every question that states that someone has made a will demands that you explain what the formal requirements are. Where a will is mentioned in a question, you are entitled to assume, in the absence of any specified indications to the contrary, that it was validly made, and you should not even mention the requirements of the Wills Act 1837 (as amended). This is the case, for instance, with all the questions which mention wills in other chapters of this book: as for instance, those in **Chapter 15 (Perpetuities and Accumulations)**.

A discussion of the formal requirements for a will is, however, needed if the question itself suggests that such requirements might not have been complied with — as is evidently the case with both the questions in this chapter.

QUESTION 1

In 1997, Croesus decided to make a codicil to his will. He drew a box at the top of a sheet of paper and made an inked impression of his right thumb inside it. He then wrote underneath that he gave Goldacre, of which he was the fee simple owner, to Delilah and Edwina jointly. Later the same day, he asked Delilah, together with Ajax and Sampson, to act as witnesses. Croesus showed them his right thumb and placed it over the inky print of it made earlier. Ajax then left the room to fetch more wine. During his absence, Delilah and Sampson (in the presence of Croesus) signed their names as witnesses at the bottom of the sheet.

Croesus's mobile telephone then rang, summoning him to an urgent meeting. Making his apologies, he immediately went to his car. The chauffeur accidentally put the engine into reverse, so that the car drew up opposite the window of the room to which Ajax had just returned, and in which, at that moment, Ajax began to sign as a witness. Ajax managed to write only the first three letters of his name, however, before suffering an asthmatic attack. He did not complete his signature.

Six months later, Sampson married Edwina. Two months after the wedding, Croesus died. The validity of 1997 document as a codicil and of the devise of Goldacre are now being challenged by Maud, who is the sole beneficiary of Croesus's entire estate under a will made in 1970.

Advise Delilah.

Commentary

This is a typical sort of examination question on the formal requirements for a will. As in other areas, you should keep a look out for important recent cases, as examination questions may well be drafted so as to demand a knowledge of them.

Suggested Answer

Delilah and Edwina will be entitled to Goldacre only if the codicil was validly executed and if the witnessing of the codicil does not cause either of them to forfeit the devise.

A will (including a codicil) must (*inter alia*) be 'signed by the testator' (Wills Act 1837, s. 9(a)). The ink print of an illiterate testator is a valid signature for this purpose (*Re Finn* (1935) 105 LJP 36). Presumably the same applies to a testator who is physically incapable of holding a pen; but it is not clear whether the ink print of a literate and physically capable testator would also be valid. We need to know whether Croesus is literate and physically capable of signing. In any event, assuming that the print comprises a signature, it does not matter that it appears at the top of the document, as the necessity for the signature to be at the foot or end was abolished for wills made after 1982 (Administration of Justice Act 1982, ss. 17, 73(6)). It is now enough that the testator 'intended by his signature to give effect to the will' (Wills Act 1837, s. 9(b)). In *Re Hornby* [1946] P 171, the placing of the signature in a box near the end of the document met the requirements of the Wills Act 1837, s. 9, in its original form, and would now probably meet the current requirements of the substituted section.

The additional problem here, however, is that, unlike the testator in *Re Hornby*, Croesus made his mark before, rather than after, the writing of the dispositive words. In *Wood v Smith* [1992] 2 All ER 556, the Court of Appeal held that, provided the document was signed and executed on one occasion, the testator's signature which preceded in time the writing of the dispositive words could still 'give effect to' them. The Court of Appeal left open the question of whether the same result would ensue if the events occurred on different occasions; but Scott LJ doubted whether it would. More evidence is needed in the problem as to the timing of the events, in order to ascertain whether they can be considered to have occurred on a single occasion.

Assuming that they did, the signature must still be 'made or acknowledged in the presence of two or more witnesses present at the same time' (Wills Act 1837, s. 9(c)). Although the drawing of a dry pen over a previously written signature is not, for this purpose, a signing (*Re Maddock* (1847) LR 3 P&D 169), it may be effective as an acknowledgement (see *Mellows: The Law of Succession*, 5th edn, London: Butterworths, 1993, para. 6.15). Croesus's actions in relation to the thumb-print may similarly comprise an acknowledgement, which was evidently properly witnessed, as Delilah, Ajax and Sampson were present at the same time.

A further requirement is that each witness must either attest and sign the will, or acknowledge his signature (which was not possible in the case of the pre-1983 requirements: *Re Colling* [1972] 3 All ER 729), in each case in the presence of the testator (Wills Act 1837, s. 9(d)). This requirement is clearly met in the case of Delilah and Sampson; and, as only two witnesses are needed, the codicil will not be void on this ground. A witness's attestation and signature can also be considered to be made 'in the presence of' the testator, even if the testator has left the room, provided he could have seen the witness sign had he chosen to look (*Casson* v *Dade* (1781) 1 Bro CC 99). A clear line of sight leads to a presumption that the attestation was good (*Winchilsea* v *Wauchope* (1827) 3 Russ 441). If, therefore, like the testatrix who retired to her carriage in *Casson* v *Dade*, Croesus could have seen Ajax signing had he looked, Ajax's signature would have been made in the presence of Croesus as the section requires.

Did Ajax, however, sign the will? In *Re Chalcraft* [1948] P 222, a testatrix close to death managed to complete only the first part of her signature. This was held to be a valid signature as she did all that she could. By analogy, this principle might be extended to signatures by witnesses, in which case Ajax might also be treated as having done enough.

Assuming that the codicil is valid, Delilah has the problem that the Wills Act 1837, s. 15, provides that a gift to a witness is void. Since Delilah, a beneficiary under the codicil, also witnessed the codicil, this section would result in her forfeiting the devise. The Wills Act 1968, s. 1, however, provides that the witnessing of a beneficiary under the will is disregarded if the will is duly executed 'without his attestation and without that of any other such person'. Sampson might appear to be another 'such person', because he married another beneficiary, Edwina, before Croesus died. This is not, however, the case, because it has been held that the Wills Act 1837, s. 15, does not invalidate a gift to a witness's spouse if the marriage took place only after the will was executed (*Thorpe* v *Beswick* (1881) 6 QBD 311).

If Ajax's signature was not valid, s. 15 will bite and Delilah will forfeit her share. The issue is then whether Edwina would take Goldacre absolutely, or whether s. 15 would sever the devise by operation of law, so that Edwina takes only a half share in Goldacre, the other half passing to Maud under the will of 1970. There is no case law on this; but the former result appears to be more in line with the intended effect of the section and the nature of a joint tenancy.

If, however, Ajax's signature is valid, Delilah does not forfeit her share as joint tenant. On this basis, assuming that the codicil is itself valid, the devise of Goldacre will be excepted from the gift to Maud under the will made in 1970 (which is, to this extent, revoked), and Goldacre will pass instead to Delilah and Edwina as joint tenants.

QUESTION 2

(a)   Potts, a 19-year-old cook in the British army, was sent to the Republic of Rubovia in 1997 as part of the British contingent of a peace-keeping force. The aeroplane that took him to Rubovia left from a military air-base in the south of England. Just before boarding the plane, Potts told his friend and fellow-cook, Pans, 'If anything happens to me, everything goes to Daisy'. Daisy was Potts' sister. Shortly after his arrival in Rubovia, Potts told Pans, 'I've been thinking. If I don't make it, I want Sally to have the lot'. Sally was Potts' girlfriend. A few months ago, Potts completed his period of service in Rubovia and returned to England. While on a few weeks' home leave, he accidentally strayed over the cliffs at his home near Hastings, and was killed.

Advise Potts' elderly widowed mother, who would be entitled to his estate (which includes the fee simple of Heavyacre) under the intestacy rules.

(b)   By his will, Quark gave the lease of a third floor flat in Boson Villas, Hammersmith, to Higgs (who was one year his junior), and the residue of his estate to Charm. Last year, the flat was completely destroyed in a massive gas explosion. Quark and Higgs, who were in the flat at the time, were both killed instantly. At the time, the lease on the flat had two years to run, and there is no possibility of Boson Villas being rebuilt before its expiration. Quark had taken out insurance on the flat with the Strange Insurance Co. Ltd, and under the policy, the sum of £15,000 has become payable to Quark's executors.

Advise Quark's executors whether they should pay this money to the executors of Higgs's estate, or whether they should hold it for Charm as part of Quark's residuary estate.

Commentary

Part (a) is a fairly standard type of problem on privileged wills. Part (b) is different: it is a somewhat eclectic fantasy, involving the doctrines of lapse and ademption mixed up with the termination of a lease by analogy with *National Carriers Ltd* v *Panalpina (Northern) Ltd* [1981] AC 675. The examiner probably had great fun setting part (b), and is more likely than not to be well disposed to anyone who has a reasonable stab at it.

Suggested Answer

(a)   Potts' mother will be entitled to his estate only if Potts died intestate. At first sight this may appear to be the case, since he died without having made a will complying with the formalities of the Wills Act 1837, s. 9. The section does not, however, apply if it can be established that Potts was entitled to make, and did make, a privileged will that remained unrevoked at his death.

Under the Wills Act 1837, s. 11, 'any soldier being in actual military service' may dispose of his personal estate as he may have done before the passing of that Act. This means that even a nuncupative (i.e., oral) will made by such a person is valid. Under the Wills (Soldiers and Sailors) Act 1918, s. 3, this privilege was extended to wills of realty. Thus, Heavyacre is also capable of being the subject of a gift under a privileged will.

A member of the armed forces (which Potts would appear to be) ranks as a soldier even if he is allocated a non-combative role, such as that of a doctor or a chaplain (*Re Wingham* [1949] P 187) or (as in the problem) that of a cook. If, however, Potts was a civilian employee, the position is less clear. In *Re White's Application* [1975] 2 NSWLR 125, an Australian court held that a British subject employed by the United States Army as a civilian engineer was doing the job of a soldier and was therefore entitled to the privilege. It remains to be seen if an English court would adopt a similarly wide interpretation.

Assuming Potts was a soldier, the next issue is whether he was 'in actual military service'. It is doubtful whether a soldier about to be sent as part of a peace-keeping force merely to a disturbed area can be said to be in actual military service (*Re Wingham*, Denning LJ). Potts might nevertheless have been in actual military service even if Britain was not at war with Rubovia. Thus in *Re Jones* [1981] 1 All ER 1, a corporal in the Parachute Regiment was shot whilst on patrol. It was held that, in aiding a civil power to put down an insurrection, he was in actual military service, and so entitled to make a privileged will. If a war was raging between various factions in Rubovia at the time when Potts was sent there, he is also likely to be held to have been in actual military service. Moreover it is not necessary for Potts to be in the war zone at the time of making the privileged will. Thus in *Re Stable* [1919] P 7, the privilege applied to a nuncupative will made in England by a soldier under orders to go to the front.

Potts was therefore capable of making a privileged will just before boarding the aeroplane: but did he in fact do so? It is not necessary that the deceased should be aware that he is making his will; it is enough if he intends that his estate should be disposed of in accordance with his statement (*Re Stable*). It is not sufficient, however, if the words are a mere statement of how the deceased believes his property will devolve in the absence of a will (*Re Knibbs'*

Estate [1962] 2 All ER 829). It is therefore a matter of evidence whether Potts' words to Pans on boarding the aeroplane were meant to be testamentary or indicated merely a misunderstanding of the intestacy laws.

Even if the former construction were found to be the correct one, however, what is the effect of Potts' further words to Pans made after their arrival? A fresh privileged will can be made provided the deceased was in actual military service at the relevant time — as Potts evidently was here. Furthermore, even though the Wills Act 1837, s. 20, requires the same formalities for the revocation of a will as for its creation, it has been held that a later privileged will revokes an earlier will (even an earlier formal will (*Re Gossage's Estate* [1921] P 194)) to the extent that it is inconsistent with it, even though the later will does not comply with the Wills Act 1837, s. 9. Potts' later words to Pans therefore appear to revoke his earlier privileged will in favour of Daisy, and to create a fresh privileged will in favour of Sally.

A privileged will does not cease to be valid merely because its maker ceases to be in actual military service, as Potts was while on leave at home. Furthermore, the manner of Potts's death is also irrelevant.

It would therefore appear that Sally is entitled to Potts' estate, and that Potts' mother (unless she can make a claim under the Inheritance (Provision for Family and Dependants) Act 1975) will receive nothing.

(**b**)   Quark's executors must pay the insurance money to the executors of Higgs's estate if Higgs died with a vested interest in the lease. This will not be the case if Higgs predeceased Quark, since the general rule is that a gift by will lapses if the beneficiary predeceases the testator. This rule does not apply if Higgs was Quark's child or remoter issue and himself left issue living at Quark's death (see Wills Act 1837, s. 33) but there is no evidence of that in the problem. Thus, in the absence of evidence indicating which of Quark or Higgs died first, the presumption in the Law of Property Act 1925, s. 184, applies. This provides (*inter alia*) that if two persons have died in circumstances rendering it uncertain which died first, for the purpose of determining title to property the younger is deemed to survive. If the section applies, the person treated as dying first is Quark. Even where it is considered likely that the deaths were simultaneous, in the absence of proof of this, the presumption applies (*Hickman* v *Peacey* [1945] AC 304).

For Higgs's estate to take, however, it is not enough that Higgs dies after Quark; the property which Higgs is to take under the will must also be in existence at the time of Quark's death. Land is generally regarded as indestructible and, strictly, so is the legal estate of an airspace, since the right to the space survives the destruction of the part of the building which encloses it. Nevertheless, the destruction of a building ends the tenant's capacity to make use of it, and it appears that the law is coming to recognise that such destruction can terminate (and thus, in effect, destroy) the lease itself. Thus, in *National Carriers Ltd* v *Panalpina (Northern) Ltd* [1981] AC 675, the House of Lords considered that the doctrine of frustration might apply to a lease if, owing to circumstances beyond the control of either of the parties to it, the tenant was unable to use the premises for the purposes contemplated. Since the lease of the third floor of Boson Villas will expire before the property can be reinstated, it is possible that the court, applying the reasoning of *Panalpina*, would hold that the destruction of the building terminated the lease.

If this is held to have occurred, the next issue is whether the destruction occurred before or after the death of Quark. If it was before, the gift adeems: if after, the lease vests in Higgs. In the absence of evidence on this point, the court will need to apply a presumption. If the testator dies in the same calamity which destroys one of his assets and it is uncertain which perished first, the asset is deemed to have been destroyed before the testator, so that the gift adeems (*Re Mercer* [1944] 1 All ER 759). This presumption was, however, developed in the context of chattels, the existence of which might be considered more precarious than that of a leasehold estate. It is therefore uncertain whether the court would apply that presumption in the problem, or, indeed, whether, in respect of leasehold property, the presumption might be reversed.

If the court were to apply the reverse presumption in the case of a leasehold estate, the combined effect of such presumption and the Law of Property Act 1925, s. 184, would be that Higgs would be treated as having acquired a vested interest in the lease on Quark's death. In these circumstances, the interest of Higgs (or, after his death, the interest of his estate) would be transferred to the rights under the insurance policy when the lease terminates on the destruction of the building (*Re Hunter* (1975) 58 DLR 175 (Ontario)).

If any of the foregoing requirements is not satisfied, Quark's executors should hold the insurance money for Charm as residuary beneficiary under Quark's will.

7 Registered Land

INTRODUCTION

Originally introduced in the nineteenth century, the system of registration of titles to land has been gradually extended throughout England and Wales. This has been done by designated areas being declared areas of compulsory registration of title. In such an area, the purchaser's title under all conveyances of freehold land, grants of leases for more than 21 years, and assignments of leases with more than 21 years unexpired, must be registered substantively (i.e., with its own separate title) at HM Land Registry.

The first time there is such a disposition of unregistered land in such an area, the conveyance, grant or assignment takes place in the normal way for unregistered conveyancing. The purchaser therefore obtains legal title under the conveyance, grant or assignment. The purchaser must, however, obtain registration of title within two months; the sanction for non-compliance being that the legal title is divested from him, and thereafter the vendor holds the legal title in trust for the transferee: Land Registration Act 1925, s. 123.

By the 1980s, most parts of England and Wales were areas of compulsory registration. All remaining areas became areas of compulsory registration on 1 December 1990. It will, of course, be some years before all titles to land are registered, so that the system of unregistered conveyancing, although in decline, will continue for some time to come. Nevertheless, the system of registered conveyancing is now significantly more important than that of conveyancing under the old unregistered system.

With the implementation of the Land Registration Act 1997, the events which give rise to compulsory registration will be considerably widened and will, therefore, hasten the process of registration. These events will include dispositions by way of gift, and those made by personal representatives or on a court order. A legal estate will also become registrable if the legal owner creates over it a first legal mortgage protected by the deposit of title deeds.

Registration, which is effected under the Land Registration Act 1925, furnishes a title guaranteed by the state; and the underlying principle is that the register at HM Land Registry should, so far as is practicable, reflect the title to the land. HM Land Registry issues the registered proprietor with a land certificate, which contains the entries recorded on the register at HM Land Registry on the date it was last compared with it. If the registered proprietor has granted a legal mortgage of the land, HM Land Registry will instead issue the mortgagee with a charge certificate. On a transfer of land with registered title, the legal title passes only when the transfer is registered at HM Land Registry.

The system of registration of titles also recognises two categories of interests which, unlike the legal estates mentioned above, are not registrable substantively. These are minor interests and overriding interests, as defined in the Land Registration Act 1925, s. 3(xv) and (xvi) respectively. Minor interests do not bind a purchaser of the registered land unless they are protected by entry on the register of title to that land. Overriding interests are interests which, although not entered on the register, are nevertheless interests subject to which registered dispositions of the land take effect. The two categories are mutually exclusive in that an interest cannot be both a minor interest and an overriding interest at the same time. However, an interest which is not protected by registration as a minor interest may, in some circumstances, nevertheless obtain protection as an overriding interest. Categories of overriding interests are set out in the Land Registration Act 1925, s. 70(1).

The existence of overriding interests is therefore an important qualification to the basic principle that the register is an accurate reflection of the title to the land. Since the decision of the House of Lords in *Williams & Glyn's Bank* v *Boland* [1981] AC 487, moreover, the scope of one category of overriding interests — that specified in the Land Registration Act 1925, s. 70(1)(g) — has been revealed to be considerably wider than had been previously realised. Paragraph (g) deems to be an overriding interest:

> The rights of every person in actual occupation of the land or in receipt of the rents and profits thereof, save where enquiry is made of such person and the rights are not disclosed.

This paragraph has led to considerable litigation and has caused many difficulties for conveyancers — difficulties which, however, they have been able largely to overcome. For these reasons, many examination questions on registered land are primarily concerned with overriding interests in general, and with paragraph (g) in particular. In this chapter, therefore, Question 1 concentrates on paragraph (g). Question 2 is broader, and perhaps more difficult, which calls for a critique of the concept of overriding interests and invites a discussion of the desirability of maintaining a balance between the different interests involved. The Law Commission's proposals for reform, contained in their *Third Report on Land Registration*, Law Com. No. 158 (1987), are useful, in that they explain and highlight the difficulties of the existing system. Question 3 demands a grasp of the remedy of rectification.

Questions on overriding interests may also arise in other types of questions, such as Questions 4 and 5 of **Chapter 5**, where there is a clear contrast between registered and unregistered titles to land.

QUESTION 1

Hector is the registered proprietor of a large Victorian house which he bought on 1 July 1990 with the aid of a loan of £50,000 from the Troy Building Society, which registered its mortgage a month later. His mother provided half the deposit and agreed to pay half the mortgage instalments. As she had been recently widowed, Hector had invited her to set up home with him. The house required some extensive redecoration and rewiring before it was habitable, so his mother did not move in immediately but took a fortnight's holiday. On her return she moved in with her furniture and possessions. During her absence, Hector had the house redecorated; the vendor allowed him to have access in advance of completion for this purpose.

In 1991 Hector converted the house into three flats. He now occupies the ground floor himself with his mother and he let the flat on the first floor to Ajax on a monthly tenancy in 1991. Hector's brother, Paris, took possession of the flat on the second floor under a seven-year lease at a rent of £3,000 per year. Paris had a friend, Helen, who had recently become unemployed, so he allowed her to share the flat free of charge. In 1993, Paris accepted an offer of a two-year contract abroad. He decided to keep the flat on, however, and has continued to pay Hector the rent. Paris had told Helen she can remain there as long as she wants provided she pays the electricity bills.

At the rear of the house, there is a large car-parking area. Hector entered into an agreement last year with his neighbour Odysseus that Odysseus could park his caravan there when not travelling abroad with it.

Hector, unbeknown to his mother, took out a second mortgage from the Sparta Bank earlier this year to prop up his failing business. As he has not been making any repayments to either the Troy Building Society or the Sparta Bank, they are both seeking to recover their loans. Hector has now fled the country and his business is insolvent.

Discuss.

Commentary

This is a question that mixes different issues relating to overriding interests. The major area of difficulty is without question that of the Land Registration Act 1925, s. 70(1)(g) and a question on overriding interests is bound to concentrate on that subsection while including some passing reference to some of the other subsections. A knowledge of the case law on s. 70(1)(g) is indispensable.

Suggested Answer

Hector's mother

Hector's mother has an equitable interest in the house by virtue of her contribution to the purchase price. The question arises as to whether her interest can override the interest of the legal mortgagees.

Under the Land Registration Act 1925, s. 70(1)(g), the rights of every person in actual occupation of land are protected as overriding interests. This includes the right of a person with an equitable interest in the land. Such a person has to be in actual occupation. Two issues arise here: what is actual occupation and when must such occupation occur?

Actual occupation naturally includes the physical presence of the person claiming the interest (*Hodgson* v *Marks* [1971] Ch 892). In *Williams & Glyn's Bank Ltd* v *Boland* [1981] AC 487, actual occupation was said to be a matter of fact to be construed in ordinary words of plain English. However, later cases have found shades of meaning within this apparently literal interpretation of the section. In *Abbey National Building Society* v *Cann* [1991] 1 AC 56, it was thought that occupation by a caretaker or company representative could satisfy the section. In *Lloyds Bank* v *Rosset* [1991] 1 AC 107, the presence of builders on the site of a semi-derelict farmhouse was held to be capable of satisfying the requirements of the section. Thus, the physical presence of the mother may not be necessary if it can be shown that the decorators were present in the property as her agents. They were, in fact, hired by Hector not his mother, so there may be an argument that they were not acting as her agents for these purposes. While it is the case that a temporary absence may not destroy the notion of actual occupation (as in *Chhokar* v *Chhokar* [1984] FLR 313 where the wife's absence while she was in hospital having a baby did not cause her to lose her status of actual occupier), Hector's mother does not begin actual occupation until a fortnight after the completion of the transaction. This would seem to be distinguishable from a case where the continuity of occupation has been broken by a temporary absence. Thus, it would be necessary for the mother to establish vicarious occupation through the decorators.

A person claiming an overriding interest under s. 70(1)(g) must establish actual occupation at the time of the disposition, that is, the date of completion of the transaction. Such claim to an overriding interest is enforceable providing the rights remain subsisting at the date of registration (*Abbey National Building Society* v *Cann*). Thus, the mother's claim to an overriding interest against the Troy Building Society will depend on her establishing her actual occupation through the decorators as her agents at the date of completion on 1 July 1990.

It might be argued, however, that she has waived her right as against the Troy Building Society as she must have known of its charge over the property and must have impliedly consented to its taking priority over her interest (*Paddington Building Society* v *Mendelsohn* (1985) 50 P & CR 244). Indeed, she had agreed to pay half the mortgage instalments. This argument will not prevail against the Sparta Building Society. Not only is she clearly in actual occupation at the time of the creation and registration of its charge, but she is unaware of it and, therefore, cannot be taken to have waived her priority.

Ajax

Ajax occupies a flat in the house under a monthly tenancy. As a legal lease granted for a term not exceeding 21 years it is protected as an overriding interest under the Land Registration Act 1925, s. 70(1)(k). Overriding interests, other than those protected under s. 70(1)(g) (*Abbey National Building Society* v *Cann*), must be in existence at the date of registration of the purchaser's interest. Thus, Ajax's interest will be enforceable against the second mortgagee but not the first.

Paris and Helen

Paris is in occupation of the second-floor flat under a seven-year lease. If this is a legal lease then it is protected under the Land Registration Act 1925, s. 70(1)(k). If it is equitable it would seem that the section does not apply and he would have to rely on s. 70(1)(g) unless it was registered as a minor interest and so protected. However, he is no longer in actual occupation himself although Helen is occupying the property in his absence. Helen is occupying the flat under an informal arrangement and her occupancy would constitute no more than a personal right to occupy as a bare licensee. As such she does not satisfy the requirement of s. 70(1)(g) (*Strand Securities Ltd* v *Caswell* [1965] Ch 958). At the time of the second mortgage, Paris is no longer in occupation himself, nor is he receiving any rent from Helen. Neither he, therefore, nor Helen have any protection under s. 70(1)(g) against the Sparta Bank. As his lease did not begin until after the acquisition of the property and the creation of the charge in favour of the Troy Building Society, he will also have no right against them.

Odysseus

Odysseus has an agreement to park his caravan on the car park. If this constitutes an easement (which could be legal only if granted by deed) then his interest is protected under the Land Registration Act 1925, s. 70(1)(a). This would apparently be the case whether his easement is legal or equitable. In *Celsteel Ltd* v *Alton House Holdings Ltd* [1985] 1 WLR 204, it was held that s. 70(1)(a), in conjunction with the Land Registration Rules 1925, r. 258, covers such equitable easements which are openly exercised and enjoyed over the land. This decision was followed and applied by the Court of Appeal in *Thatcher* v *Douglas* (1995) 146 NLJ 282. There might, therefore, be a question as to the availability of the protection if Odysseus's caravan is not in the car park at the time of the registration of the second charge. It would clearly not affect the first charge since the agreement was only entered into last year.

If s. 70(1)(a) does not apply, then it may be necessary to consider s. 70(1)(g). In *Epps* v *Esso Petroleum Co. Ltd* [1973] 1 WLR 1071, the parking of a car on a strip of land did not suffice to establish actual occupation. However, in *Kling* v *Keston Properties Ltd* (1985) 49 P & CR 212, the parking of a car in a garage by agreement was held to constitute sufficient occupation to satisfy the section as regards a right of pre-emption of the garage. Indeed, it was suggested in that case, that had the car not actually been parked at the time, its intermittent presence in the garage would have sufficed.

In the problem, the caravan is not parked in any defined area such as a garage. It may be possible, therefore, to distinguish *Kling* v *Keston Properties Ltd.* In any case, the overriding interest would only be exercisable against the second mortgagee on the same grounds as before.

QUESTION 2

'In the interests of certainty and of simplifying conveyancing, the class of rights which may bind a purchaser otherwise than as a result of an entry on the register should be as narrow as possible but interests should be overriding where protection against purchasers is needed, yet it is either not reasonable to expect or not sensible to require any entry on the register.' (Third Report on Land Registration (Law Com. No. 158).)

Discuss.

Commentary

An account of the different types of overriding interests will not suffice for a question of this type. It requires a critical analysis of the problems to be encountered in the system of registered conveyancing brought about by a group of interests which, despite their failure to appear on the register, still bind the purchaser. Familiarity must, of course, be shown with the different types of interests but as they can simply be looked up in the statute do not waste time presenting a complete list. You will need to be very familiar with the case law so that you can juggle with it to bring out the various points you are making. If you have not broadened your mind by reading the Law Commission Report, all is not lost. There is sufficient information in the extract to permit you to develop the critique of overriding interests on which it requires you to focus. Needless to say, some account of the Law Commission proposals will propel your answer skywards.

Suggested Answer

The fundamental principle of registered conveyancing is that the purchaser is bound by everything on the register which is a mirror of the title to the land. As part of the 1925 legislation, the Land Registration Act was concerned to simplify conveyancing and provide certainty for the purchaser. Once the title is registered it is thenceforth guaranteed by the state.

Under the system of registration, legal titles to land are registered and there is a provision for other interests to be protected on the register. Interests which are capable of subsisting at law under the Law of Property Act 1925, s. 1(2), are registrable. Other interests can be protected on the register as minor interests by means of notice, caution, restriction or inhibition. Thus, the register should also provide a mirror of interests affecting the land. There is one limitation to this mirror principle which is the category of overriding interests. These are interests which, although not registered or protected on the register, bind a registered proprietor regardless of his state of knowledge as to their existence (Land Registration Act 1925, s. 3(xvi)).

The list of overriding interests is contained in the Land Registration Act 1925, s. 70(1). It includes a range of interests such as rights of way, rights under local land charges and leases not exceeding 21 years. The most controversial of the overriding interests is the protection given by s. 70(1)(g) to the rights of persons in actual occupation of the land or in receipt of rent.

The justification for having a category of interests which exists outside the register is that they will be discoverable on inspection. A balance between the interests of a purchaser and the objective of the 1925 legislation, and that of the person who, for some social or technical reason, requires the additional protection of an overriding interest, should therefore be struck. The purchaser, simply by carrying out an inspection of the property, as might be expected during the process of the conveyance of a legal title, can discover the interest. The person with the interest is not vulnerable because of any failure to have the interest unprotected on the register. The difficulty with this theory is that it presupposes that overriding interests are all discoverable by inspection. This may not necessarily be the case. In the first place, there is a question as to the date when an overriding interest may arise. A purchaser may be supposed to have inspected the property before completion of the transaction. In registered land completion does not transfer the legal title. This only occurs on registration. Should overriding interests be allowed to arise during the time between completion and registration? The majority of the House of Lords in *Abbey National Building Society* v *Cann* [1991] 1 AC 56, decided that the critical time was the date of registration. They decided, however, that interests arising under s. 70(1)(g) were a special case when the date should be the date of the completion of the transaction. This does mean that in all other types of overriding interests, they can be created unbeknown to the purchaser, between completion and registration. Although this may, in practice, be unlikely, it does mean that such interests as easements and short leases could be created which irrevocably bind the purchaser. It was for this reason that Lord Bridge in the *Abbey National* case dissented on this point, preferring the date of disposition.

The concept of overriding interests within the system of registered conveyancing contrasts remarkably with the effect of the Land Charges Act 1972 in unregistered conveyancing. Any registrable interest left unprotected under that Act is void, (*Midland Bank Trust Co.* v *Green* [1981] AC 513). This applies regardless of the state of knowledge of the legal owner and was considered by the court in *Midland Bank Trust Co.* v *Green* to reflect the intention of the legislature in keeping the process of conveyancing simple and in protecting the purchaser.

The most difficult overriding interests have been those protected under s. 70(1)(g). The impact of this was noted in the case of *Williams & Glyn's Bank Ltd* v *Boland* [1981] AC 487 where the equitable interest of Mrs Boland was held to prevail as an overriding interest against the legal mortgagee. This case reflects the social policy of the legislature in protecting this type of interest. There was, in fact, nothing to prevent Mrs Boland protecting her interest as a minor interest on the register. The fact that she did not is symptomatic of the nature of these interests which arise unknown to the individuals concerned, who are likely to be unaware of the need or manner of their protection. For this reason the legislature deemed that they should be protected regardless of their appearance on the register. For purchasers in the position of the Williams and Glyn's Bank, this involves a heavy burden of inspection and inquiry prior to the completion of the transaction. It is not sufficient for the purchaser to make inquiries of the vendor; the section is specific in requiring inquiries to be made of the person benefiting from the overriding interest (*Hodgson* v *Marks* [1971] Ch 892). The concept of actual occupation is wide in that it includes occupation through an agent as in *Lloyds Bank* v *Rosset*, where builders employed by Mrs Rosset who were occupying the property at the relevant date were held to be in actual occupation as her representatives. Although the occupation must in general be continuous, a temporary absence from the property will not cause the interest to be lost, as in *Chhokar* v *Chhokar* [1984] FLR 313, where Mrs Chhokar was absent from the property while giving birth to a child. However, preparatory acts such as laying carpets in readiness for occupation will not be sufficient to establish actual occupation under the section (*Abbey National Building Society* v *Cann* [1991] 1 AC 56).

One practice adopted by professional mortgagees to protect themselves from the priority of an overriding interest may be ineffective. In *Woolwich Building Society* v *Dickman* (1996) 72 P & CR 470, the Court of Appeal held that a document signed by the occupiers of property purporting to subordinate any rights they might have as tenants to the interest of the mortgagee, was ineffective. If this decision were to be applied to the interest of an equitable owner and occupier, it would further limit the self-help available to mortgagees.

Solutions may be found in the doctrine of overreaching, as was demonstrated in the case of *City of London Building Society* v *Flegg* [1988] AC 54, where the doctrine was triggered by the fortuitous presence in the circumstances of the case of two legal owners who both gave a receipt for the mortgage moneys. The purchaser may also seek to identify the claimants and require that waivers should be signed before proceeding with the transaction. This route, commonly used by institutional lenders, may be successful, provided that the pitfall of undue influence is avoided.

Clearly, the situation is not as clear-cut as the ethos of the 1925 legislation sought to achieve. Proposals for reform have been made by the Law Commission. These include narrowing the list of overriding interests, providing that the critical date for the establishment of the overriding interest is the date of disposition, and introducing an indemnity scheme. In respect of the present s. 70(1)(g), it is proposed to narrow the category so as to exclude the rights of those who are in receipt of rents or profits; only those in actual occupation should be included. This would avoid the problem of a virtually undiscoverable group of claimants. In the meantime, while registered conveyancing has undoubtedly simplified the procedure for the conveyancer, much caution is required in undertaking a careful inspection and making appropriate inquiries to discover any overriding interests.

QUESTION 3

'Rectification and overriding interests share the feature that they each provide a means of asserting an unregistered interest against the proprietor of registered land. Together they merely represent different ways in which reliance on the register may ultimately prove to be misplaced.' (Gray, K., *Elements of Land Law*, 2nd edn, London: Butterworths, 1993.)

Explain and discuss this statement. How might the situation be reformed?

Commentary

This question pulls together the two aspects which have the potential for undoing the mirror principle in the system of registration of title. The impact of overriding interests and of the decision in *Williams & Glyn's Bank Ltd* v *Boland* [1981] AC 487 is well-known. There is an early Law Commission paper on the implications of this case which recommends that the purchaser should be favoured (Law Com. No. 115). However the Third and Fourth Reports on Land Registration (Law Com. No. 158 and Law Com. No. 173) make some radical and far-reaching recommendations which form the basis of the draft Land Registration Bill (Law Com. No. 173, Appendix).

Suggested Answer

The principle underlying registration of title is that the purchaser is bound by everything which appears on the register; it mirrors the title. The principle is imperfect both in respect of the category of overriding interests and the remedy of rectification. Overriding interests are listed in the Land Registration Act 1925, s. 70 and constitute a closed list. They include such categories as rights of way, leases not exceeding 21 years, rights in the course of acquisition by adverse possession and the rights of those in actual occupation of land. Once the existence of an overriding interest has been established, then it is binding on the purchaser of the legal estate regardless of notice.

The power of rectification is also statutory and is contained in the Land Registration Act 1925, s. 82. There are eight grounds in s. 82 and once one of the grounds has been established then the court has a discretion whether to order rectification. Thus, there is a distinction between the effect of overriding interests and the remedy of rectification in that the latter is discretionary while the former is not.

The effect of an overriding interest is that a purchaser is deemed to take the land subject to it regardless of his state of knowledge. Thus, where a person has an overriding interest they may seek rectification of the register. In *Chowood Ltd* v *Lyall* [1930] 2 Ch 156, the land in question had been transferred to another person. However, the land had been adversely possessed for a sufficient period for the adverse possessor to succeed in extinguishing the title of the original transferor. Rectification of the register was granted against the transferee and in favour of the adverse possessor.

Where, an existing entry on the register has been obtained by fraud or misrepresentations, or an entry has been wrongly omitted or included, or there is some subsisting unregistered entitlement such as that of an adverse possessor or other claimant with an overriding interest, then the court (and, in some cases, the registrar) has a discretion to order rectification. In addition, there is an apparently wide ground in s. 82(h) that the court may rectify in any case in which it is deemed just to do so. In *Argyle Building Society* v *Hammond* (1985) 49 P & CR 148, the court indicated that this subsection gave a very broad discretionary power. However, in *Norwich and Peterborough Building Society* v *Steed* [1992] 3 WLR 669, the Court of Appeal rejected this approach and held that the effect of this subsection was to provide for the rectification of such errors as were not covered by the preceding specific subsections.

The power to rectify is limited by the provisions in s. 82(3) (as amended by the Administration of Justice Act 1977, ss. 24 and 32). This section protects the proprietor in possession by providing that rectification can only be ordered where it is to give effect to an overriding interest or an order of the court, or where the proprietor has caused or substantially contributed to the error or omission by fraud or lack of proper care, or where, for any other reason, it would be unjust not to rectify the register against him. So, in *Epps* v *Esso Petroleum Co. Ltd* [1973] 1 WLR 1071, the court refused to order rectification where a strip of land had been wrongly conveyed to the defendants' predecessors in title and then to the defendants. The court considered that the error would have been discovered had the plaintiffs undertaken appropriate enquiries before completion of their purchase, and that the justice in the case lay wholly with the defendants. However, in *Argyle Building Society* v *Hammond* (1984) 49 P & CR 148, the court held that there was power to rectify. In this case, a transfer of a house took place, by way of a forged deed, to the original registered proprietor's sister and her husband, who then charged the house to the plaintiffs. It was held that it would be a proper exercise of the court's discretion for an order for rectification to be made. The deed was a complete nullity for which the original proprietor was not responsible in any way.

Where the register is rectified, there is a provision which enables a person who has suffered loss to seek compensation from a central fund (s. 83). The compensation is intended to cover the value of the estate lost and any other reasonable costs or expenses. It is not available where the claimant has contributed to the loss by fraud or negligence (s. 83(5)(a)). This does, to some extent, alleviate the fact that the register may prove to be defective. However, it has been held that where the loss has been caused by the existence of an overriding interest, then this provision for indemnity is not available. In such a case, the loss is caused by the fact that the purchaser has acquired property which is subject to all entries on the register and any overriding interests. The register is then rectified to give effect to an interest which is already subsisting, so the loss is caused by this subsisting interest and not by the order for rectification. This decision was reached in *Chowood Ltd* v *Lyall* [1930] 2 Ch 156 and applied in *Re Boyle's Claim* [1961] 1 WLR 339. Thus although a person suffering loss by reason of an order for rectification (or a failure to rectify) may seek an indemnity, a person suffering loss as a result of the existence of an overriding interest may not do so. There is, therefore, some protection for a person who relies on the register only to find that that reliance has been misplaced except in the case of an overriding interest. The existence of such an interest leaves the injured person completely vulnerable as in the case of *Hodgson* v *Marks* [1971] Ch 892 where the registered proprietor was deprived of the entire estate as a result of the rectification in favour of a person with an overriding interest under the Land Registration Act 1925, s. 70(1)(g).

There are clearly important differences between the effect of the existence of an overriding interest and the effect of the remedy of rectification. However, it is also clear that they may both have the effect of depriving someone of an estate or interest in the land which they believed they were entitled to as a result of their reliance on the register.

The Law Commission has proposed changes to the system of registered land both in relation to the system of overriding interests and to the remedy of rectification and the availability of an indemnity. In its Third Report on Land Registration: B. Rectification and Indemnity 1987 (Law Com. No. 158) it recommends that in a case where there is a *bona fide* purchaser for value who has exercised the standard of care of a prudent purchaser and is in actual occupation, then the remedy of rectification should not be available. However, the exception is retained in respect of an overriding interest or a claim by a trustee in bankruptcy except that the indemnity provisions would be extended to cover the former cases. In addition, it is recommended that the ground on which rectification may be sought where it is deemed just should be repealed since it creates too great a degree of uncertainty in the provisions of registered land.

In respect of overriding interests, the Law Commission recommended that the list of interests should be narrowed but the availability of the indemnity provisions should be extended. In particular, the provisions which have caused the greatest degree of uncertainty, that is, those contained in the Land Registration Act 1925, s. 70(1)(g), should be narrowed so as to exclude the rights of those in receipt of rents and profits from the land. The need to retain a category for short leases is acknowledged, and legal easements and profits, rights acquired by adverse possession, rights of persons in actual occupation and customary rights are retained. Clearly, the major problem with the present operation of the category of overriding interests is that it can deprive the estate owner of any interest in the land without compensation. The Law Commission, in an attempt to reconcile the need to protect the claimant and to provide some greater degree of certainty for the estate owner, has recommended the compromise that the indemnity provisions should be made available in respect of this new and narrower class of overriding interests. In respect of the other rights which are contained in s. 70(1), it is proposed that they should either be reclassified as 'general burdens' on registered land, or be reduced to minor interests only. It is not proposed that they should benefit from the indemnity provisions.

8 Trusts of Land

INTRODUCTION

The founding of a family dynasty was a feature of English social life amongst the landed gentry for many centuries. Land represented power, status and wealth, and they sought to retain that wealth within their own families for future generations. Most of the larger text books on land law give some account (in varying degrees of detail) of its historical development, and indeed this is necessary for a true understanding of the subject. Our land law developed from a feudal society organised around the manorial system where the chief landowner was the lord of the manor. Land was one of the most important things in that society.

A study of the history of land law (in more depth than you will require) reveals a constant conflict between the desire of landed gentry to keep the land in their families for future generations, and the concern of the legal system to ensure that land was freely alienable and not locked away and kept for one generation after another by means of a device called a strict settlement.

Settlements had been in existence since the early thirteenth century, and in 1925 much land was subject to a strict settlement. The Settled Land Act 1925 was yet a further attempt by the legal system to make land more freely alienable, and s. 106 expressly provided that there could be no fetter on the powers of the person currently enjoying and managing the land (the tenant for life), including his power of sale. A need to sell the land often arose in order to raise money to pay taxes on the death of the previous life tenant, so that settled estates were systematically broken up and settlements are not common today. Their comparative rarity compared with the other form of settlement before 1997 (the trust for sale), and the cumbersome legal machinery required to create a settlement, led to their abolition and replacement with a trust of land under the Trusts of Land and Appointment of Trustees Act (TLATA) 1996. The abolition is of any future settlements, however, and there is a saving for settlements in existence on 1 January 1997 which are allowed to continue under the Settled Land Act until they come to an end.

Settlements under the Settled Land Act were also used by the courts to give effect to informal family arrangements supported by an estoppel or a constructive trust. A recent example of the courts' use of a settlement for these purposes is *Costello* v *Costello* (1995) 27 HLR 12.

For a discussion of its application in this way in *Costello* and other cases, see M. P. Thompson [1994] *Conv* 391. This type of arrangement will in future probably take effect under a trust of land. Question 4 in this chapter considers the kind of arrangement which could give rise to a settlement in this way. It also considers some of the provisions of the Settled Land Act which gave protection to a purchaser of settled land, and it is interesting to see that s. 16 of the TLATA contains not entirely dissimilar provisions with regard to a purchaser of land subject to a trust of land under the 1996 Act.

Settlements under the Settled Land Act are very rarely dealt with in any detail in land law courses nowadays. Presumably their total extinction will be accelerated by the TLATA 1996 and they will soon be consigned to legal history. The type of family arrangement for which a settlement was used will now take effect under a trust of land. Question 1 in this chapter considers the reasons for the demise of settlements and trusts for sale, and looks generally at the new regime introduced by the 1996 Act. Question 2 looks at the impact of the new Act on certain specific dispositions.

Question 3 considers the provisions of the Act as they will apply to a trust creating successive interests in land. This type of arrangement, if professionally created, was to be found behind a trust for sale, but if contained in a homemade will would often inadvertently create a settlement. This was very inconvenient because s. 13 of the Settled Land Act (the 'paralysing section') provided that there could be no dealings with the land until a vesting deed under the Act had been executed, thus causing a delay to any sale of the property. The Administration of Justice Act 1982 relieved the problem to some extent by providing that certain wills leaving land in succession should take effect as absolute dispositions, but it did not cover all situations where a settlement was created inadvertently.

Although settlements will become increasingly rare after 1996, and trusts for sale under the LPA 1925 are virtually extinct, their machinery may still remain relevant to matters of title for a few years yet. It is conceivable therefore that conveyancers will have to have some knowledge of their operation for a few years to come.

It remains to be seen how the new Act will work in practice and how the courts will interpret certain sections. Many of the sections are similar to provisions in the Law of Property Act 1925 which applied to trusts for sale. Others (such as s. 16 referred to above) have a similarity to provisions found in the Settled Land Act. These similar sections have been referred to in the suggested answers both in this chapter and in **Chapter 9** on Co-ownership. The next few years, as we see cases on the TLATA reaching the courts, will be very interesting for land lawyers!

QUESTION 1

What problems with regard to trusts of land were addressed by the Trusts of Land and Appointment of Trustees Act 1996? What are the main provisions of the Act with regard to future trusts of land?

Commentary

Although questions on the old regime of settlements and trusts for sale will obviously become increasingly rare, it was thought worthwhile to include this comparison of 'before and after' to give some idea of the purpose of the TLATA 1996. There are no cases as yet on its interpretation, but many of its sections vary the recognisably similar provisions of the Law of Property Act or the Settled Land Act, and these variations have been pointed out. It is hoped that the comparisons which have been made will give you a flavour of the new thinking on trusts of land.

Suggested Answer

Under the 1925 legislation, a trust of land *had* to be in one of two forms — either a settlement under the Settled Land Act (SLA) 1925 or a trust for sale under the Law of Property Act (LPA) 1925. The overreaching provisions, whereby a purchaser got a good title to the land if he obtained a receipt for the purchase moneys from two trustees and the beneficial interests attached to the proceeds of sale of the land instead, were common to both.

The SLA 1925 was designed primarily for trusts of large estates which were to continue for some time. The legal estate in the land and all the powers of management were given to the tenant for life (usually the person of full age for the time being entitled to possession of the land). The trustees (who had to give a receipt for capital moneys) were generally what was described as the 'watchdogs' of the settlement, although in practice their control over the tenant for life's exercise of his powers was minimal. The equitable interests were 'off the title' and a purchaser generally had no right to enquire about them. This arrangement required two legal documents — a vesting deed (or assent) and a trust instrument — and s. 13 of the SLA (the 'paralysing' section) provided that there could be no dealings with the settled land until a vesting deed had been executed.

The legal machinery for setting up a settlement was therefore quite cumbersome. There were fewer and fewer large estates for which the device was suitable. However, because a trust of land *had* to take effect behind either a trust for sale or a settlement, and the two were mutually exclusive, a trust of land created without the express provision of a trust for sale took effect as a settlement. Section 1 of the SLA was a general 'mopping up' provision under which a settlement often arose accidentally, usually from a home-made will where a husband would leave his house to his wife and then to his children without imposing any trust for sale. (The Administration of Justice Act 1982 ameliorated the situation to some extent by providing that in certain cases, such as where an interest given to the wife was not specifically stated to be a life interest, such dispositions should not create successive interests in land but should operate as an absolute disposition to the wife.)

The trust for sale under the LPA 1925 was a much simpler device requiring only one document to create it — a conveyance of the legal estate to the trustees for sale on trust for the beneficiaries' equitable interests. Because of its comparative simplicity, it was often used to give effect to successive interests in land rather than a settlement. Moreover, because the LPA 1925 allowed a settlor to require the trustees to obtain certain consents before the land could be sold, whereas the SLA 1925 provided that there could be no restrictions whatsoever on the powers of the tenant for life (including the power of sale), there was a curious paradox whereby it was possible to make land less freely alienable under a trust for sale than under a settlement. There had to be an express trust for sale imposed, however, as otherwise successive interests in land automatically took effect behind a settlement.

The legislation also provided that a trust for sale would arise under statute in certain circumstances, the two most significant ones being under s. 34(2) and s. 36(1) of the LPA 1925 wherever there was co-ownership of land, and under s. 33(1)(a) of the Administration of Estates Act 1925 wherever there was an intestacy of land.

The trust for sale was not without its problems, however. Because the essence of a trust is that it imposes a binding obligation, and equity 'looks on that as done which ought to be done', the equitable doctrine of conversion applied to it. This meant that in equity there was a notional sale of the land, so that the interests of the beneficiaries were interests in personalty (the proceeds of sale) and not in land. There were some curiously inconsistent decisions where the courts were often understandably reluctant to apply the doctrine when it led to an unintended and undesired result.

Moreover, the rights of beneficiaries under a trust for sale were often limited and it was sometimes difficult for them to oppose the decisions of the trustees. They had no rights of occupation of the property (*Re Power* [1947] Ch 572) unless an express trust for sale gave them such rights. They had rights of consultation only if the trust for sale were a statutory one, or (in the case of an express trust for sale) if they were specifically given such rights. This meant that the trustees for sale could ignore the wishes of the beneficiaries if they were so minded. Moreover, because there was a trust for sale and only a power to postpone sale, the trustees had to be unanimous to postpone, and even one trustee alone could insist on a sale of the property (*Re Mayo* [1943] Ch 302). The whole thrust of a trust for sale was towards a sale of the property, and s. 30 of the LPA 1925 provided that any person interested in the property could apply for a sale, which the court had power to order; there was no corresponding provision, however, whereby the court could order a stay of sale.

The TLATA 1996, which came into force on 1 January 1997, abolished settlements as from that date by providing that after then no new settlements could be created, although existing ones might continue. It also provided that any trusts of land (or of land and personalty) created after 1996 would take effect as trusts of land under the Act, and that trusts for sale in existence on 1 January, including statutory ones, would become trusts of land under the Act. The Act therefore operated retrospectively on existing trusts for sale with the one exception mentioned below of trusts for sale arising under wills of certain testators who died before 1 January 1997. The most central point of the new trust for land is that it is not possible for a settlor to negative the power which the trustees have to postpone a sale of the land. Under s. 14 (which replaces s. 30 of the LPA) the court may also make an order to retain the land.

Section 3(1) abolishes the application of the equitable doctrine of conversion to trusts for sale, so that the interests of the beneficiaries under a trust of land are in the land itself and not in the proceeds of sale of the land. The one exception to this is under the will of a testator who died before 1 January 1997. This was to allow for a testator who specifically disposed of 'personalty' and 'realty', as property held under a trust for sale would pass to the beneficiary entitled to personalty and not realty under such a will, and the testator is presumed to have intended this. Consistent with recognising that the beneficiaries have an interest in the land itself, beneficiaries entitled to an interest in possession are also given a right to occupy the land in certain circumstances (s. 12(1)), and under s. 11(1) a right to be consulted by the trustees on the exercise of the trustees' functions, although this right does not appear to operate retrospectively to trusts for sale created before 1997 unless adopted by deed.

Like s. 26(3) of the LPA, which applied only to statutory trusts for sale, there is a requirement to have regard to the wishes of the beneficiaries or the majority of them in value.

Trustees for sale and a tenant for life under the SLA had only certain specified and limited powers of dealing with the land, although the settlor could enlarge these powers. Section 6 gives to the trustees all the powers of an absolute owner of the land (including the power to sell the land and buy other land, which it was doubtful whether former trustees for sale could do). The settlor may limit these powers, but if he does not then s. 6 will apply to give the trustees very wide powers indeed. If the settlor does place restrictions on the exercise of the trustees' powers, such as the necessity to obtain the consents of certain persons to a sale of the property, there are savings for a purchaser in s. 16 of the 1996 Act (which is not dissimilar to ss. 18 and 110 of the SLA 1925). If the purchaser does not have actual notice of the restriction, the transaction cannot be invalidated. (It is a relief to see that *actual* notice is required to invalidate the transaction after all the cases following the House of Lords decision in *O'Brien* on constructive notice!) The trustees are to exercise their functions 'as trustees' and 'not in contravention of any rule of law or equity' (s. 6(6)), and their powers are still subject to any enactment applying to trustees, such as the Trustee Investments Act 1961. They are therefore subject to the usual fiduciary obligations of trustees, and the standard of care which applies to trustees.

Those beneficiaries of full age and capacity, and collectively entitled to the beneficial interests, are given powers to appoint new trustees and to require a trustee to retire (ss. 19–21). These provisions apply generally to all trusts and not just to the new trusts of land, but again do not apply to pre-1997 trusts for sale unless adopted by deed. There is a corresponding power for the trustees to terminate the trust in favour of such beneficiaries by conveying the land to them (s. 6(2)), or by partitioning the land between them (s. 7(1)).

The circumstances which gave rise to a statutory trust for sale before the Act now give rise to a trust of land under the Act (Sch. 2 amending the previous sections), and its provisions apply to such trusts.

The 1996 Act is comprehensive in that it sets out to create a general 'umbrella' for trusts of land of any kind, and s. 1(2) specifically states that it includes bare trusts and implied, resulting and constructive trusts and trusts for sale. It is still possible to create a trust for sale, although as the power to postpone sale cannot be abrogated, there is little point in this.

The Act provides, in effect, a new framework for trusts of land, replacing the old settlement and trust for sale with a more realistic, and (it is hoped) more workable, trust over which the beneficiaries will have far more control. It remains to be seen how the courts will interpret its sections, and how much of the old case law — for example, on when to order a sale under s. 30 of the LPA — will still be regarded as relevant.

QUESTION 2

(a)   Lucinda, who died in December 1996, left a will appointing Tom and Tessa as her executors and trustees and including the following dispositions:

'(i)   I devise my house Redroofs to my nephew Maurice for life, and on his death to his son Leopold absolutely;

(ii)   I devise my house Greengates to my nieces Annie (aged 22), Beryl (aged 20), and Connie (aged 16) in equal shares absolutely;

(iii)   I give my house Whitegables to my trustees Tom and Tessa upon trust to sell and to hold the proceeds of sale for the same persons to whom I give, devise and bequeath my residuary estate.

I gave devise and bequeath my residuary personalty to Jane and my residuary realty to Peter.'

Advise Tom and Tessa as to the effect of these dispositions.

(b)   How would your answer differ if Lucinda had died in January 1997?

Commentary

This question is designed to illustrate the changes made in practice by the TLATA 1996. As mentioned in the introduction to this chapter, although the pre-1997 law will become increasingly unimportant, it may still be relevant to title for some years to come. The type of disposition in (a)(i) is one which is sometimes found in home-made wills (and there is no reason to think that this will change); and there must be many co-ownership situations as in (a)(ii) which arose before 1997 to which the Act applies. The disposition in (a)(iii) highlights a specific saving for trusts for sale which arose under a will where the testator died before 1 January 1997.

Suggested Answer

(a)(i) Lucinda's disposition of Redroofs would create a settlement under s. 1 of the SLA 1925. Where a disposition limited land to persons by way of succession without imposing a trust for sale, a settlement automatically arose. The tenant for life to whom the legal estate was conveyed was the person of full age entitled to possession of the settled land, namely, Maurice. Although the TLATA 1996 provides that no settlements can be created after 1996, it does not convert existing settlements into trusts of land, and they continue. The tenant for life has only the old SLA powers, however, and does not acquire the new and more extensive powers given to trustees of a trust of land.

(ii) This disposition created co-ownership of land which, before 1997, had to take effect behind a statutory trust for sale. As a minor cannot hold a legal estate in land, the legal estate would be vested by the executors in Annie and Beryl as joint tenants and trustees. There would be a statutory trust for sale under s. 34(2) of the LPA 1925 for Annie, Beryl and Connie, who would be tenants in common in equity as there are words of severance in the disposition ('in equal shares').

The operation of the TLATA 1996 was retrospective as regards trusts for sale, however, so that even on such a pre-1997 disposition, on 1 January 1997 the statutory trust for sale becomes a trust of land under the Act.

(iii) Before 1997, the equitable doctrine of conversion applied to a trust for sale. Because the trust imposed an obligation to sell, the beneficiaries' interests were regarded as personalty (the proceeds of sale) and not realty (*Fletcher* v *Ashburner* (1779) 1 Cro CC 497). Whitegables would therefore have gone to Jane and not to Peter. Although the TLATA 1996 is retrospective on trusts for sale in its abolition of the doctrine of conversion, there is a saving for trusts for sale under the will of a testator who died before 1 January 1997, so that there would be no change to this disposition.

(b)(i) Although the TLATA 1996 does not operate retrospectively to convert existing settlements into trusts of land, it is not possible to create a settlement under the SLA 1925 after 31 December 1996. This disposition will take effect as a trust of land under the new Act. The trustees will be Lucinda's personal representatives.

(ii) The TLATA 1996 abolishes the statutory trusts for sale which arose wherever there was co-ownership of land. This was done by amending s. 34(2) and s. 36(1) of the LPA 1925. Otherwise, the law of co-ownership is not changed. Schedule 1, para. (2) provides that wherever land is conveyed to a minor and an adult, the adult becomes a trustee of a trust of land for himself and the minor. This means that Annie and Beryl will be trustees of a trust of land for themselves and Connie, and they will all be tenants in common in equity (as before).

(iii)   Although it is still possible to create a trust for sale after 1996, s. 3(1) of the TLATA 1996 abolishes the application of the equitable doctrine of conversion to a trust for sale as regards dispositions of land on or after 1 January 1997. There is therefore no notional conversion of Whitegables into proceeds of sale and it will pass with Lucinda's residuary realty to Peter.

QUESTION 3

James, who died earlier this year, appointed Tick and Tack as executors and trustees of his will and left all his property in trust for his wife Emma for life, and then to his two children John and Jane absolutely. His property included the Owl House, a listed building, and his will provided that this should not be sold without the consent of John and Jane.

Polly, who has always liked the house, made a good offer for it to the trustees which was in excess of its likely market value. She knew that Jane did not want to sell the house, but did not know of the restriction on sale in James's will. Tick and Tack consulted Emma, who was keen to sell, but overlooked the fact that they should have consulted John and Jane. The trustees have now conveyed the house to Polly.

Advise John and Jane.

Commentary

This question requires you to have a knowledge of the different sections of the TLATA 1996 relating to the powers of trustees and the effect of a restriction on the exercise of those powers. It also requires consideration of the effect on a purchaser of a breach of the restriction. Because the sections impose a general fiduciary duty on the trustees, you also need to be aware of the general standard of care which applies to trustees.

Suggested Answer

The disposition in James's will creates a trust of land under the TLATA 1996, which, by its definition in s. 1(1), is a trust of any property which 'includes' land, even though it also includes personalty. The trustees, Tick and Tack, have all the powers of an absolute owner for the purpose of exercising their functions 'as trustees' (s. 6(1)), but must have regard to 'any rule of law or equity' (s. 6(6)). These provisions suggest that trustees are under a general fiduciary duty and that the general standard of care applicable to all trustees applies to them. This is the standard of care established in the case of *Speight* v *Gaunt* (1883) 9 App Cas 1, and it requires a trustee to exercise the care which an ordinarily prudent man of business would apply in managing his own affairs.

The policy of the Act is to give trustees very wide powers of management which may then be restricted by the settlor, and s. 8(2) states that the powers under s. 6 shall not be exercised without obtaining any specified requisite consents. Section 8(1) states that there must be a provision that these sections do not apply. One interpretation of this subsection is that there needs to be an express exclusion, but a better view may be that a direction to the contrary will have the effect of excluding ss. 6 and 7. (There is a provision also in s. 10(1) similar to s. 26(1) of the LPA 1925, that as regards a purchaser, any two consents shall be sufficient, but this of course will not apply to the present circumstances.) Section 6(5) requires trustees to have regard to the rights of the beneficiaries in exercising their powers, and Tick and Tack have acted in breach of these sections.

Section 11(1) of the TLATA 1996 requires trustees to consult beneficiaries of full age and entitled to an interest in possession in the land. This general duty to consult would apply to Emma, but not to John and Jane who do not have an interest in possession. Section 11(1)(b) requires trustees to give effect to the wishes of such beneficiaries, or the majority of them in value, but only 'so far as consistent with the general interest of the trust'. It may be that Emma has compelling reasons for wanting to sell the Owl House, which would perhaps override the requirement for obtaining consents to the sale from John and Jane. Section 14 allows the trustees to make an application to the court for an order (*inter alia*) 'relieving them of any obligations to obtain the consent of ... any person in connection with the exercise of any of their functions'. Tick and Tack are therefore in breach of trust in selling without the consents of John and Jane or an order dispensing with them.

So far as the purchaser Polly is concerned, s. 16(1) relieves a purchaser of ensuring that the trustees have in fact had regard to the rights of any beneficiaries under the trust (s. 6(5)), or any requisite consents (s. 7(3)). Section 16(2) and (3) provides that a contravention of s. 6(8) or s. 8 shall not invalidate the conveyance, however, if the purchaser does not have actual notice of it. Polly knew that Jane did not want to sell the Owl House and has made a very good offer for it, suggesting that she might have had constructive notice (i.e., the notice she would have had if she had made enquiries) of the restriction, or that as regards Jane she might not have acted entirely in good faith. Section 16 refers specifically to *actual* notice, however, which Polly did not have, and the transaction is therefore valid. It seems that a purchaser who knows that beneficiaries are opposed to a sale or other transaction is wiser not to ask too many questions!

Although this does not invalidate the conveyance, it does not of course relieve Tick and Tack from their statutory obligations under ss. 6(5) and 8(2) towards the beneficiaries. They are also in breach of s. 16(3)(a), which requires them to take all reasonable steps to bring any limitation on their powers to the notice of a purchaser. To have overlooked the requirement of consents to a sale of the Owl House was probably also a breach of the common law standard of care imposed upon trustees in *Speight* v *Gaunt* (*supra*), and they will therefore be liable to John and Jane for breach of trust.

QUESTION 4

Answer both parts.

(a)   Sidney, who died in 1996, was the registered proprietor of a house. In his will he left his house to his son Bert, 'subject to the right of my aunt Agnes to live in it during her lifetime'. Agnes now wishes to sell the house and use the proceeds to buy a small flat.

Discuss.

(b)   By a settlement dated 1 January 1990, Larry settled his freehold house on himself for life with remainder to his brother Ronald. Last year, Larry's business fell into difficulty and he sought a loan from Sam. Sam required some security for this loan so Larry handed him an old set of title deeds to the house which he had kept. These show Larry to be the fee simple owner of the house and Sam, unaware of the settlement, accepted them as security for the loan. Larry has now died and Sam wishes to recover his loan. Larry's estate is insolvent.

Discuss.

Commentary

Note carefully the dates in this question. These dispositions pre-date the implementation of the Trusts of Land and Appointment of Trustees Act 1996 which applies to all settlements made after 1 January 1997. Here, therefore, the Settled Land Act 1925 applies. Frequently, the Settled Land Act is described as a well-oiled machine and, in general, this is true. The Act itself is comprehensive and clear and if you have access to the statutes in the exam, there is no difficulty about making reference to the specific powers of the tenant for life, for example, or the role of the trustees of the settlement. A working knowledge of the Act, contrary to popular opinion, makes many questions on settlements quite straightforward. There are really only two problem areas within this field and this question raises both of them. One relates to the informal creation of a settlement as evidenced in such cases as *Bannister* v *Bannister* [1948] 2 All ER 133. The other relates to the protection of an innocent purchaser and the difficulties of reconciling ss. 18 and 110 of the Act. Each of these areas could form a question in its own right. One that mixes them, as this one does, is really not cricket. You should also be aware that the Law Commission Report on Trusts of Land (Law Com. No. 181) makes certain unfavourable comments about the informal creation of strict settlements. There are numerous articles to read on these thorny areas.

Suggested Answer

(a)   As Sidney dies prior to the implementation of the Trusts of Land and Appointment of Trustees Act 1996, it is necessary to consider the effect of the Settled Land Act 1925.

Under the Settled Land Act 1925, s. 1(1)(i), where land is limited in trust for persons by way of succession, a settlement arises. In Sidney's will, he purports to leave land to Bert subject to the right of Agnes to live in it during her lifetime. The question arises, therefore, whether this is sufficient to bring into play the Settled Land Act 1925. If it does, then Agnes becomes the tenant for life and, as such, is entitled to have the legal estate vested in her, and, in addition, acquires all the powers of the tenant for life under the Act. These include the power to sell the property, to lease and mortgage it.

In order to create a settlement expressly two documents are required. Where a settlement is created by will, a vesting assent is required to convey the legal estate by the personal representatives to the tenant for life. The will itself constitutes the trust instrument, i.e., the document setting out the terms of the settlement. The issue in this problem is whether the words of gift in the will constitute the creation of a strict settlement. The words are loosely formulated and such a result may have been unintended by Sidney.

There are precedents where an informal arrangement has triggered the application of the Settled Land Act 1925 but they are usually to give effect to a constructive trust or an estoppel. In *Bannister* v *Bannister* [1948] 2 All ER 133, the defendant sold two cottages to her brother-in-law at a price below the market price and there was an arrangement that she could live in one of them rent-free for as long as she liked. It was held that the oral agreement created a constructive trust under which she was entitled to a life interest determinable on her ceasing to live in the property. The Court of Appeal held that the effect of creating a trust in this form was to make the defendant a tenant for life under the Settled Land Act 1925. This result is extraordinary in that an informal oral agreement was deemed sufficient to create a settlement, a result clearly unintended by the parties concerned. In *Binions* v *Evans* [1972] Ch 359, the ruling in *Bannister* v *Bannister* was applied by two of the Court of Appeal judges. In *Binions* also, an informal agreement to permit the occupation of a property rent-free for the remainder of the defendant's life was held to create a settlement under the Act in order to give effect to a constructive trust which arose when the property was sold to the plaintiffs at well below the market price because of the defendant's occupation. In *Binions* v *Evans*, Lord Denning MR dissented on the ground that s. 1(1)(i) required an express limitation of the land to persons in succession and an informal arrangement could not satisfy the requirement. He also felt that the agreement was never intended to give to the defendant the extensive powers of management, including the power to sell or lease the property, given to a tenant for life under the Settled Land Act. Therefore, in the particular circumstances of the case, he would have protected the interest of the defendant by imposing a contractual licence. Lord Denning MR's approach was criticised in *Griffiths* v *Williams* (1977) 248 EG 947, where the Court of Appeal found that the interest of the defendant amounted to a lease determinable on death which was protected under the doctrine of estoppel. They specifically avoided the award of a life interest as it would create a strict settlement under the Act, a result unintended by the parties. Similarly in *Dodsworth* v *Dodsworth* (1973) 228 EG 1115, the court declined to protect the equity raised by an estoppel by imposing a life interest which might have created a Settled Land Act settlement since that would have awarded the defendants a greater interest than was envisaged. Whilst the results of *Bannister* v *Bannister* have been unfavourably received, they have been applied more recently in *Ungurian* v *Lesnoff* [1990] Ch 205 where an informal grant to a cohabitee of a right of residence for life in a flat, on the strength of which she had carried out much work to the flat, was held to create a tenancy for life under the Settled Land Act 1925. The Act was also applied in *Costello* v *Costello* (1995) 27 HLR 12, to give effect to a family arrangement between a mother and a son.

These cases concern informal grants. In the problem, the grant is in the form of a will and, albeit it is loosely worded, it does apparently create a succession of interests which could have constituted a settlement for the purposes of the Settled Land Act 1925, s. 1(1), particularly if Aunt Agnes were able to plead an estoppel or a constructive trust arising in her favour as a result of dealings between her and Sydney during Sydney's lifetime. Presumably such informal arrngements might now take effect under a trust of land under the TLATA 1996 and the courts may well use this form of trust to give effect to them in future.

   (b)   It would appear that the 1990 settlement has been properly created and is, therefore, a perfect settlement. Larry has acted fraudulently in masquerading as the fee simple owner and inducing Sam to take the title deeds on that basis as security for the loan. The question therefore concerns the respective rights of Sam, the innocent purchaser, and Ronald, the remainderman. As the settlement was created prior to the implementation of the Trusts of Land and Appointment of Trustees Act 1996, it will be subject to the provisions of the Settled Land Act 1925.

Section 18 of the Settled Land Act 1925, deals with the situation where a settlement has been perfectly created. It provides that where there is an unauthorised dealing by the tenant for life with the land, that transaction 'shall be void'. This would seem to answer the question summarily. Larry has sought to pledge the estate as though he is entitled to the fee simple. This is outside his powers. He is only entitled to deal with his own equitable interest which amounts to a life interest. On a straightforward interpretation of the Act, this means that the loan arrangement with Sam is void. This view was supported in *Weston* v *Henshaw* [1950] Ch 510 where a tenant for life happened to have an old deed in his possession which purported to show that he was the fee simple owner of the estate. He fraudulently used it to gain a mortgage. It was held that as the mortgage had been unauthorised according to s. 18(1)(a), it was void.

Whilst a logical conclusion on a literal interpretation of s. 18, this decision does ignore the general protection afforded throughout the land law system to the innocent purchaser who has no notice of any equitable interest. In particular,

s. 110(1) provides that a purchaser dealing in good faith with a tenant for life shall, as against all other beneficiaries, be taken to have complied with the requirements of the Act. In the problem, this would imply that the capital money representing the loan had been paid to two trustees as required by s. 18(1)(c) of the Act. In *Weston* v *Henshaw* the judge took the view that s. 110(1) only applies to cases where the purchaser knows that he is dealing with a tenant for life. This leaves the purchaser most in need of protection (that is, one who is dealing with a fraudulent tenant for life) completely vulnerable.

This argument was acknowledged in *Re Morgan's Lease* [1972] Ch 1 where it was stated *obiter* that such knowledge is irrelevant. In this case reference was made to the earlier case of *Mogridge* v *Clapp* [1892] 3 Ch 382 which was not cited in *Weston* v *Henshaw*. In *Mogridge* v *Clapp* it was accepted without question that s. 110 applies to a person regardless of whether they knew or did not know that the other party was a tenant for life. The only consideration as to the application of s. 110 was whether they were in 'good faith' and this would apply equally to the purchaser who knows the true status of the tenant for life as to one who does not.

Thus, there is a difference of view as to whether Sam would be protected by s. 110 in preference to Ronald as remainderman. The preferred view would seem to accept the argument in *Re Morgan's Lease* on the ground that it is consistent with the general scheme of the 1925 legislation, which is concerned to ensure that a purchaser in good faith is able to take legal title to land free from incumbrances.

9 Co-ownership

INTRODUCTION

This chapter deals with co-ownership of land which, before January 1997, took effect under a statutory trust for sale. After 31 December 1996, all co-owned land is held on a trust of land under the new regime introduced on 1 January 1997 by the TLATA 1996. This Act is retrospective as regards trusts for sale (with one exception), which no longer exist unless expressly created. Even then, the provisions of the Act will apply to them and it will not be possible to exclude the implied power to postpone sale.

The chapter covers co-ownership arising expressly and from the conveyance of land to co-owners, as well as co-ownership under constructive and resulting trusts, which are also now included within the new regime of trusts of land under the TLATA 1996. Because there is a large area of overlap between these topics, they should ideally be studied together, and you should be prepared for questions which demand an ability to apply them together. Some of the questions in this chapter contain such overlaps. A general question on the aims and effects of the TLATA 1996 is to be found as Question 1 of **Chapter 8** on Trusts of Land.

Question 1 of this chapter deals with the mechanisms for governing co-ownership as a trust of land. It considers the rights of the beneficiaries, the functions of the trustees and the statutory guidance now given to the court under s. 15, TLATA 1996 in dealing with applications concerning the land held on trust for co-owners.

Question 2 is a longer-than-would-be-expected examination question which explores many issues of a joint tenancy and a tenancy in common, including severance of an equitable joint tenancy. In doing so, it picks up some of the points dealt with in Question 1. The law relating to the operation of the two forms of co-ownership has been left unchanged by the new Act.

Questions 3 and 4 are essentially on implied, hidden co-ownership. If you have read the area of law covered by the questions 1, 2 and 4 in **Chapter 5**, you will have realised that this type of co-ownership is of comparatively recent judicial development. The courts are keeping abreast of changing social patterns which have thrown up many problems, often involving an adjudication between the purchaser of land and a third party with rights in it. It is, of course, the achievement of a correct balance between the interests of a purchaser and a third party which is central to any system of land law.

QUESTION 1

A testator who died recently devised his freehold four-bedroom house 'Dunroamin' to trustees upon trust for his three children Susan, Tom and Ursula in equal shares. The will provides that should any of the three children wish to do so, they may live in the house.

Advise the trustees under the following circumstances:

(a) Tom, who is married with five children, would like to live in the house, but Susan and Ursula would like it to be sold and the proceeds of sale to be divided between them;

(b) If Tom and his family do go to live in the house, whether Susan and Ursula would be entitled to any rent for his occupation;

(c) Tom is single and aged 17 and wishes to occupy the house with his aunt and guardian, with whom he is now living.

How would your answer differ if there had been no provision in the will for any of the three children to live in the house if they so wished?

Commentary

This is a fairly straightforward question on the powers of the trustees and the rights of the beneficiaries under a trust of land. It requires a knowledge of the relevant sections of the TLATA 1996. As yet, there is no case law on the Act and it remains to be seen how some of its sections will be applied by the courts. Comparisons have been made in the suggested answer with the previous law on trusts for sale under the Law of Property Act 1925, as it is not inconceivable that the courts may refer to this when resolving disputes under the 1996 Act.

Suggested Answer

(a) This disposition will take effect under the TLATA 1996 which came into force on 1 January 1997. Because there is no requirement to sell the property, it takes effect as a trust of land. It is recognised that the interests of the beneficiaries under trusts of land are interests in land rather than in the proceeds of sale of land as under the trust for sale under the Law of Property Act 1925 which the trust of land replaces.

Section 12(1), TLATA 1996 gives a beneficiary who has an interest in possession the right to occupy the land if the trust makes it clear that the property is to be available for occupation (as here), or the trustees hold land that is so available, and the land is not for any reason unsuitable. A four-bedroom house might be regarded as reasonably suitable for a family with five children.

Section 11 requires the trustees to consult the beneficiaries of full age entitled to an interest in possession in the land and to give effect to their rights or the wishes of the majority of them in value. (In this respect, it is similar to s. 26(3) of the 1925 Act as it applied before 1997 to a statutory trust for sale, although narrower because it only requires consultation with the beneficiaries with an interest in possession.) This requirement of consultation may be excluded by the settlor, but does not appear to have been here.

The trustees may not unreasonably exclude any beneficiary's entitlement to occupy land (s. 13(2)), but may impose reasonable conditions with regard to his occupation (s. 13(3)), including obligations with regard to the use of the land and payment of outgoings (s. 13(5)). It has been pointed out by commentators on the Act that these provisions will almost certainly require the trustees to give to a beneficiary a written licence to occupy the property setting out the terms of occupation. Section 9 also allows trustees to delegate any of their functions (other than the receipt of capital money) to a beneficiary of full age entitled in possession, and if Tom is to occupy the house the trustees may wish to consider this. Any delegation must be done by a power of attorney to the beneficiary for a fixed or indefinite period.

Section 6 of the Act, which gives the trustees all the powers of an absolute owner of the land, also requires them to have regard to the rights of the beneficiaries in exercising those powers (s. 6(5)). They must also act 'as trustees' and not contrary to 'any rule of law or equity'. However, there is no presumption in favour of a right of sale under the new Act, but only a power of sale. As the testator has specifically mentioned occupation by the beneficiaries as a possible purpose of the trust, it seems probable that they could decide to allow Tom and his family to occupy 'Dunroamin'. If Ursula and Susan are aggrieved by this decision, they can apply to the court under s. 14, whereby the court may make any order, including one not to sell (unlike the old s. 30 of the 1925 Act, where sale was often the required way to resolve any dispute unless the purposes for which the property was acquired were still extant). The matters to which the court must have regard in deciding what order to make are set out in s. 15 and include the intention of the settlor, the purpose of the property (as under s. 30), and the welfare of any minor. Presumably this might include Tom's five children, and possible occupation by a beneficiary being stated as a purpose might tilt the decision in Tom's favour.

(b) One of the conditions which the trustees may impose for occupation of the property under s. 13(5) is the payment of compensation to any beneficiary who is excluded from occupation, or that the beneficiary who occupies the property should forego other benefits under the trust. Under the old case law on co-ownership it was recognised that if one co-owner was effectively excluded from occupation, he could be awarded rent from the occupying co-owner (*Dennis* v *McDonald* [1981] 1 WLR 810, *Bernard* v *Josephs* [1982] Ch 391). It is probable, therefore, that Susan and Ursula could require Tom to pay a rent — presumably of two-thirds of the rack rent value of the house.

(c) If Tom were a minor and the aunt's house were unsuitable for him to live in for any reason, the trustees should consider very seriously allowing Tom and the aunt to occupy 'Dunroamin', bearing in mind that the welfare of any minor is specifically mentioned in s. 15(1) as a factor which the court should consider in making any order. Susan and Ursula may be able to argue that a four-bedroom house is unsuitable for only two people, though, and that consideration of Tom's minority would only be for a further 12 months (although there are provisions in the Act for protecting a beneficiary who has taken up occupation from being disturbed: s. 13(7)).

Had there been no specific provision in the will allowing any of the three children to live in the house if they so wished, and the duty to consult and to have regard to the wishes of the majority in value under s. 11(1) applies, the trustees might have to do what Susan and Ursula wish and exercise their power of sale. The trustees, or Tom's guardian on his behalf, could apply to the court under s. 14, but s. 15(2) specifically requires the court to have regard to the wishes of other beneficiaries entitled to occupy (Susan and Ursula), as well as to the welfare of any minor who 'might reasonably be expected to occupy [the property] as his home' (s. 15(1)). Given that Tom is a minor for only another year, and that a four-bedroom house may not be entirely suitable, it is possible that the wishes of Susan and Ursula might prevail.

QUESTION 2

In 1995 Angus, Belinda, Connie and David, who were medical students, decided to buy a large house in which to live while they were studying. They contributed to the purchase price equally. Connie was only 17 at the time.

At the end of his first year at University, Angus unfortunately failed his examinations and, having decided that medicine did not suit him, went to Spain to train as a toreador. He wrote enthusiastically to Belinda and Connie (then 18) about his life in Spain, but not to David. He said that as he did not feel he would have much use for the house in future, he would like them to buy his share or to sell the house.

In December 1996, Belinda was tragically killed in a riding accident. She had made a will leaving all her realty to her sister Iris and all her personalty to her brother James.

David recently married, and while Angus was staying with them to attend the wedding, David took the opportunity to have dinner with Angus and Connie to discuss the future of the house. The occasion was a convivial one, and all three agreed that their shares in the property should be separate and distinct in future, although nothing was put into writing to this effect.

Sadly, Angus recently perished on the horns of a bull.

David would like the house to be sold; but Connie, who has not yet finished her studies, would like to keep it.

(a)　If the house is sold, how should the proceeds of sale be split?

(b)　If the house is sold, who will be able to give a good title to it?

(c)　Advise Connie as to whether she might successfully oppose a sale.

Commentary

This is a fairly typical examination-type question on co-ownership. Before you can say who will be entitled to the proceeds of any sale and who will be able to convey the legal estate to a purchaser, you will have to trace logically the devolution of both the legal estate and the equitable interests. You should do this in the answer to the question, of course, but you may find it easier to set it out first in diagrammatic form in rough, as follows:

Legal Estate	Trust for Sale	Equitable Interests
ABD	ditto	ABCD (JTs)
AD	ditto	ACD (JTs)
1 January 1997		
AD	in trust for	ACD
AD	ditto	ACD (JTs or Ts in C)
D	ditto	CD equally or CD and A's heir equally

In case your transcription to essay form is erroneous, it might be preferable to put only two or three lines through your rough working but still leave it legible! A kind-hearted examiner might be prepared to give some credit for a correct rough working erroneously transcribed.

Such questions will often involve circumstances which are problematic as to whether there has been an effective severance or not of the equitable joint tenancy. If so, you should be prepared to answer the question in the alternative, i.e., showing how the equitable interests devolve if there has been a severance and if there has not been. After all, you can hardly be expected to predict what the judge would decide in any particular circumstances!

Before 1 January 1997, co-ownership of land had to take effect behind a trust for sale under the Law of Property Act 1925. All such statutory trusts for sale were abolished by the TLATA 1996 and become trusts of land instead. The question illustrates how the new Act would operate on an existing co-ownership situation. Apart from amending the form of trust under which co-ownership takes effect, the law of co-ownership is unchanged.

Suggested Answer

(a) As Connie was only 17 when the house was purchased in 1995, she could not hold a legal estate in land, and the legal estate will therefore be vested in Angus, Belinda and David as joint tenants at law.

The Law of Property Act 1925, s. 36(1), imposed a statutory trust for sale wherever land was conveyed to joint tenants, so that Angus, Belinda and David held it as joint tenants and trustees for sale for themselves and Connie in equity. Assuming that there are no words of severance in the conveyance (such as 'in equal shares') then they will be joint tenants in equity also as they contributed equally to the purchase price.

On 1 January 1997, the TLATA 1996 came into force and all existing trusts for sale of land were converted into trusts of land by amendment of ss. 34(2) and 36(1) of the Law of Property Act 1925, and this is retrospective. Apart from this, the law of co-ownership is basically unchanged by the 1996 Act.

It is possible that the content of Angus's letter to Belinda and Connie might be sufficient to constitute a notice of severance for the purposes of the Law of Property Act 1925, s. 36(2). The section requires any such notice to be given to 'the other joint tenants', however, so that notice to only two of them would not be sufficient to sever Angus's share with regard to any of them, and the joint tenancy would continue in equity.

It is possible also that the letter might qualify as an act of severance being 'an act of any one of the persons interested operating on his own share' (*per* Page-Wood V-C in *Williams* v *Hensman* (1861) 1 John & H 546). A declaration of intention to sever by one party was accepted by Havers J in *Hawkesley* v *May* [1956] 1 QB 304 as a sufficient act of severance, and this was approved by Plowman J in *Re Draper's Conveyance* [1969] ChD 486, where he found that a summons and affidavit in support filed by a wife asking for the sale of the matrimonial home and division of the proceeds was sufficient to sever the joint tenancy held by her and her husband. The problem remains, however, that the letter to only two of the joint tenants cannot effect a severance with a third to whom there has been no 'declaration', as it would still lack the necessary element of mutuality for severance. If Angus's share is to be severed, it must be severed with all of them, and the letter, again, would therefore be ineffective.

Connie's attaining her majority did not automatically make her a co-trustee and owner of the legal estate, which continued to be vested in Angus, Belinda and David. For Connie to become a trustee and joint tenant at law, there would have to be a deed of appointment by the existing trustees vesting the legal estate in her and them as joint tenants.

When Belinda died, she was a joint tenant of both the legal estate and the equitable interest, so that the right of survivorship applied to both. Angus and David therefore held the legal estate on trust for themselves and Connie as joint tenants in equity. It is not possible to sever an equitable joint tenancy by will, so that Belinda's will was ineffective to do this. (Note that had there been a severance and had Belinda's share been held by her as a tenant in common, it would have passed under the will as personalty to James. This is because the equitable doctrine of conversion operated before 1996 and a person's interest under a trust for sale was for many purposes regarded as personalty. Although s. 3(1), TLATA 1996 abolishes the application of the doctrine to trusts for sale of land, there is a saving for trusts for sale of land created by will where the testator died before 1 January 1997.)

Although the legal joint tenancy cannot be severed, as a tenancy in common cannot exist at law after 1925, the equitable joint tenancy may be severed either by notice (Law of Property Act 1925, s. 36(2)), or by any of the three ways described by Page-Wood V-C in *Williams* v *Hensman* (*supra*). (*Note*: the first has already been considered in relation to the letter from Angus.) The two ways of severance which should be considered in relation to the dinner party are severance by mutual agreement between the joint tenants, or a course of dealing sufficient to intimate to all the joint tenants that their interests were mutually to be regarded as being held under a tenancy in common in future.

Although all three joint tenants appear to have agreed upon a severance of the equitable joint tenancy, it is a purely oral agreement. In *Burgess* v *Rawnsley* [1975] Ch 249, Lord Denning MR expressed the opinion that severance of the equitable joint tenancy could be oral as it was not a contract for the sale or other disposition of land, and so did not have to comply with the Law of Property Act 1925, s. 40 (now repealed), or be a specifically enforceable contract. This was probably justified only by regarding the interests of the joint tenants as personalty because of the operation of the doctrine of conversion. After 1 January 1997, the joint tenants have an interest under a trust of land, so that severance by agreement will probably have to comply with s. 2, Law of Property (Miscellaneous Provisions) Act 1989 as being 'a contract for the sale or *other disposition* of an interest in *land*'. Any such agreement will then have to be in writing and signed by all parties, so that the oral agreement over dinner would not suffice.

Even if the oral agreement is not effective, it may still operate as a severance if it can be regarded as a sufficient course of dealing to sever. This would essentially be a matter for the court to decide.

Assuming that there was no effective severance of the equitable joint tenancy, when Angus died the right of survivorship would operate to vest his legal share in the surviving joint tenant, David. His equitable interest would pass, again by the right of survivorship, to Connie and David equally. If there was a severance of the equitable joint tenancy, when Angus died the right of survivorship would still operate to vest his legal share in David, but his equitable interest would pass under his will or intestacy.

The proceeds of sale would be split equally as to one-third each between Angus's heir, Connie and David if there had been a severance of the equitable joint tenancy; if there was no effective severance (which seems likely) then the sale proceeds would be split equally between David and Connie.

(b) Although David is the sole remaining trustee and owner of the legal estate, there is still co-ownership in equity. In order to overreach the equitable interests, therefore, a purchaser should require the appointment of a second trustee (who may be Connie or someone else) to give a good receipt for the purchase moneys.

(c) One of the main purposes of the TLATA 1996 was to abolish the presumption in favour of a sale which applied to a trust for sale under the Law of Property Act 1925. Section 11(1), TLATA 1996 requires trustees to consult the beneficiaries as to the exercise of their extensive powers and to have regard to the wishes of the majority in value (as s. 26(3) of the 1925 Act required in the case of a statutory trust for sale before 1997). If there had been an effective severance and both David and Angus's heir wanted the property sold, this would suggest that the property should be sold. However, s. 11(3) states that the duty of consultation under s. 11(1) does not apply to 'a trust created before the commencement of this Act by a disposition' (as here) unless adopted by deed. This appears to reverse s. 26(3) LPA, and the only remedy would therefore be an application to the court under s. 14, TLATA.

If there was no severance so that David and Connie have equal shares, s. 14 of the 1996 Act allows a trustee or a person with an interest in property to apply to the court for an order. The section is wider than s. 30 of the 1925 Act which it replaces, because whereas s. 30 allowed an application for sale, a s. 14 application can be for any order and would presumably allow Connie to apply for an order resisting sale.

Section 15, TLATA 1996 sets out statutory criteria which the court should consider when making an order under s. 14, and the two relevant ones here would appear to be 'the interests of the persons who created the trust' (s. 15(1)(a)), and 'the purposes for which the property subject to the trust is held' (s. 15(1)(b)). This latter subsection reflects the case law on s. 30 of the 1925 Act, and it remains to be seen how applicable that will still be in construing the new s. 15.

QUESTION 3

Would you agree that the decision of the House of Lords in *Lloyds Bank plc* v *Rosset* [1991] 1 AC 107 has adopted an unduly restrictive approach to the possibility of the protection of interests through the imposition of a constructive trust?

Commentary

A thorough understanding of the principles established by Lord Bridge in *Lloyds Bank plc* v *Rosset* and in the preceding case law is a prerequisite for this question. It requires an analysis of the elements required to establish a constructive trust and a thorough-going discussion of the cases. In particular, the analysis needs to be aimed at the elements highlighted by Lord Bridge, which he regarded as essential, and the way in which they might be shown to rein back some other judicial trends. The question is provocatively phrased and might be similarly answered either in agreement or disagreement.

Useful additional reading might include *Constructive Trusts and Unjust Enrichment* by Sir Nicholas Browne-Wilkinson (Holdsworth Club of the University of Birmingham, 1991). *Constructive Trusts*, by A.J. Oakley, 3rd edn, London: Sweet & Maxwell, 1997, provides an excellent insight into the development of the constructive trust. You should also refer to the case notes in the *Conveyancer*, in particular at [1996] *Conv* 154. The Law Commission has recently commented on the uncertainty surrounding this area of law (*Sixth Programme of Law Reform* (Law. Com. No. 234)).

Suggested Answer

A constructive trust may be imposed where there is some prior bargain or agreement between the legal owner of the property and some other person by which the legal owner has conceded some equitable entitlement to the other person. The circumstances surrounding the agreement are deemed to have affected the conscience of the legal owner so that it would be inequitable to deny the existence of the equitable interest. Such an agreement will not have been created so as to satisfy the requirements of the Law of Property Act 1925, s. 53(1)(b). It will, however, be enforceable because constructive trusts are exempted under the Law of Property Act 1925, s. 53(2), from the requirement of formal writing. This very exemption has ensured that the difficulties of establishing a constructive trust in order to satisfy the court as to the need to protect the beneficial interests have resulted in a long line of cases. *Lloyds Bank plc* v *Rosset* is an important pronouncement by the House of Lords as to the principles on which the remedy will be made available.

A primary element in the constructive trust is the establishment of the bargain as between the parties or, as it is sometimes expressed, a 'common intention'. Once the common intention is discovered, then where the equitable owner has changed his position in reliance on it, the conscience of the legal owner is affected and he would be culpable in equity should he seek to renege on the agreement.

In *Lloyds Bank plc* v *Rosset*, Lord Bridge stated that there must be some agreement, arrangement or understanding reached between the parties that the property is to be shared beneficially. Such an agreement may be deduced from express discussions or be an implied bargain. Where the common intention is founded on express discussions then the existence of such discussions must be clearly established. 'Our trust law does not allow property rights to be affected by telepathy' (*Springette* v *Defoe* (1993) 65 P & CR 1, per Steyn LJ at p. 8). Thus there must be express evidence of these discussions. Lord Bridge emphasised that evidence of such discussions must be set out with some particularity so that there is no vagueness about the assertions. Examples of such agreement or understanding, can be found in the cases of *Eves* v *Eves* [1975] 1 WLR 1388 and *Grant* v *Edwards* [1986] Ch 638. In the former case, the plaintiff had been led to believe that the property would belong to them jointly and it had only been vested in the defendant's sole name because she was under 21. In *Grant* v *Edwards*, the property was put into the name of the man and his brother but here the reason given was that the plaintiff was involved in divorce proceedings which would be prejudiced by the property being put in their joint names. Lord Bridge in *Lloyds Bank plc* v *Rosset* considered these cases to be examples of the express agreement or understanding.

The time when such an agreement would normally arise was considered by Lord Bridge in *Lloyds Bank plc* v *Rosset* to be the date of the acquisition of the property. He thought that it would only arise exceptionally at a date later than this. This is an example of the more restrictive approach of that case since earlier cases such as *Bernard* v *Josephs* [1982] Ch 391, have not imposed such a limitation.

The possibility of founding a constructive trust on the basis of an implied bargain deduced from the conduct of the parties has been acknowledged in earlier case law (e.g., *Gissing* v *Gissing* [1971] AC 886 and *Burns* v *Burns* [1984] Ch 317). Lord Bridge did not cut back on this feature although he emphasised the importance of the nature of the evidence which must be brought to bear.

The existence of such a bargain is to be deduced objectively and must be a demonstrable fact. The decision in *Lloyds Bank plc* v *Rosset* merely confirms the judgment on this matter in *Gissing* v *Gissing* decided 20 years earlier, which itself operates restrictively on the establishment of a constructive trust in many family situations. *Pettit* v *Pettit* [1970] AC 777 also illustrates the requirement for a prior agreement to be present before an interest could be obtained. There had, however, been a development of some case law which indicated that an implied agreement could be founded on evidence which demonstrated that the parties had adopted a principle of sharing everything including the home (*Midland Bank plc* v *Dobson* [1986] 1 FLR 171). In this respect, the decision in *Rosset* has been restrictive. In that case, a dilapidated farm had been purchased in the husband's sole name. Mrs Rosset had undertaken improvements to the property and had supervised the builders herself. This was discounted by the House of Lords (overruling the Court of Appeal on this point) as evidence of a common intention as to the sharing of the beneficial ownership. The common intention to renovate the property as a joint venture and share it as the family home with the children was deemed to be irrelevant to the establishment of a common intention as to ownership. In this respect the decision reverts to the approach in *Gissing* and halts the trend towards a more liberal approach in the inference of a constructive trust. This approach was also applied in *Ivin* v *Blake* (1994) 67 P & CR 263, where the Court of Appeal held that a contribution to the running of a business did not give rise to a beneficial interest in the absence of an express agreement. However, the more recent Court of Appeal decision in *Midland Bank* v *Cooke* [1995] 4 All ER 565 again adopts an agreement 'attributed' to a married couple to share everything as sufficient to fund a constructive trust of one half of the matrimonial home.

A further requirement for the establishment of a constructive trust is evidence that the person who is seeking to establish equitable ownership has relied in some way on the bargain so as to change his position. In this respect the constructive trust has many similarities to the doctrine of proprietary estoppel. Indeed, in *Rosset*, Lord Bridge treated the concepts as interchangeable. The evidence required to establish detriment varies according to whether the common intention has been established on the basis of an express agreement or an implied bargain. In the latter case, more rigorous standards of proof are required (*Hammond* v *Mitchell* [1991] 1 WLR 1127). The conduct relied upon will furnish evidence both of the bargain and of the detrimental conduct. In *Rosset*, Lord Bridge stated that the nature of the detriment required in such circumstances was unlikely to be anything less than a direct contribution to the purchase price, whether initially or by the payment of mortgage instalments. In this respect, the House of Lords' decision in *Rosset* has demonstrated a tendency towards a much stricter evidential requirement than the earlier cases. Thus it would seem that only money payments (normally considered, at least in respect of a direct contribution, to give rise to a resulting trust) will do. It would seem, therefore, that, in cases where the common intention is to be implied from conduct, such contribution as renovatory work, such as was carried out in *Eves* v *Eves*, will not suffice. Neither will indirect contributions to household expenses be sufficient detrimental conduct, nor domestic labour. The decision in *Rosset* returns to and hardens the approach taken 20 years before in *Gissing* v *Gissing* where contributions to household expenses and domestic labour were not considered to be evidence of detrimental conduct in reliance on a common intention to share beneficially in the property.

Further, this detrimental conduct must be referable to the implied agreement. In other words, a link was required between the indirect contributions and a bargain in *Gissing*, and a link between the improvement work and such an agreement in *Rosset*. This need for the link was established by Lord Diplock in *Gissing* and followed by Lord Bridge in *Rosset*.

It would seem, therefore, that only in certain respects has the decision in *Rosset* further restricted the application of the constructive trust. The basis for the principles set out by Lord Bridge were clearly foreshadowed by the House of Lords in *Gissing* v *Gissing*. However, in the intervening 20 years, a more liberal approach in the form of a constructive trust of a new model was beginning to develop under the auspices of Lord Denning MR with decisions in such cases as *Heseltine* v *Heseltine* [1971] 1 WLR 342; *Cooke* v *Head* [1972] 1 WLR 518; *Hussey* v *Palmer* [1972] 1 WLR 1286 and *Eves* v *Eves* [1975] 1 WLR 1338. This trend appears to have been brought firmly to a close with the decision in *Lloyds Bank plc* v *Rosset* which picks up where *Gissing* v *Gissing* left off.

QUESTION 4

In 1980, Nancy bought a house of which she was the sole registered proprietor. Her father, who had been recently widowed, moved in with her. He gave her £10,000 for the deposit on the house and spent £5,000 of his life insurance money on adapting part of the ground floor so that he had a bedroom with *en suite* bathroom for his own use. In 1985, Nancy met and fell in love with Bill, who moved in with her. Bill, who was unemployed, spent a good deal of time on improving and renovating the house. He also did all the housework and cooking. He spent most of his £5,000 redundancy money on the renovations and also contributed to the housekeeping bills. Last year, Nancy took out a mortgage on the house with the Fagin Finance Emporium in the sum of

£25,000. Tiring of Bill's obsessive housekeeping, she bought a round-the-world air ticket and left. The Fagin Finance Emporium is now seeking possession of the house.

   (a)   Advise Bill and Nancy's father.

How would your answer differ if:

   (b)   Nancy and Bill had been married?

   (c)   Nancy had been declared bankrupt?

Commentary

This question requires the application of resulting and constructive trusts which raises the initial difficulty of the judicial confusion between the two. It is best to try and analyse the distinctions between the two rather than ignore the issue (even if that is what some of the judges seem to do). David Hayton in Hayton and Marshall, *Commentary and Cases on the Law of Trusts and Equitable Remedies*, 10th edn, London: Sweet & Maxwell, 1997, provides a convincing argument for the importance of making the distinction, as does the Court of Appeal in *Drake* v *Whipp* (1995) 28 HLR 531. Avoid launching off into a discussion while forgetting the problem. This is a problem question, so take advantage of that and use the points in it as hooks on which to hang your argument.

Suggested Answer

   (a)   There are two potential claimants: Bill and Nancy's father. Either may have acquired an equitable interest in the house which is registered in Nancy's name as the sole legal owner. There is no written evidence of an express trust; therefore it is necessary to consider whether either has acquired an interest under a resulting trust (inferred from the actual or presumed intention of the parties) or a constructive trust (imposed by law). The Law of Property Act 1925, s. 53(2), provides that there is no requirement for writing in such cases.

The distinction between resulting and constructive trusts has become blurred. In *Gissing* v *Gissing* [1971] AC 886, it was considered that it was unnecessary to make the distinction. However, the traditional view is that a resulting trust tends to be implied in those circumstances where there is a contribution of money made to the acquisition of a property regardless of the source of that contribution (*Tinsley* v *Milligan* [1993] 3 WLR 126) in circumstances where it is not a gift or a loan, or where the presumption of advancement applies. Where the parties contribute unequally to the purchase price they are presumed to hold beneficially as tenants in common in proportion to their respective contributions (*Bull* v *Bull* [1955] 1 QB 234). At the time of the acquisition of the house, Nancy's father makes a contribution of £10,000 for the deposit. By making that contribution, it can be argued that, in the absence of any evidence that the contribution was a gift or a loan, for example, there was an intention that he would share in the beneficial interest in proportion to the extent of his contribution (*Bull* v *Bull*). A presumed resulting trust will, in these circumstances, arise. There is a further complication in this case in that the relationship between father and daughter usually gives rise to a presumption of advancement. This would presume that an advance made for his daughter's benefit by her father is a gift. The effect of this is that it shifts to the father the onus of proving that the £10,000 payment was *not* a gift (*Murless* v *Franklin* (1818) 1 Swan 13). In *McGrath* v *Wallis* [1995] 2 FLR 114 however, the Court of Appeal held that a presumption of advancement may be easily refuted where money has been contributed to the purchase of a house where occupation is to be shared with the contributor.

The second question relates to the £5,000 which Nancy's father spent on the bedroom with *en suite* bathroom. If, Nancy's father succeeds in establishing that the first payment was referable to the acquisition of a share in the beneficial ownership, then it becomes easier to prove that the subsequent expenditure was similarly referable. However, the concept of the resulting trust is less likely to be successful in cases where there is something less than a direct contribution to the purchase price at the time of the acquisition. In such situations, it is more likely that a constructive trust would be the appropriate remedy. To establish constructive trust liability, it is necessary to show first that there was a common intention that the beneficial ownership would be shared. In the father's case this could be evidenced by the establishment of the resulting trust at the outset. In *Lloyds Bank plc* v *Rosset* [1991] 1 AC 107, Lord Bridge thought it would only be in exceptional cases that a constructive trust could be founded on an agreement entered into at a point later than the acquisition. To establish a common intention of shared beneficial ownership it is necessary to show that a bargain was entered into between the parties, whether expressly or impliedly. A verbal agreement, in reliance upon which the father undertook the expenditure, would be sufficient to found a claim under a constructive trust. If the father can point to no express bargain, then it may be possible to infer an agreement based on the conduct of the parties. In *Lloyds Bank plc* v *Rosset* it was said that the conduct must provide a basis from which to infer a common intention. In addition, it was necessary to show that the beneficial owner had changed her position in reliance on the agreement. In *Gissing* v *Gissing* [1971] AC 886, it was said that one party must have been induced by the other to act to their detriment. Thus, the father could argue that by spending his insurance money on the conversion of the bedroom he had acted in reliance on the agreement entered into at the time of the acquisition of the house. Clearly, this will be easier to establish if he can show an express agreement at the time of the acquisition of the house. If, however, it is established that his payment of the deposit was a gift or loan, then it will prove singularly difficult to show that his expenditure on the conversion of the bedroom was based on an implied common agreement that the beneficial ownership should be shared.

In respect of Bill, the situation is different since he did not make a contribution at the outset. According to Lord Bridge in *Lloyds Bank plc* v *Rosset*, it is in exceptional cases that a common intention can be deduced to share in the beneficial ownership at a date later than the time of acquisition. Bill's contribution is £5,000 to the renovation of the house and the payment of the housekeeping costs. It would seem extremely unlikely that a resulting trust would be implied in the case of either of the contributions. The cost of the renovations and the housekeeping expenses would not amount to direct contributions to the purchase price, nor would they amount to the equivalent of purchase money (*Burns* v *Burns* [1984] Ch 317 and *Pettit* v *Pettit* [1970] AC 777). Similarly, in the context of constructive trusts the outcome is scarcely more positive for Bill. In the absence of an express agreement, it is necessary to show detrimental reliance on an implied bargain. Bill could argue that the use of his redundancy money is clear evidence of detrimental conduct. His labour alone is unlikely to be sufficient to establish detrimental conduct. In *Eves* v *Eves* [1975] 1 WLR 1338, the woman's arduous work of renovation was held to have been carried out in reliance on a common intention that she should share the beneficial ownership. The conduct of the man in inducing her to agree that the property should be put in his name alone was clear evidence of a common intention and her work would not have been carried out without such an agreement. However, in the present case, Bill's work may not fall into the same category. On its own, without any express agreement as to beneficial ownership, it might be viewed as solely an anxiety on his part to improve his living conditions. In *Lloyds Bank plc* v *Rosset* the woman's work in assisting in the renovation of the house was simply attributed to her anxiety to move the family in quickly. It was not sufficient evidence to point to an agreement as to shared beneficial ownership. On the other hand, Bill's work, coupled with his expenditure, might increase his chance of a successful claim. It would seem apparent, however, that his payment of the housekeeping expenses would have no relevance in establishing beneficial ownership. In *Gissing* v *Gissing*, it was held that the wife's contribution to the household expenditure and her labour in caring for the family was insufficient evidence of detrimental conduct in reliance on a common intention to share beneficially in the ownership. Therefore, whilst it may well be possible for the father to rebut the presumption of advancement and establish a resulting trust in his favour, at least in respect of his payment of the deposit, it seems less likely that Bill will be able to establish a constructive trust.

The difference between a resulting trust and a constructive trust may well be important as regards their enforceability against a third party. A resulting trust is more likely to bind a third party than a constructive trust as it arises initially when the property is purchased, and is for money or money's worth. A constructive trust can arise only when a party has acted to his detriment, which must necessarily be some time after the acquisition of the property, and may also include some element of voluntary disposition.

The different effects are well illustrated by the case of *Densham* v *Densham* [1975] 1 WLR 1519. In that case, a wife had contributed one-ninth of the original deposit on a house which was conveyed into the name of her husband only. The husband later became bankrupt. It was held that the one-ninth share which she had under a resulting trust was binding on the trustee in bankruptcy, as it preceded the bankruptcy in time and was for value. A further share which she claimed under a constructive trust was voidable by the husband's trustee in bankruptcy as it involved an element of voluntary distribution.

Drake v *Whipp* (1995) 28 HLR 531, emphasised the importance of the distinction between resulting and constructive trusts even as between the parties themselves. In particular, it affected the size of the share. In relation to constructive trusts, 'a broad brush approach' is to be adopted which could take account of contributions to the overall cost of the property. Resulting trusts, on the other hand, permitted the size of the share to be quantified only by reference to the cost of acquisition.

If either party has an equitable interest in the house, then, as they are both in actual occupation, this will constitute an overriding interest under the Land Registration Act 1925, s. 70(1)(g). As the capital money is paid to only one trustee (Nancy) by the Fagin Finance Emporium, the doctrine of overreaching will not operate. The Fagin Finance Emporium will, therefore, take subject to the rights of any beneficiaries.

(b) The law relating to a share acquired in the matrimonial home by a spouse whose name was not on the legal title was originally also determined under a resulting or constructive trust, and indeed *Gissing* concerned a married couple. The case law has been superseded as regards married couples, however, by the Matrimonial Proceedings & Property Act 1970, s. 37, and the Matrimonial Causes Act 1973 (as amended by the Matrimonial and Family Proceedings Act 1984).

The former provides that the beneficial interest of either spouse in 'real or personal property' may be enlarged by that spouse contributing substantially in money or money's worth to the improvement of such property.

Section 37 applies in the absence of any agreement to the contrary, and has been described by Lord Denning MR as purely declaratory of the previous case law (*Davis* v *Vale* [1971] 1 WLR 1021). The answer is therefore unchanged, but as far as Bill is concerned, his share may be determined by an application to the court under the Act.

The Matrimonial Causes Act 1973 applies only on divorce and so would not apply here. Where it does apply it gives a court very extensive powers of property disposition between the spouses, taking into account circumstances relevant to their conduct in the marriage as well as their contributions to the property.

The answer is unchanged as regards Nancy's father.

(c) Had Nancy been declared bankrupt, then, where an application is made by the trustee in bankruptcy to a court with jurisdiction over the bankruptcy, the Insolvency Act 1986, s. 335A (inserted by Sch. 3 of the Trusts of Land and Appointment of Trustees Act 1996) applies. The court shall make such order as it thinks just and reasonable having regard to the criteria set out in s. 335A(2). These criteria include the interests of the bankrupt's creditors and, where a dwelling-house is involved which is or has been the home of the spouse or former spouse, then the conduct of that spouse in contributing to the bankruptcy is to be considered. Further matters include the needs and financial resources of that spouse and the needs of any children, and all the circumstances of the case other than the needs of the bankrupt. This might presumably include the fact that the house is also Nancy's father's home. After one year, however, the interests of the creditors are to become paramount unless there are exceptional circumstances.

It is likely that the same considerations will be applied if Nancy and Bill are unmarried. In *Re Domenico Citro* [1991] Ch 142, Nourse LJ said that the case law relating to unmarried couples is the same as the statutory law relating to married couples, so the same considerations may well be taken into account by the court if Nancy and Bill are unmarried.

There is no indication in the statute of the relative weights to be given to the competing interests of the creditors and other parties with an interest. Each case must depend on its facts (*Abbey National* v *Moss* [1994] 1 FLR 307, and *Re Domenico Citro* (above)). In a recent Court of Appeal decision (*Bank of Baroda* v *Dhillon and another* (1997) *The Times*, 4 November), the priority to be given to the interests of the creditors in preference to those of a spouse with an overriding interest, was recognised where an application for an order for sale under s. 30, Law of Property Act 1925 (now s. 14 of the Trusts of Land and Appointment of Trustees Act 1996) was made.

10   Proprietary Estoppel and Licences

INTRODUCTION

There is a difficulty in seeking to establish separate categories for such topics as estoppel and licences and, indeed, constructive trusts, since in many of the cases they seem to be inextricably linked. Question 3, a mixed question, attempts to tackle this overlap. In so far as the doctrine of proprietary estoppel has a separate existence it deals with the situation where a party attempts to renege on an agreement in breach of equitable principles. There is no single judicial pronouncement on the doctrine, although the classic exposition is normally considered to have been that of Lord Kingsdown in *Ramsden* v *Dyson* (1866) LR 1 HL 129 at 170. There are further developments of the doctrine in *Crabb* v *Arun District Council* [1976] Ch 179 and *E.R. Ives Investment Ltd* v *High* [1967] 2 QB 379. There is a development of the case law which has evolved the doctrine, so that the modern approach, confirmed by *Taylors Fashions Ltd* v *Liverpool Victoria Trustees Co. Ltd* [1982] QB 133, shows a broader direction without the requirement of satisfying a number of strict prerequisites established in some of the earlier cases. However, it remains necessary to know the essentials for establishing the doctrine, i.e., the assurance of entitlement given by the owner, the reliance on the assurance by the claimant, and the detriment caused by that reliance.

Questions relating to the topic of licences usually bear upon one (or both) of two issues. The first is the question of the nature of the interest. Does it create a mere personal permission to use land in a certain way or does it have a proprietary dimension? The second question flows from the first. Can a licence bind third parties? It is necessary to be able to distinguish between the different types of licences — bare, coupled with an interest and contractual. Then there follows the question of the manner of protection of the equity raised by the estoppel, and an abundance of case law providing a variety of examples of the way that this dilemma can be resolved. This is an area where there is much judicial doctrinal debate and the precedents need to be read with care.

QUESTION 1

'The more recent cases indicate that the application of the *Ramsden* v *Dyson* principle — whether you call it proprietary estoppel, estoppel by acquiescence or estoppel by encouragement is really immaterial — requires a very much broader approach which is directed rather at ascertaining whether, in particular individual circumstances, it would be unconscionable for a party to be permitted to deny that which, knowingly, or unknowingly, he has allowed or encouraged another to assume to his detriment than to enquiring whether the circumstances can be fitted within the confines of some preconceived formula serving as a universal yardstick for every form of unconscionable behaviour.' (*per* Oliver J in *Taylors Fashion Ltd* v *Liverpool Victoria Trustees Co. Ltd* (1982).)

Discuss.

Commentary

This essay question requires a knowledge of the historical development of the doctrine of proprietary estoppel. As with the development of constructive trusts, the ambit of the doctrine has been ill-defined and it probably remains that way. Oliver J's dictum has been described as a watershed in the judicial approach to the doctrine and is pivotal to the discussion. However, as with all equitable doctrines, the parameters remain vaguely drawn and the essay should include reference to any dissent from Oliver J's view.

This topic probably has a glowing future since it seems able to replace the doctrine of part performance which was abolished by the Law of Property (Miscellaneous Provisions) Act 1989, s. 2.

There are numerous articles on this topic which include: Battersby [1991] *Conv* 36 and Evans [1988] *Conv* 346.

Suggested Answer

Proprietary estoppel is an equitable doctrine whereby a person is prevented from insisting on his strict legal rights when it would be inequitable for him to do so having regard to the dealings which have taken place between the parties (*Hughes* v *Metropolitan Railway Co.* (1877) 2 App Cas 439). According to the modern case law on the subject, it would seem to be essential to show that there has been some assurance of an individual's rights and some detrimental reliance on those rights. This approach is referred to in Oliver J's *dictum*. Earlier cases took a stricter approach to the establishment of the doctrine.

The equitable doctrine of 'encouragement and acquiescence', now called proprietary estoppel, appeared in the dissenting opinion of Lord Kingsdown in *Ramsden v Dyson* (1866) LR 1 HL 129. This case was followed by *Willmott* v *Barber* (1880) 15 ChD 96, which established strict criteria (or tests) for the application of the doctrine of proprietary estoppel. These criteria were necessary, according to Fry J, in order to establish that it would be tantamount to fraud for individuals to assert their strict legal rights. This fraudulent conduct comprised the legal owner remaining silent in the face of someone else's mistaken belief. In this case it was considered that the mistake must be unilateral; i.e., only that of the person who believes he has a right.

The strict criteria were fivefold:

(a)   the plaintiff must have made a mistake as to his legal rights;

(b)   the plaintiff must have spent money or done some act on the faith of his mistaken belief;

(c)   the defendant, as holder of the legal right, must know of the existence of his own right which is inconsistent with the right claimed by the plaintiff;

(d)   the defendant must know of the plaintiff's mistaken belief; and

(e)   the defendant must have encouraged the plaintiff in his expenditure of money or the other acts performed, either directly, or by abstaining from asserting his legal right.

Originally, these criteria were followed diligently and it was considered necessary to establish them in every case before the doctrine could be applied. However, as the statement of Oliver J suggests, the attitude towards them has changed, and in some later cases they have been followed whilst in others, they have been selectively ignored. In *Inwards* v *Baker* [1965] 2 QB 29, there was no mistaken belief on either side. Each knew the state of the title, but the defendant had built a bungalow on his father's land in the expectation that he would be allowed to remain living there. The court held that, although the strict criteria in *Willmott* v *Barber* had not been satisfied, this was a case where the person who made the expenditure had been induced by an expectation, and equity would protect him to prevent an injustice. All that was considered necessary was that the licensee should, at the request or with the encouragement of the owner of the land, have spent the money in the expectation of being allowed to stay there. The court expressed the view that it would not allow that expectation to be defeated if it would be inequitable to do so. This represented a considerable relaxation of the *Willmott* v *Barber* criteria.

In *E.R. Ives Investment Ltd* v *High* [1967] 2 QB 379, again, the strict criteria were not adhered to. There was an agreement upon which the defendant acted and the plaintiff's predecessor in title acquiesced. Neither party was mistaken as to the rights intended to be created. Nevertheless, the acquiescence in the defendant's expenditure under the agreement was held to give rise to an estoppel binding upon the plantiff.

The basis for this broader application of principle might be considered to be the opinion of Lord Kingsdown in *Ramsden* v *Dyson* (1866) LR 1 HL 129. In this case, he considered that the doctrine of estoppel could arise where there was the fostering of an expectation in the minds of both parties at the time, which, once acted upon, it would be unconscionable to deny later.

In *Crabb* v *Arun District Council* [1976] Ch 179, the plaintiff altered his legal position in the expectation, encouraged by the defendants, that he would have a right of access to his land over a road owned by the defendants. There was no mistaken belief on either part. The defendants even erected a gate to provide for the plaintiff's access. It should, however, be noted that Scarman LJ, did rely on the five criteria and must have considered them satisfied because he concurred with the other judges in allowing the claim of estoppel to succeed.

In *Taylors Fashions Ltd* v *Liverpool Victoria Trustees Co. Ltd* [1982] QB 133 the mistake made was not unilateral. It related to the enforceability of an option to renew a lease. It had not been thought necessary to register such an option as it was contained in the lease and ran with the land. However, it had been decided in another case that such options required registration. In *Taylors Fashions* the plaintiffs had incurred considerable expenditure in reliance on the option, which had not been registered. When the defendants refused to renew the lease, the plaintiffs argued that they were estopped from doing so as they had acquiesced in the expenditure. The plaintiff's claim was, in fact, refused, although the refusal was not on the basis of failing to comply with the strict criteria established in *Willmott* v *Barber*. Oliver J held that the doctrine of proprietary estoppel required a broader approach which depended on the particular circumstances of the individual case. It was necessary to demonstrate that it would be unconscionable for a party to deny that which he had allowed or encouraged another to assume to his detriment. This was more pertinent to any particular case than seeking to confine the doctrine within some 'preconceived formula serving as a universal yardstick for every form of unconscionable behaviour'.

Thus, *Taylors Fashions* indicates that the five tests (which are, in any event, more relevant to cases based on unilateral mistake) are no longer to be slavishly followed. Where there is no unilateral mistake, but an encouragement by acquiescence or a common expectation, this relaxation of the doctrine is clearly important. It is noteworthy, however, that in cases as recent as *Crabb* v *Arun District Council* [1976], there is still evidence of a judicial determination to fit any case of proprietary estoppel into the straitjacket of *Willmott* v *Barber*.

QUESTION 2

Cyril was the registered proprietor of Acacia Lodge. Five years ago, he told his Aunt Agatha that she could live there rent-free for as long as she wanted provided she did any necessary repairs. Agatha gave up her council flat and moved in. Agatha was very nervous about intruders so she spent £2,000 on security locks and a burglar alarm. Cyril only found out about this when he visited her one day and accidentally set off the alarm.

Last year, Cyril sold Acacia Lodge to Derek at half the market value for a vacant property of that type. Cyril told Derek about the arrangement with Aunt Agatha and Derek assured him that he was looking at the property as a long term investment.

Earlier this year, Aunt Agatha decided to replace the windows as the house was very cold. She had double-glazed units installed at a cost of £5,000 which absorbed practically all of her life-savings. When Derek came to visit Acacia Lodge, he told her he was absolutely delighted about the windows. He said: 'As long as you carry on paying for all the outgoings and repairs you can do what you want with the place as we agreed'.

Derek was killed in a road accident last week. The devisee of Acacia Lodge now wishes to sell it with vacant possession. Advise Aunt Agatha.

Commentary

This is a question which cuts across the areas also covered in **Chapter 11**. It can be difficult to decide whether the circumstances presented give rise to a resulting or constructive trust, to a contractual licence or to the doctrine of proprietary estoppel. If in doubt, go in with all guns firing. Separate out the arguments for each type of equitable remedy or you might shoot yourself in the foot. There are overlaps, but it is easier to handle the issues if you keep the points separate. This is a question that requires the inclusion of a lot of case law to illustrate the points.

Suggested Answer

There are several potential causes of action based upon a contractual licence, a constructive trust and the doctrine of proprietary estoppel.

Contractual licence

Agatha was told by Cyril that she could live in the property rent-free provided she undertook repairs. Such an agreement is capable of forming the subject-matter of a licence. However, the property was subsequently transferred to Derek so the issue is whether this licence is enforceable against Derek's devisee as a successor in title who was not a party to the licence agreement. The facts suggest that when Acacia Lodge was sold to Derek, it might have been sold subject to her rights, as reflected by the low price. In *Binions* v *Evans* [1972] Ch 359, it was agreed between the trustees of the Tredegar Estate that Mrs Evans should occupy a cottage on the estate for the rest of her life. The trustees sold the cottage to purchasers who bought at less than the market price because they took expressly subject to Mrs Evans' rights of occupation. Because of this, all three judges agreed that a constructive trust arose for Mrs Evans, but they disagreed as to the nature of the rights given to Mrs Evans under her agreement with the trustees. The majority took the view that she was a life tenant under the Settled Land Act 1925, but Lord Denning MR considered that she had a licence which was protected by the constructive trust. Lord Denning MR's view is inconsistent with the earlier House of Lords' authority of *King* v *David Allen & Sons (Billposting) Ltd* [1916] 2 AC 54, and the *dicta* in *Ashburn Anstalt* v *Arnold* [1989] Ch 1, that a licence cannot be an interest in land, although it is in line with the Court of Appeal decision in *Errington* v *Errington* [1952] 1 KB 290. Since the judicial authorities are in some disarray on this matter, the argument could be made (despite the recent judicial disapproval) that Agatha has a contractual licence which binds Derek if he took the land expressly subject to her rights — a matter which is clearly demonstrated since he took the property at half its vacant value. Derek's devisee, being a volunteer, can be in no better position.

Constructive trust

A constructive trust will be imposed by the court to prevent unjust enrichment or injustice. The constructive trust will arise where the holder of the legal estate cannot in good conscience take the beneficial interest (*per* Cardozo J in *Beatty* v *Guggenheim Exploration Co.* 225 NY 380 at 386 (1919) quoted by Lord Denning MR with approval in *Binions* v *Evans*). In *Bannister* v *Bannister* [1948] 2 All ER 133 an oral agreement was made whereby the defendant was permitted to stay in a cottage which she had sold to the plaintiff, 'as long as you like, rent-free'. The sale was at a considerably lower price than the market value. The Court of Appeal held that she was entitled under a constructive trust to a life interest determinable on her ceasing to live in the cottage. Again, in *Re Sharpe* [1980] 1 WLR 219, an elderly aunt lent money to her nephew to buy a house on the understanding that she could move in and live there for the rest of her life. After the aunt had moved in, the nephew went bankrupt and the trustee in bankruptcy sought possession. A constructive trust was imposed under which the aunt was entitled to remain in the house until she was repaid.

Aunt Agatha is told, as in *Bannister* v *Bannister*, that she may stay in Acacia Lodge for as long as she wants rent-free. However, she does not contribute money to the purchase although she does undertake some considerable expenditure — £2,000 for security systems and £5,000 for double-glazing. Recent cases such as *Lloyds Bank plc* v *Rosset* [1991] 1 AC 107 have emphasised the necessity of showing some bargain between the parties whether expressly agreed or to be implied from conduct. It is not apparent that there is any express agreement in this case so the evidence of expenditure would need to be very compelling to establish any intention that the parties intended that Aunt Agatha should share in the beneficial ownership. At best, her contribution might be viewed as a loan to be protected, as in *Re Sharpe*, by a constructive trust protecting her continuing occupation until such time as she is repaid. However, in *Re Sharpe*, the loan was made for the purpose of acquiring the property. In the present problem, the contribution is made firstly for installing security systems — a cost she might have incurred if she had remained in her council home, and secondly in respect of double glazing to which the same argument applies. Again, Derek's devisee, who is a volunteer, cannot be in any better position than Derek as regards any claim of Agatha's.

Proprietary estoppel

To rely on the doctrine of proprietary estoppel, Aunt Agatha must show that it would be unconscionable for her to be evicted from the property when she has been encouraged or allowed to assume to her detriment that she will be permitted to remain there for as long as she wished (*Taylors Fashions Ltd* v *Liverpool Victoria Trustees Co. Ltd* [1982] QB 133). She could rely on the promise made by Cyril and the assurance given her by Derek. Her actions in giving up her council flat and spending money on Acacia Lodge could amount to the detrimental conduct in reliance on the representations, which is necessary for her to establish to succeed under this head (*Crabb* v *Arun District Council* [1976] Ch 179).

The court will take account of the proportionality between the remedy and the detriment it is designed to avoid. In *Sledmore* v *Dalby* (1996) 72 P & CR 196, the plaintiff, an elderly woman in need of a home, sought possession of a house which her son-in-law had occupied for 30 years undertaking improvements in the belief that it would be left to his wife. The son-in-law had other accommodation, however, and was not in such need of the house as the plaintiff. The Court of Appeal held that it was inequitable to allow any expectation raised earlier to be defeated in the circumstances of the case. It would therefore be appropriate to consider the balance in Aunt Agatha's case between her interest and that of the devisee of Derek's estate.

Once Aunt Agatha has established the doctrine, the court would seek a way to satisfy her claim. In *Dodsworth* v *Dodsworth* (1973) 228 EG 1115, the defendants spent £700 on improvements to a bungalow in the expectation that they would be able to remain there for as long as they wished. The Court of Appeal held that the defendants would be allowed to remain in occupation until their expenditure was reimbursed. A more extreme example can be found in *Pascoe* v *Turner* [1979] 1 WLR 431, where the Court of Appeal ordered that the fee simple should be conveyed to the defendant who had spent £1,000 on the property in reliance on the promise that the property was hers.

Thus, Aunt Agatha may seek to rely on the doctrine of proprietary estoppel and any interest so protected would bind a volunteer such as Derek's devisee.

QUESTION 3

'The Court of Appeal [in *Ashburn Anstalt* v *Arnold* [1989] Ch 1] put what I hope is the quietus to the heresy that a mere licence creates an interest in land. They also put the quietus to the heresy that parties to a contractual licence necessarily become constructive trustees.' (*per* Sir Nicholas Browne-Wilkinson in *IDC Group Ltd* v *Clark* [1992] 1 EGLR 187, at 189.)

Discuss.

Commentary

This is one of those academic arguments which have huge practical conveyancing implications. You need to be completely familiar with all those property concepts that you studied early in your course such as personal rights and proprietary rights, rights *in personam* and rights in *rem* and so on. The cases are difficult, not least because the judgments may contain different arguments with which you need to be familiar. There are also differences between the cases which may mean that they are distinguishable and there may be room for reading into some of the judgments a more profound interpretation than they are sometimes accorded. The Court of Appeal judgment in *Ashburn Anstalt* v *Arnold* is sometimes said, for instance, to have brought an end to Lord Denning's development of the contractual licence. Read Fox LJ's judgment for yourself and form your own view.

For additional reading see 'Licences and Third Parties', Wade (1952) 68 *LQR* 337; Sheridan (1953) 17 *Conv* 440; Crane (1967) 31 *Conv NS* 332; Thompson [1983] *Conv* 50; Moriarty (1984) 100 *LQR* 376; Dewar (1986) 49 *MLR* 741, to name but a few articles from the many written on this subject. This is an erudite topic which has spawned many commentaries.

Suggested Answer

The original concept of a licence was that it created a right *in personam* which bound the immediate parties. A gratuitous or bare licence is one that gives a mere permission to use land in a certain way. Such permission may be withdrawn at any time by the licensor. A contractual licence is one that is supported by consideration. Again, it was originally thought only to bind the parties to the contract under the doctrine of privity of contract. If it were withdrawn, then an action for damages might lie. It may be possible that an injunction would be available where, on the proper construction of the contract, the licence was irrevocable (*Winter Garden Theatre (London) Ltd* v *Millenium Productions Ltd* [1948] AC 173). Thus, as between the parties to the contract, equity might intervene in order to preserve the bargain.

However, such equitable intervention in itself does not necessarily extend to the creation of an interest in land. Such a development would lead to the result that a contractual licence would bind a third party. Earlier cases are clear on the point that a contractual licence is not capable of being a proprietary right and cannot, therefore, bind third parties. The earliest statement of this view was in *Thomas* v *Sorrell* (1674) Vaugh 330. The more recent decision of the House of Lords in *King* v *David Allen & Sons (Billposting) Ltd* [1916] 2 AC 54, concluded that a licence to affix advertisements to the side of a cinema wall did not bind the successors in title to the original contracting party. This view was followed by the Court of Appeal in *Clore* v *Theatrical Properties Ltd* [1936] 3 All ER 483. The subsequent development of judicial authority on this point has, unfortunately, not followed the clarity of this line of reasoning and there are two cases which can be cited as standing for the proposition that a contractual licence can bind a third party.

The first of these is *Errington* v *Errington* [1952] 1 KB 290. In this case the Court of Appeal held that a son and daughter-in-law were licensees of a house subject to the condition that they paid the mortgage instalments. Since the breach of this contractual licence could have been restrained by the intervention of equity, this had the effect of creating an interest in equity which was vested in the licensees. This equitable interest bound third parties, in this case, the licensor's widow who had inherited the house. This principle was also followed in *E.R. Investment Ltd* v *High* [1967] 2 QB 379, where a licence was created which was binding on a purchaser for value and this decision has recently been referred to with approval in *Thatcher* v *Douglas* (1995) 146 NLJ 282.

Secondly, the case of *Binions* v *Evans* [1972] Ch 359, further strengthened this development of the contractual licence. In this case, a contractual licence was enforced against a purchaser who took a conveyance of land expressly subject to it. Mrs Evans had entered into a written agreement with the Tredegar Estate trustees whereby she was permitted to remain in a cottage on the estate for the rest of her life free of rent and rates. The conveyance to purchasers was expressed to be subject to this condition and this was reflected in the price. The purchasers then sought to gain possession of the cottage on the ground that they were not bound by her interest. The Court of Appeal were unanimous in deciding that Mrs Evans was protected as a constructive trust arose. Two of the judges considered that the agreement entered into created a settlement under the Settled Land Act 1925 and Mrs Evans was the tenant for life. Lord Denning MR, however, argued that since the purchasers took expressly subject to her rights, her contractual licence was protected. A licence bound a third party where a constructive trust arose and such a trust would arise where a person took land expressly subject to it. He distinguished the earlier decisions in *King* v *David Allen & Sons (Billposting) Ltd* and *Clore* v *Theatrical Properties Ltd* on the ground that actual occupation would be required before a contractual licence could bind a third party. This viewpoint was accepted in *DHN Food Distributors Ltd* v *Tower Hamlets London Borough Council* [1976] 1 WLR 852 where an irrevocable contractual licence was said to give rise to a constructive trust which gave the licensees a sufficient interest in land to qualify for compensation for disturbance. In addition, in *Re Sharpe* [1980] 1 WLR 219 an irrevocable licence to occupy a house until a loan was repaid was held to bind the trustee in bankruptcy.

Although there is no House of Lords decision which is a direct authority in this area, views have been expressed in various cases. In *National Provincial Bank Ltd* v *Ainsworth* [1965] AC 1175 the view that a contractual licence could be converted into a proprietary interest was treated with reluctance. In *National Provincial Bank Ltd* v *Hastings Car Mart Ltd* [1964] Ch 665 the Court of Appeal took the traditional view that a contractual licence creates no more than a personal right and, as such, cannot bind a purchaser regardless of notice. In *Ashburn Anstalt* v *Arnold*, Fox LJ obiter could not accept that, where land was sold expressly subject to a licence a constructive trust should, as a general proposition, be imposed. The fact that a purchaser may have notice of a contractual licence was not, he considered, enough to subject him to it. He considered that the decision in *Errington* v *Errington* was in conflict with earlier authority including the decisions of the House of Lords in *King* v *David Allen & Sons (Billposting) Ltd* and *Clore* v *Theatrical Properties Ltd*. However, Fox LJ does appear to leave open the possibility that there may be occasions where the conscience of the purchaser is affected and that in a situation where a purchaser takes title subject to another's rights and, in consequence, takes at a lower price (as in *Binions* v *Evans*), a constructive trust will be imposed. Fox LJ's remarks, although obiter, have been referred to as authoritative in *Habermann* v *Koehler* (1996) 72 P & CR D10.

Thus, the status of contractual licences remains in some doubt. It would seem unlikely that it could be said with certainty that there are no circumstances where a contractual licence would create a proprietary interest and, thus, be capable of binding third parties. The strict view of the earlier cases has clearly been eroded. The effect of the decisions in *Errington* v *Errington* and *Binions* v *Evans* has not been clearly laid to rest by the *dicta* in the more recent cases such as *Ashburn Anstalt* v *Arnold* [1989] Ch 1. (Although *Ashburn Anstalt* was overruled by *Prudential Assurance Co. Ltd* v *London Residuary Body* [1992] 2 AC 386 on other grounds, the dicta were not discussed and may be considered as authoritative.)

11 Leases and Licences

INTRODUCTION

The questions in this chapter have caused the writers a considerable headache! The reason for this is that it is difficult to know exactly what should be included under this heading and what may safely be left out.

You will doubtless have seen on the library shelves whole textbooks on the subject of landlord and tenant, and land law courses vary enormously as to the depth in which they deal with the subject. Most text books on landlord and tenant divide the subject into the general law of leases and the statutory law. Some land law courses may include some of the statutory law, although the majority will probably only touch lightly upon it, if at all.

Even the general law of leases is very wide however as it deals with the effect of a number of different covenants which are frequently found in leases. The advice on this topic must therefore be to *listen to your lecturer*! If your lecturer deals in depth with repairing covenants and practically ignores covenants against assignment, then you should do the same. You must be guided by the lectures and tutorials you are given as to which covenants you should pay attention to, and the depth in which the lecturer expects you to know some particular aspect of the subject. Be sure, too, that you look at the current year's lectures and tutorials — lecturers may get bored with a topic they have covered in some depth for a year or two and decide to have a change!

Having said that, Questions 1 and 3 are old favourites for examiners in some form or another. A perusal of Question 2 and its answer should give you a basic understanding of the nature of different types of leases; Question 6 and its answer give some idea of the complexity (and injustices) of the rules which did govern the enforceability of covenants against the original parties to a lease and between successors in title to the original parties; new rules have replaced them for leases made after 1 January 1996 to which the Landlord and Tenant (Covenants) Act 1995 applies. So it is in Questions 4 and 5 that we have dealt with the different forfeiture procedures and selected some particular covenants in leases for consideration. Therefore it is in answering these two questions that you need to consider the extent to which your lecturer has dealt with these particular covenants.

Both Question 4 and Question 5 deal with the assignment or sublease of the term of a lease, and Question 5 deals with the assignment of the landlord's reversion. It is quite possible for a truly sadistic examiner, perhaps labouring under the stresses of academic life, to dream up an extremely complicated problem involving the devolution of title to the lease and the reversion and the consequent enforceability of covenants between different parties. Although such a question may sound totally confusing on a first reading, *keep calm*! It is usually possible to reduce such questions to a diagrammatic form which clarifies the situation immediately. You should therefore do a rough diagram before embarking upon your answer. Once you have achieved this, you may be surprised at how comparatively simple the whole question becomes.

The diagrammatic form (used in some text books also) is to indicate a lease or a sublease by a vertical line and an assignment by a horizontal one. Thus the following sequence of dispositions is represented by the diagram below it.

L leases to T. T assigns to T1. T1 assigns to T2. T2 sublets to S. S assigns to S1. L assigns the reversion to L1.

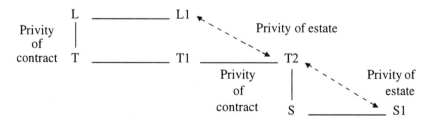

(It may, of course, also be important to note the order in which the dispositions occur.)

The significance of this diagram is that wherever two parties are joined by a vertical line, there will be privity of contract between them; wherever it is possible to join two parties by a single diagonal line, there will be privity of estate on the lease or sublease (or its reversion) assigned. If it is necessary to draw two diagonal lines however, then there will be no privity of estate or of contract. In the diagram on p. 134, there is privity of contract between L and T and between T2 and S. There is privity of estate on the headlease between L1 and T2, and on the sublease between T2 and S1. There is no privity of contract or estate between L1 and S or S1.

Once you have identified what privity, if any, exists between the parties, then you will be well on the way to determining what covenants are enforceable between them. The diagram should also help you to consider what possible indemnities may arise between the parties. You should remember, however, that these rules have changed for leases made on or after 1 January 1996, and there is now a very much more limited liability under the Landlord and Tenant (Covenants) Act 1995.

Question 5 is one where a diagram of this sort helps to clarify the situation and one has been included in the introduction to the question.

QUESTION 1

A year ago, George inherited a large Victorian house which he decided to convert into three flats from which he might derive an income. He therefore made the following arrangements:

(a)   He completed the conversion of the ground floor flat. On 1 May he signed a 'licence' giving Annie the right to occupy the flat for a payment of £200 per month. On 2 May, he signed an identical 'licence' giving Bob the right to occupy the flat with Annie or any other person whom George should select for a payment of £225 per month.

(b)   He completed the conversion of the small one-bedroomed attic flat and gave Joe and Linda a licence to occupy it at a fee of £400 per month. They both signed identical licence agreements which bore the same dates. The licence agreement also reserved the right to George to nominate another occupier or to occupy the flat himself. Linda recently vacated the flat, since when George has accepted only £200 fee per month from Joe.

(c)   The conversion of the basement flat is not yet completed but his niece, Marie, who recently left her husband and had nowhere to live, moved in last month and is paying a rent of £20 per week. George has kept a key to the premises in order to supervise the workmen and has entered the premises a few times for this purpose.

George has now received a very attractive offer for the freehold of the house from Horace. Advise Horace as to whether he will be able to obtain vacant possession of the flats.

Commentary

This question is on an area of law which has been the source of much litigation. The reason for this was the extensive rent control and security of tenure given to tenants for many years by legislation. The courts recognised that this could affect a landlord unfairly as he could find that he had inadvertently created a tenancy, which became protected, by letting an occupier into his premises under circumstances of exigency or kindness on his part.

With the demise of strict security of tenure and rent control, it is possible that we shall see fewer of these types of cases. The fundamental distinction between a lease and a licence (that the former is an interest in land whilst the latter is not) will nevertheless remain important in determining whether rights granted to an occupier will bind a third party or not. Moreover, a licence will not give a business tenant a right to extend his occupation under the Landlord and Tenant Act 1954, Part II, whereas a lease will generally do so.

Suggested Answer

(a) In *Street* v *Mountford* [1985] AC 809 Lord Templeman said that wherever exclusive possession of premises is granted for a term at a rent, then *prima facie* a lease will be created. He warned that judges must be wary of 'sham' agreements, where a lease is disguised as something else, such as a licence or a service occupancy. In *Street* v *Mountford* itself, the agreement purported to be a licence and the landlord expressly reserved the right to enter the room to inspect and maintain it and to read the meters. It was held however that the reality was that a lease had been created whereby the tenant had exclusive possession for a term at a rent. The landlord's express reservation of rights of entry for certain purposes merely emphasised the tenant's right to exclusive possession.

Exclusive possession means however that the tenant may exclude everyone else, including the landlord, from the premises. Where premises are shared therefore, it is necessary to consider the nature of the sharing arrangements to decide whether the occupiers all have equal rights and interest in the whole of the property, in which case they may be joint tenants, or whether they all have different individual rights to parts of the property, which would be incompatible with a joint tenancy. Again, it is the reality of the arrangement which should be considered if this differs from the arrangement which the agreement purports to create.

In *Antoniades* v *Villiers* [1988] 3 WLR 1205 the two occupiers of a small one-bedroom flat paid equal contributions to payments of rent. It was held that the landlord's purported right to occupy was merely a sham, so that they had together exclusive possession and were tenants. On the other hand, in *AG Securities* v *Vaughan* [1988] 3 WLR 1205 four occupiers who signed different licence agreements on different dates and for different terms and different individual payments were held to be licensees of a four-bedroom flat as the necessary four unities were not present to make them joint tenants. Although they each had an exclusive right to occupy the flat with the other three, they did not collectively have a total exclusive possession.

Although Annie and Bob between them occupy the whole of the flat, the different agreements on different dates and for different payments would suggest that, as in *AG Securities* v *Vaughan*, they are licensees rather than joint tenants. George's right to select another occupier would also suggest that they do not have the necessary exclusive possession for a tenancy, unless this is in reality a 'sham'.

(**b**)   The fact that the agreement between George and Joe and Linda is called a licence is inconclusive (*Addiscombe Garden Estates* v *Crabbe* [1957] 3 WLR 980). Where possession of premises is given for a term at a rent, it will *prima facie* create a lease (*Street* v *Mountford*). Moreover, the intention of the parties is to be determined from the reality of the arrangement rather than any formal agreement. In his judgment in *Street* v *Mountford*, Lord Templeman warned the judges that they must be wary of 'sham' agreements.

One of the essentials of a valid lease is that the lessee must have exclusive occupation. If there are joint tenants, then they may collectively have exclusive occupation between them. If this is the situation, then if one joint tenant leaves the premises, the other joint tenants will be able to choose a successor if they so wish. If, however, there is a right reserved for the landlord to share the accommodation, or to put in another occupier, then this would tend to negate the notion of a joint tenancy. In *Antoniades* v *Villiers*, where a landlord reserved the right to occupy a small one-bedroom attic flat, it was held that this was unrealistic, and the arrangement therefore amounted to a tenancy and not a licence. The identical licence agreements to commence on the same date, and the fact that Joe and Linda pay equal contributions to the 'fee' of £400 per month, all suggest that they are joint tenants.

In *Mikeover* v *Brady* [1989] 3 All ER 618 however, identical licence agreements required two occupiers to take responsibility for their own payments of £86.66 per month. Although the fee was exactly the same for both of them, the Court of Appeal held that as it was not a joint liablity, the necessary unity of interest for a joint tenancy did not exist. The fact that George has accepted only the original £200 which Joe was liable to pay suggests that Joe and Linda were separately liable for a share of the 'fee', and this could mean that they were indeed licensees and not joint tenants.

(**c**)   The fact that George retains a key to the basement flat might suggest that Marie does not have exclusive possession, but only exclusive occupation. In *Luganda* v *Service Hotels Ltd* [1969] 2 Ch 209, where the landlord retained a key to enter a room and carry out certain minimal services such as cleaning, the occupier was held to have exclusive occupation, which enabled him to exclude everyone except the landlord, but he did not have exclusive possession as against the landlord, and did not therefore have a tenancy. In *Abbeyfield (Harpenden) Society Ltd* v *Woods* [1968] 1 WLR 374, although the occupier had exclusive possession of a room, the various services provided made the agreement as a whole a licence.

In *Family Housing Association* v *Jones* [1990] 1 All ER 385 however the retention of a key for purposes not related to shared occupation, but in order to discuss rehousing and inspect the state of repair of the premises, was not sufficient to negate exclusive possession. It may well be therefore that George's retention of a key for purposes not relating to his agreement with Marie does not detract from her exclusive possession so that she could have a lease.

Although Lord Templeman said in *Street* v *Mountford* that exclusive possession of premises for a term at a rent would *prima facie* create a lease, he did recognise that the circumstances of certain arrangements might mean that they were not intended to create legal relations at all. These could well be the types of agreement referred to earlier by Lord Denning MR in *Facchini* v *Bryson* [1952] 1 TLR 1386 which are affected by 'circumstances such as of family arrangement, and an act of friendship or generosity or such like'. If the rent which Marie pays is substantially below the market rent, and in fact is merely a nominal rent, then the arrangement may fall within this category. However, a small rent paid to a relative is not necessarily conclusive of a licence rather than a tenancy (see *Ward* v *Warnke* [1990] 22 HLR 496, where a son-in-law who paid a small rent to his parents-in-law was held to be a tenant of a holiday cottage which he occupied). In *Ashburn Anstalt* v *Arnold* [1989] Ch 1 the Court of Appeal confirmed that rent is not essential for a lease, so that presumably such an arrangement without any rent at all could still constitute a lease. In practice however, the higher the rent, the more difficult it will be to draw the inference that the agreement was in fact affected by any of Lord Denning MR's circumstances.

If the arrangements made by George have merely created licences then, because as the Court of Appeal confirmed in *Ashburn Anstalt* a licence is not an interest in land, the licensees will not have any rights binding upon Harold. As the premises are dwelling-houses however, the Protection from Eviction Act 1977, s. 5 requires that Harold should nevertheless give 28 days' notice to vacate the premises.

If the arrangements created leases, then these would be periodic tenancies and would be legal interests under the Law of Property Act 1925, s. 54(2). As such, they would be binding on Horace as purchaser.

The type of periodic tenancy is determined by the period by which the rent is expressed to be payable rather than the periods when it is actually paid, so that Annie and Bob would have a monthly tenancy terminable by one month's notice to terminate at the end of the month, and Marie would have a weekly tenancy, terminable by a week's notice. The Protection from Eviction Act 1977, s. 5, which applies to the occupation of dwelling-houses, requires however that Marie should be given 28 days' notice.

QUESTION 2

Consider the effect of the following dispositions:

(a)   A grants to B a lease of a flat for one day;

(b)   The grant of a lease to B for 20 years 'if he so long lives' at a rent of £1,000 per annum;

(c)   A lease of Black House to B for 20 years or until A should marry;

(d)   A grants B a lease for seven years with an option to renew on exactly the same terms as the present lease;

(e)   An oral agreement to grant a lease of Red House to B for two years at a market rent of £5,000 per annum to take effect in possession;

(f)   A grants B a yearly tenancy of White House not to be terminated by A unless B becomes unemployed.

Commentary

This is a straightforward question on leases if you know your general basic law on the subject well.

The different parts of the question require a knowledge of the operation of case law and statutory provisions on certain grants. It is the type of question to which you will either know the answer or not.

You would be unwise (unless desperate!) to attempt a question with six parts unless you are fairly sure of the answer to at least four parts of it. Unless your exam paper specifically states that all parts of the question merit equal marks, some parts may be worth more than others. Part (c) of this question, for instance, is a very short point on the wording of the Law of Property Act 1925, s. 149(6), whereas part (f) involves a fundamental point of law on the nature of leases, recently reaffirmed by the House of Lords, upsetting the decision in *Re Midland Railway Co.'s Agreement* [1971] Ch 725 which had stood since 1971. Part (f) gives a student the opportunity to show an understanding of the decision and its effect, and to pick up more marks than may be possible on part (c). It would be a strange examiner who did not regard an explanation of this as deserving of more marks than the short point in part (c)!

Suggested Answer

(a) One of the essential requirements of a lease is that it must be for a certain term. Although the technical name for a lease is 'a term of years' the Law of Property Act 1925, s. 205(1)(xxvii) specifically defines it as including 'a term for less than a year'. It is therefore possible to have a lease for just one day. The same definition section also says 'whether or not at a rent', so that it could still be a lease if no rent were reserved, although this is a factor which might suggest that it is instead a licence.

As the lease is for less than three years, it may also be a legal lease provided that it fulfils the other requirements of the Law of Property Act 1925, s. 54(2), i.e., it is at the best rent obtainable (a market rent) and takes effect in possession.

(b) A lease determinable upon death is for an uncertain duration and is therefore *prima facie* void. The Law of Property Act 1925, s. 149(6), states that a lease 'determinable with life or lives' at a rent or for a fine shall become a term of 90 years terminable by one month's written notice on the death. Although the section states that consideration for the lease is necessary, in *Griffiths* v *Williams* (1977) 248 EG 947 it was applied to a gratuitous lease in order to satisfy an estoppel. Presumably consideration would be necessary however for it to apply to an expressly created lease. Lack of any consideration would give B a life tenancy under a settlement before 1 January 1997, and presumably a life interest under a trust of land on or after that date (TLATA 1996).

The grant to B for 20 years determinable on his death is therefore converted to a term of 90 years, which may be determined by the grantor or B's personal representatives by one month's written notice on B's death.

Note that s. 149(6) was applied in *Skipton Building Society* v *Clayton* (1993) 66 P & CR 223 to an agreement which called itself a 'licence' but which the court found in reality to be a lease.

(c)   This grant is also for an uncertain duration and is therefore *prima facie* void. Although the Law of Property Act 1925, s. 149(6) rescues leases terminable on the *tenant's* marriage and converts them into a term of 90 years, it does not apply apparently to leases terminable on the marriage of anyone else. It would not therefore apply here and the grant would be void.

(d)   The grant of a lease containing an option to renew on exactly the same terms gives to B the right to require another lease with the same option to renew, and therefore contains the seeds of its own perpetual reproduction.

The Law of Property Act 1922, s. 145 converted such leases into terms of 2,000 years. The tenant alone has a right to terminate the lease by giving 10 days' notice to terminate on a date when the lease would have terminated but for its conversion into a 2,000-year term. The tenant must give notice of any assignment to the landlord, and such leases differ from other leases with regard to the privity of contract rule. Once the tenant has assigned the lease, he is no longer liable to the landlord on the covenants in the lease under privity of contract.

In construing a renewal option in a lease however, the courts will lean against interpreting it as giving a right to perpetual renewal. In *Marjorie Burnett Ltd* v *Barclay* (1980) 258 EG 642 the provision for review of rent on renewal was said to be inimical to the creation of a 2,000-year term and the lease was construed as giving only one further right to renew after the first renewal.

(e)   A lease for two years at a market rent which takes effect in possession will be a legal lease within the Law of Property Act 1925, s. 54(2), notwithstanding that it is 'parol'.

Before the Law of Property (Miscellaneous Provisions) Act 1989 there was an anomaly in that even though such a lease could be validly granted orally, an agreement for such a lease had to satisfy the Law of Property Act 1925, s. 40, and was only enforceable if evidenced in writing or supported by part performance. Section 2(5)(a) of the 1989 Act removes this anomaly by providing that an agreement for such a lease does not have to comply with s. 2(1) of the 1989 Act and is therefore valid even though oral.

(f) A periodic tenancy satisfies the requirement that a lease must be for a fixed and definite duration as it is regarded as being a lease for the period which is automatically renewed and runs on from one period to the next unless notice is given by either party. In *Breams Property Investment Co. Ltd* v *Stroulger* [1948] 2 KB 1 a restriction prohibiting the landlord from giving notice to quit during the first three years was, however, accepted as valid.

In *Re Midland Railway Co.'s Agreement* [1971] Ch 725, a provision that the landlord would not give notice to quit unless it required the demised premises for the purposes of its undertaking was also accepted as valid. In *Prudential Assurance Co.* v *London Residuary Body* [1992] 2 AC 386, however, the House of Lords affirmed the rule in *Lace* v *Chantler* [1944] KB 368 that the duration of a lease must be certain. They expressed the opinion that *Re Midland Railway* had been wrongly decided as the restriction on one party to give a notice to quit was governed by events which were uncertain, thus rendering the duration of the whole term uncertain. In *Prudential Assurance Co.*, a local authority had granted a lease of land until it was 'required by the Council for the purposes of the widening of Walworth Road and the street paving rendered necessary thereby'. It was held that the grant was void as a lease as the term granted was of uncertain duration. The tenant therefore had a yearly tenancy, which arose by reason of his occupation and payment of rent on a yearly basis.

A's grant of the yearly tenancy would therefore be void for uncertainty of term, although B might acquire an implied yearly periodic tenancy if he occupies the White House and pays rent annually.

QUESTION 3

(a) 'There is now no distinction ... between a lease and an agreement for a lease' (Field J in *Re Maughan* (1885) 14 QBD 958). Discuss.

(b) Leslie is the registered proprietor of two cottages, Nos. 1 and 2 Sycamore Terrace, which he inherited from his aunt.

A year ago, he agreed in writing to let No. 1 to Abigail for five years at a rent of £2,500 per annum. Both he and Abigail signed the agreement. Abigail took possession and has paid rent monthly. However, Abigail has been away visiting relatives in Australia for the last three months.

Six months ago, Leslie alone signed an agreement to let No. 2 to Bodgem Ltd for two years at £20 per month, the term to begin one year thereafter. The low rent was because the agreement stated that Bertram, the managing director of Bodgem Ltd, was to occupy the cottage and that he would carry out certain modernisations. Leslie allowed Bertram to move into the cottage three months ago, in order to begin the work.

Leslie has now sold the freehold of both the cottages to Percy who wants to know whether the agreements are binding upon him.

Would your answer differ if the title to the two properties were unregistered?

Commentary

Part (**a**) of this question is a straightforward book question, the answer to which is to be found in most textbooks on land law. It does however illustrate the vital differences between a legal estate in land and an equitable one, and so is quite fundamental to an understanding of land law.

In the course of your answer, you would probably mention the case of *Walsh* v *Lonsdale* (1882) 21 ChD 9, which was one of the first cases to apply the Judicature Act 1875, s. 25(11) (now the Supreme Court Act 1981, s. 49(1)). This provides that in the event of a conflict between common law and equity, equity shall prevail. The result is that where there is a valid contract to create or transfer an interest in land of which equity will grant specific performance, the contract itself creates an equitable interest. The principle is not confined to leases, but is generally applicable in land law, and a reference in your answer to the broader principle would be appropriate as showing a general understanding of property law.

Part (**b**) of the question gives you an opportunity to apply this fundamental knowledge. Although the question asks about the binding effect of different arrangements on a purchaser, it is essential to decide first what interests, if any, the agreements or arrangements create before you are able to decide whether they will bind a purchaser or not. So your answer should address this question first.

It is not unusual for questions on land law papers to ask about the effect of a transaction in both registered and unregistered title, and you should be prepared for this.

Suggested Answer

(a) A deed must be used in order to create, or to convey, a legal estate or a legal interest in land (Law of Property Act 1925, s. 52(1), re-enacting an earlier provision in the Conveyancing Act 1881). The exception to this is a lease not exceeding three years which complies with the requirements of the Law of Property Act 1925, s. 54(2) (at the best rent obtainable without a fine and taking effect in possession), which may be legal notwithstanding that it is created by parol.

A *contract* for the 'sale or other disposition' of land will be enforceable however if it complies with certain formal requirements. Before 27 September 1989, such a contract had to be evidenced in writing to satisfy the Law of Property Act 1925, s. 40, although equity would be prepared to enforce a purely oral contract if there was a sufficient act of part performance. The Law of Property (Miscellaneous Provisions) Act 1989, s. 2, requires such contracts, created after 26 September 1989, to be actually in writing and signed by both parties, or in two parts with one part signed by each party, and the two parts exchanged, as in a normal conveyancing transaction. The 1989 Act repeals the Law of Property Act 1925, s. 40, and it probably also abolishes the doctrine of part performance, although it may well be that a purely oral estoppel will be recognised as making a contract enforceable where it is affected by this.

Where the actual lease, conveyance, or other document purporting to create or to convey a legal estate or interest is in writing but has not been executed as a deed, then provided it complies with s. 2 of the 1989 Act as to signatures, it will create a valid contract to create or convey the estate or interest. Under the doctrine of *Walsh* v *Lonsdale* (1882) 21 ChD 9 the grantee has an equitable estate or interest, that is, one which equity will recognise and protect.

A legal lease must therefore be created either by deed, or fall within the Law of Property Act 1925, s. 54(2). Equity may be prepared to grant specific performance of a valid contract for a lease, however, requiring the lessor to execute a valid legal lease.

It should be remembered, however, that the equitable remedy of specific performance is discretionary and will be awarded only according to equitable principles. One of these is the well-known equitable maxim that the party seeking an equitable remedy 'must come to equity with clean hands'. Therefore if the tenant is at fault in any way, for example, in arrears with the rent or in breach of some other covenant in the agreement, then the remedy will not be available to him. Thus in *Coatsworth* v *Johnson* (1886) 54 LT 520 a tenant who was in breach of his covenants under an equitable lease was unable to obtain specific performance of it. Nor will the remedy be granted if the order would cause the lessor to be in breach of an agreement with a third party. In *Warmington* v *Miller* [1973] QB 11 the court refused to grant a decree of specific performance of an agreement for a sublease where the headlease contained a covenant against subletting, as an order to execute a sublease would necessarily have caused the tenant to be in breach of his covenant with the head lessor in the headlease.

As between the two contracting parties to an agreement for a lease, the agreement will in most respects be as good as a lease itself. The Law of Property Act 1925, s. 62, will not apply, however, to give to the tenant as easements the benefit of rights previously enjoyed by the demised premises. This is because s. 62 applies only to a 'conveyance', and it was held in *Borman* v *Griffith* [1930] 1 Ch 493 that a contract for a lease is not within the definition of a conveyance in the Law of Property Act 1925, s. 205, as 'an assurance of property or an interest therein'. It could not therefore operate to pass to an equitable lessee a right of way over a drive; although, on the facts of the case, it was held that he obtained the right under the rule in *Wheeldon* v *Burrows* (1879) 12 ChD 31, which will apply to a contract, such as an equitable lease. In *Wright* v *Macadam* [1949] 2 KB 744, s. 62 was held to apply however to a two-year written agreement for a lease within the Law of Property Act 1925, s. 54(2), as this was within the definition of a conveyance in s. 205.

Furthermore, on the assignment of an equitable lease or the landlord's reversion, the equitable lease may not be as good as a legal lease as regards the passing of the benefit and burden of its covenants. If the equitable tenant assigns his equitable lease, he is merely assigning the benefit of a contract and not a legal estate. There cannot therefore be any relationship of privity of estate where there is an assignment of the equitable lease or of the reversion on it.

The general rule is that it is possible to assign the benefit of a contract, but not the burden. So in *Manchester Brewery* v *Coombs* [1901] 2 Ch 608, the purchasers of a brewery became the assignees of the reversion of an hotel. They were able to enforce a covenant by the *original* tenant to buy beer only from the brewery, as the benefit of the covenant passed to them. In *Purchase* v *Lichfield Brewery Co.* [1915] 1 KB 184, however, the plaintiff landlords were unable to claim rent against the assignee by mortgage of an equitable tenant, as the burden of the covenants in the equitable lease did not pass to the mortgagee.

As regards equitable leases created on or after 1 January 1996, however, the Landlord and Tenant (Covenants) Act 1995, which applies also to equitable leases, will change this situation as it provides for the benefit and burden of all covenants (other than purely personal ones) to pass to assignees.

In unregistered title, legal leases are rights *in rem* which bind everyone. This position pertains in registered title also, where legal leases exceeding 21 years are registrable substantively, and legal leases not exceeding 21 years are overriding interests under the Land Registration Act 1925, s. 70(1)(k).

A further disadvantage of an equitable lease is the one common to all equitable interests — that it may not necessarily bind a purchaser of the legal freehold estate in the land.

In unregistered title, the equitable lease is an estate contract and is registrable as a Class C(iv) land charge under the Land Charges Act 1972. If it is so registered, it will be binding against a purchaser of the legal estate for money or money's worth; if it is not so registered, it will not be binding, even if the purchaser has *actual notice* of the equitable lease (*Midland Bank Trust Co.* v *Green* [1981] AC 513).

In registered title, an equitable lease is neither registrable substantively, nor an overriding interest under the Land Registration Act 1925, s. 70(1)(k). This section refers to the 'grant' of a lease not exceeding 21 years, and so has been held to include legal leases, but not equitable ones arising from a contract (*City Permanent Building Society* v *Miller* [1952] Ch 840). An equitable lease is a minor interest and may be protected as such by notice or caution on the register. It may, of course, also become an overriding interest under the Land Registration Act 1925, s. 70(1)(g), if the tenant is in actual occupation or in receipt of the rents and profits, so that it is more likely to be binding than in unregistered title.

Nevertheless, it is possible under both systems for an equitable lease not to bind a purchaser of the legal estate.

(b)   Leslie's agreement to let No. 1 to Abigail cannot be a legal lease as it was not made by deed, and so did not comply with the formality requirement to create a legal estate in the Law of Property Act 1925, s. 52. As the agreement is in writing and signed by both of them however, it will be a valid agreement complying with the Law of Property (Miscellaneous Provisions) Act 1989,

s. 2(1). Assuming that equity will grant specific performance of the agreement, then Abigail has an equitable lease.

If such equitable lease is registered as a minor interest, then it will bind the purchaser, Percy. Even if not so registered, it would bind Percy if Abigail were in occupation for the purposes of the Land Registration Act 1925, s. 70(1)(g). It is not entirely clear what degree of occupation is necessary to claim an overriding interest under s. 70(1)(g). The underlying rationale for the section, however, is that in most cases actual occupation of property will amount to notice to a purchaser of the occupier's interest. If Abigail's furniture and personal possessions are still in the cottage, therefore, this might well be sufficient occupation to give her an overriding interest under s. 70(1)(g), notwithstanding that she is not physically present when Percy buys.

In addition to her equitable lease, Abigail would also have a periodic tenancy by reason of occupying premises and paying rent. The type of periodic tenancy would be determined by reference to the period by which she pays rent (*Adler* v *Blackman* [1953] 1 QB 146). The rent is expressed as a figure per annum, and she would therefore have a yearly periodic tenancy. All periodic tenancies are legal under the Law of Property Act 1925, s. 54(2), and are overriding interests under the Land Registration Act 1925, s. 70(1)(k), being legal leases not exceeding 21 years. The legal periodic tenancy would therefore be binding in any event on Percy, who would have to give six months' notice to terminate it at the end of the year.

If the title to the cottages were unregistered, the five-year equitable lease would be binding on Percy if it were registered as a Class C(iv) land charge under the Land Charges Act 1972, but not otherwise. The legal periodic tenancy would however be binding, as legal estates and interests are rights *in rem* and binding against everyone. It could, of course, be determined by six months' notice as before.

Percy will not be bound by the agreement to let No. 2 to Bodgem Ltd if the agreement is void for non-compliance with the formalities of the Law of Property (Miscellaneous Provisions) Act 1989, s. 2(1). It is clear that such formalities are not satisfied, since the agreement was not signed by both parties.

A contract for a lease for a term of three years or less without taking a fine and at the best rent reasonably obtainable is not, however, subject to the formalities of s. 2(1), and can be made informally: Law of Property (Miscellaneous Provisions) Act 1989, s. 2(5). The only doubt in the problem is in regard to the rent. Although the monetary sum to be paid by Bodgem Ltd is low, at common law 'rent' can include the performance of services. The undertaking of the work by Bodgem Ltd can therefore comprise part of the rent, and so bring the agreement within s. 2(5) as being an agreement for a lease within s. 54(2), LPA 1925.

In that event, Bodgem Ltd has a valid estate contract with Leslie, which will bind Percy if protected by registration as a minor interest. Even if it is not so protected, it may bind Percy as the right of a person in actual occupation under the Land Registration Act 1925, s. 70(1)(g). Under the doctrine of separate corporate personality, Bodgem Ltd ranks as a person, albeit an artificial one. It can also be treated as being in actual occupation through Bertram, its managing director (*London & Cheshire Insurance Co. Ltd* v *Laplagrene* [1971] Ch 499).

QUESTION 4

Frieland Ltd is the freehold owner of a shop and separate flat above it.

In 1990 Frieland Ltd granted a 14-year lease of the shop to Curlywig, a firm of hairdressers. The lease includes covenants not to assign, sublet or part with the possession of the whole or any part of the property without the consent in writing of the landlord, to pay the rent of £20,000 per annum, and not to use the premises for any purpose other than that of a hairdressing business.

In 1991 Frieland Ltd granted a yearly tenancy of the flat above the shop to Susie.

In 1992 Curlywig applied in writing to Frieland Ltd for consent to assign the lease of the shop to Kingpin, a hairdresser, but some four months later had received no reply, in spite of repeatedly reminding Frieland Ltd of their application. Kingpin refused to wait any longer, so Curlywig assigned the lease to him, and Kingpin has paid the rent ever since to Frieland's agents.

A year ago, Kingpin started to have financial problems and so allowed Minnie to use part of the shop premises in the evenings as a massage parlour in return for a money payment. Kingpin is now three months in arrears with the rent.

Susie has been disturbed by unpleasant clients of the massage parlour ringing her bell and leaving the shop premises as late as 2.00 am.

Kingpin has now fallen into arrears with the rent, but has been offered a mortgage to purchase the freehold of the building, which he would like to do.

The staircase to Susie's flat is in a bad state of repair and the metal window frames are badly rusted through condensation.

Advise

(a)   Frieland Ltd

(b)   Susie

as to what possible remedies they may have.

Commentary

This question requires you to consider the effect of certain covenants commonly found in leases. It requires a consideration of the forfeiture procedure for non-payment of rent and for breach of any other covenant in a lease. You also require some knowledge of landlord's covenants which are implied into a lease, including the statutory obligations relating to dwelling-houses. Although most land law courses will include these, this is one of the more peripheral areas of the subject (mentioned in the introduction to this chapter) and it is possible that some may omit it. You will have to be guided on this by your lecture notes and tutorials.

Although there is an assignment, it is not an immensely complicated question with a series of dispositions, so that a diagram is probably unnecessary. A diagram, following the technique suggested in the introduction to this chapter, would appear as follows:

The question concerns a lease made before 1 January 1996 to which most of the Landlord & Tenant (Covenants) Act 1995 will not apply. Had the lease been made on or after that date, the benefit and burden of the covenants would still have passed as 'landlord covenants' and 'tenant covenants' under that Act, rather than under ss. 141 and 142, LPA 1925 and the rule in *Spencer's Case*.

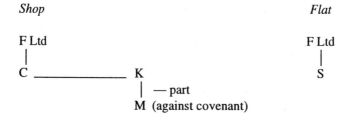

Suggested Answer

(a) A covenant not to assign or sublet without the consent of the landlord is a qualified form of such a covenant and is therefore subject to the Landlord and Tenant Act 1927, s. 19(1), which implies that such consent shall not be unreasonably withheld. The Landlord and Tenant Act 1988 provides that where a tenant applies in writing for such consent, the landlord must give his decision in writing to the tenant within a reasonable time, stating any reasons for refusing consent. The burden of proof to show that he has complied with the Landlord and Tenant Act 1988 is on the landlord, and Curlywig could have had a claim for damages for breach of the statutory duty imposed by the Act if Frieland Ltd have delayed unreasonably in replying.

However, Curlywig have gone ahead and assigned the lease, so that they may not have suffered any actual loss giving rise to a claim for damages. As Frieland Ltd's agents have accepted rent from Kingpin, Frieland Ltd will be deemed to have waived any breach of covenant. The assignment, in any event, is effective to dispose of the lease, and the landlord must proceed against the assignee Kingpin, for any breach of covenant and not against Curlywig (*Old Grovebury Manor Farm* v *W. Seymour Plant Sales & Hire Ltd (No.2)* [1979] 1 WLR 1397).

In allowing Minnie to use part of the premises, Kingpin is in breach of the covenant not to part with possession of the whole or any part of the premises without the landlord's consent. This is a covenant which touches and concerns the land. Frieland Ltd have privity of estate with Kingpin and the burden of the covenant, will therefore pass to Kingpin under the rule in *Spencer's Case* (1583) 5 Co Rep 16a. Frieland Ltd may therefore sue Kingpin for damages or forfeiture, or both.

If they decide to sue for forfeiture, they must first serve a notice under the Law of Property Act 1925, s. 146, informing Kingpin of the breach complained of, requiring it to be remedied and requiring compensation for it. The notice need not require the breach to be remedied if it is irremediable (*Scala House & District Property Co. Ltd* v *Forbes* [1974] QB 575) and need not require compensation if the landlord does not want this (*Governors of Rugby School* v *Tannahill* [1935] 1 KB 87). An immoral user of the premises may well be irremediable (*Rugby School* v *Tannahill*). Kingpin may apply for relief against forfeiture under the Law of Property Act 1925, s. 146(2), although he would be unlikely to obtain it. Breach of a covenant against assignment without consent is an irremediable breach.

The covenant not to use the premises for any purpose other than that of a hairdresser's business is a restrictive covenant. It is therefore binding upon anyone who occupies the premises, including a squatter, other than a *bona fide* purchaser for value of the lease without notice of it. (*Re Nisbet and Potts' Contract* [1905] 1 Ch 391). Frieland Ltd may therefore seek an injunction against Minnie to restrain the breach of the covenant. Under the Supreme Court Act 1981, the court may award Frieland Ltd equitable damages against Minnie either in lieu of, or in addition to, an injunction.

Frieland Ltd may also forfeit the lease for non-payment of the rent, but the procedure here is entirely different from that for forfeiture for breach of any other covenant. It is not necessary to first serve a s. 146 notice, as it is for breach of any other covenant.

Forfeiture for non-payment of rent is governed by the Common Law Procedure Act 1852. Unless the lease provides otherwise (as most leases do) the landlord must first make a formal demand for rent. Such demand is however unnecessary if at least half a year's rent is in arrear, and there are insufficient goods on the premises available for distress to satisfy the amount due (Common Law Procedure Act 1852, s. 210 (High Court); County Courts Act 1984, s. 139 (county court)).

If Frieland Ltd brings its action in the High Court, and at least half a year's rent is in arrear, Kingpin has an automatic right to relief if, before the trial, he pays off all the arrears and costs. Failing this, if Frieland Ltd re-enters under an order of the court, Kingpin has six months after re-entry in which to pay off the arrears and costs and to apply for relief. The court has a discretion to grant relief, and it would not be granted if this will prejudice the position of a *bona fide* purchaser of the lease without notice of Kingpin's right to seek relief. After six months, any application for relief is barred (Common Law Procedure Act 1852, s. 210).

If Frieland Ltd brings its action in a county court, the procedure, though differing in detail, is broadly similar in effect. If Kingpin fails to pay off the arrears and costs within the period specified by the court, he may apply for discretionary relief for six months after Frieland Ltd's re-entry (County Courts Act 1984, s. 138(9A)). If Kingpin does not apply within this time, he is barred from all relief both in the county court and in the High Court (*Di Palma* v *Victoria Square Property Co. Ltd* [1986] Ch 150).

If Frieland Ltd peaceably re-enters without a court order, the High Court has an inherent equitable jurisdiction to grant relief (*Howard* v *Fanshawe* [1895] 2 Ch 581). Although there is no statutory time limit, in practice the court will not be prepared to grant relief unless the application is made within six months (or a few days exceeding six months) of the re-entry (*Thatcher* v *C.H. Pearce & Sons (Contractors) Ltd* [1968] 1 WLR 748).

Frieland Ltd also have privity of contract with Curlywig, against whom they may also bring an action for recovery of the rent. Under s. 17, Landlord & Tenant (Covenants) Act 1995 (which is one of the sections which applies to pre-1996 leases as well as to post-1995 ones), Frieland Ltd is required to serve a notice on Curlywig within six months of the assignee's default on payment informing him of their intention to recover the rent from him. Curlywig would then have a right to the grant of an overriding lease under s. 19 of the Act.

(b) Susie's lease, being a yearly tenancy, is within the Landlord and Tenant Act 1985, s. 11(1), which applies to residential leases of less than seven years. The section requires a landlord to maintain the structure and exterior of a dwelling-house, and installations for water, gas, electricity, sanitation and space and water heating. The section was extended by the Housing Act 1988, s. 116, to include the common parts of a building of which the dwelling-house forms only part, and any installations used by all the tenants, such as a central heating boiler. The staircase would now be within this section and Frieland Ltd would be liable to repair this.

Frieland Ltd would also be liable under the principle of *Liverpool City Council* v *Irwin* [1977] AC 239. In this case, the House of Lords said that there is an implied obligation on a landlord to maintain essential access and services to premises without which the premises would be unusable.

In *Quick* v *Taff Ely BC* [1986] QB 809, however, condensation caused by metal window frames was held to be outside s. 11, as it was due to a design fault rather than to any lack of repair.

A tenant's remedies for breach of a repairing covenant are damages, which might include the cost of temporary accommodation elsewhere, storage of furniture if necessary while the repairs are carried out, and cleaning and redecoration afterwards (*McGreal* v *Wake* (1984) 269 EG 1254). Susie may also carry out the repairs herself and set off the cost against future rents (*Lee-Parker* v *Izzet* [1971] 1 WLR 1688) although she should first give notice to Frieland Ltd that she intends to do this. She may also sue Frieland Ltd for specific performance of the covenant, which extends to common parts of the building (Landlord and Tenant Act 1985, s. 17). Under the Environmental Protection Act 1990, a tenant of premises which are in such a bad state of repair as to make them 'prejudicial to health' and a public nuisance may apply to a magistrates' court for an order to repair the premises, but it has been said that only reasonable orders should be made (*Southwark LBC* v *Ince* (1989) 21 HLR 504, dealing with noise abatement), and in view of the decision in *Quick*, it is unlikely that Susie would obtain such an order with regard to the windows.

As regards the disturbance from the use of part of the shop premises as a massage parlour, Susie would have had an action for breach of the landlord's implied covenant for quiet enjoyment of the premises if the user were by the landlord himself or the breach of the covenant was due to the lawful user by another tenant of the landlord's. The covenant does not extend to the illegal user of another tenant however (*Sanderson* v *Berwick-upon-Tweed Corporation* (1884) 13 QBD 347) and such an action will probably not be available. She would of course have an action in tort against Kingpin himself.

QUESTION 5

Leonora, the freehold owner of an old house in an area of London which has recently become more fashionable, leased the house to Tony for 40 years in 1985. The lease included a covenant to keep the house in good repair, to use it only as a private dwelling-house, and an option for Tony to purchase the reversion.

In 1986 Leonora assigned the reversion to Rita. In 1987 Tony assigned the lease to Alice and in 1988 Alice assigned it to Albert. Last year, Albert sublet the house to Sam for three years.

A garden wall belonging to the property and a shed leaning against it have collapsed and require completely rebuilding. The other houses in the street have been renovated and improved over the last few years and Rita would like to replace the windows and the door so that the house is more in keeping with the neighbourhood.

Rita has recently discovered that Sam is running a mail order business from the house.

Advise Rita what causes of action she may have, and what rights of relief, if any, the parties may have.

Consider whether anyone may exercise the option to purchase the freehold reversion.

Commentary

This question requires first a consideration of the enforceability of covenants in leases against the successors in title to the original parties to the lease, and secondly a discussion of the scope and extent of repairing covenants. As mentioned in the Introduction to this chapter, a landlord's right to sue an original tenant or guarantor has been largely abrogated as regards post-1995 leases by the Landlord and Tenant (Covenants) Act 1995. Also, the Act applies to all 'landlord and tenant' covenants and not just to those 'touching and concerning the land' or 'having reference to the subject-matter of the lease'.

The enforceability of covenants against successors in title is dealt with more fully in essay form in Question 6, but it arises in this question in problem form. It is therefore a question on which you might usefully apply the type of diagram given in the introduction to this chapter. It should then look something like this:

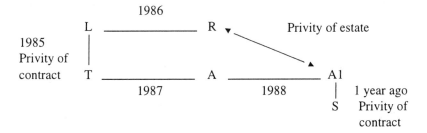

Suggested Answer

On assignment of the reversion, the benefit of covenants 'having reference to the subject-matter' of the lease pass to the assignee of the reversion (Law of Property Act 1925, s. 141), as does the burden (s. 142).

There is privity of estate between Rita, the landlord for the time being, and Albert, the tenant for the time being. The benefit and burden of covenants which 'touch and concern the land' pass to Albert (*Spencer's Case* (1583) 5 Co Rep 16a). The statutory phrase 'having reference to the subject-matter of the lease' means much the same as the words used in *Spencer's Case*, so that where there is privity of estate between the parties, the benefit and burden of covenants which affect the user and enjoyment of the demised property and the relationship of landlord and tenant, will pass. This will include the repairing covenant and the user covenant, but not the option to purchase the reversion, which is a purely personal covenant.

Rita may therefore sue Albert on the repairing covenant and on the user covenant. If there is a forfeiture clause (and it would be a very badly drawn lease which did not include a right of re-entry for breach of covenant!) then before forfeiting, she must first serve a notice on Albert under the Law of Property Act 1925, s. 146, informing him of the breach, requiring it to be remedied and requiring any compensation.

The lease, being for at least seven years with three years left to run, is within the provisions of the Leasehold Property (Repairs) Act 1938. Any s. 146 notice for breach of the repairing covenant would therefore have to inform Albert of his right to serve a counter-notice under the 1938 Act. If Albert does so, then Rita may not proceed any further in an action for forfeiture without the consent of the court. To obtain this consent, Rita will have to show that one of the five circumstances set out in s. 3(5) of the Act apply, and since *Associated British Ports* v *Bailey plc* [1990] 2 AC 703, the landlord needs to show more than just a *prima facie* case.

If Rita were to seek forfeiture on the breach of the user covenant, she would similarly have to serve a s. 146 notice. If Albert was unaware of Sam's breach of the covenant however, and immediately took steps to stop it, it is likely that he would obtain relief against forfeiture under the Law of Property Act 1925, s. 146(2) (*Glass* v *Kencakes Ltd* [1966] 1 QB 611).

Rita could also sue for damages for breach of the covenant, but any damages for breach of the *repairing* covenant would be limited to the diminution in the value of the reversion (Landlord and Tenant Act 1927, s. 18(1)). Moreover, as the lease is within the 1938 Act, Rita must comply with the procedure under the Act also in order to claim damages.

Even though there is no privity of contract or estate between Rita and Sam, Rita could sue Sam directly for an injunction or for damages in lieu for breach of the user covenant, which, although expressed positively, is a restrictive covenant. A restrictive covenant binds any occupier of the land, which includes a subtenant (*Mander* v *Falcke* [1891] 2 Ch 554). Restrictive covenants in leases are not registrable under the Land Charges Act 1972 or on the freehold title of registered land, but are binding nevertheless.

If the sublease includes the same covenants as the headlease (which it will certainly do if it has been well drafted) then Albert will be able to sue Sam on the covenants in the sublease as there is privity of contract and privity of estate between them. He may recover damages and forfeit the lease if there is a forfeiture clause.

It is uncertain whether the rebuilding of the wall and shed and the replacement of the windows and door would be within the scope of the repairing covenant anyway. In *McDougall* v *Easington DC* (1989) 58 P & CR 201, the Court of Appeal reviewed the cases on what is within the scope of a repairing covenant. The court identified three guidelines for deciding whether any particular work was a 'repair' or not. First, the work should not affect the whole, or substantially the whole, of the building. Secondly, the work should not result in the building being a totally different building from that leased. Thirdly, the cost of the work should not be a disproportionate part of the value of the building when repaired.

'Repair' was defined by Buckley LJ in *Lurcott* v *Wakeley & Wheeler* [1911] 1 KB 905, as 'renewal of a part ... restoration by renewal or replacement of subsidiary parts of a whole'. A total rebuilding of a structure might be outside this definition, although it is of course only part of the premises as a whole. In *Halliard Property Co. Ltd* v *Nicholas Clarke Investments Ltd* (1984) 269 EG 1257 a tenant was held not liable under a repairing covenant to reconstruct a jerry-built structure at the rear of the premises which had collapsed. To require him to do so would have been to give the landlord a very different building from that leased.

The replacement of the windows and the door to fit in with the neighbourhood may well be outside the scope of the repairing covenant, as this would seem to be the substitution of something different. The standard of repair imposed by a repairing covenant was laid down in *Proudfoot* v *Hart* (1890) 25 QBD 42, and is to be determined by the age, character and locality of the demised property *when the lease was granted*. Rita will only be able to expect the standard of repair which would have been appropriate therefore in 1985, and not a higher standard because the neighbourhood has improved. A curious anomaly (noted by the Law Commission) is that any repairing covenant contained in the sublease granted last year would therefore require a different standard of repair from the one contained in the headlease.

Although the option to purchase the reversion is a personal covenant and the benefit will not pass to Albert under privity of estate, it creates an equitable interest which may be assigned to him. In *Griffith* v *Pelton* [1958] Ch 205, the lease defined 'lessee' to include 'her executors administrators and assigns', and it was held that the benefit of an option to purchase the reversion therefore passed to an assignee of the lease. Even if there is no such definition in the lease, it was held in *Re Button's Lease* [1964] Ch 263 that such an option may be assigned to an assignee of the lease, provided that it is not expressed to be personal to the tenant only. Provided that the option to purchase is given to the tenant under the lease and not to Tony personally, then Albert will probably obtain the benefit of it.

As Rita is an assignee of the reversion, it will not be exercisable against her unless it has been registered as an estate contract Class C(iv) land charge under the Land Charges Act 1972 in unregistered title. In registered title, it will be binding if it has been registered as a minor interest, or will become binding as an overriding interest under the Land Registration Act 1925, s. 70(1)(g), if the tenant is in occupation (*Webb* v *Pollmount Ltd* [1966] Ch 584) or is in receipt of the rents and profits. Here, presumably, Albert is in receipt of the rents and profits, and the option would therefore be an overriding interest under the section which would be binding on Rita.

QUESTION 6

(a) Describe the rules relating to the passing of the benefit and the burden of covenants in leases made before 1 January 1996, indicating the problems which led to the passing of the Landlord and Tenant (Covenants) Act 1995.

(b) Describe the provisions of the Act applicable to:

(i) leases created on or after 1 January 1996; and

(ii) leases created before 1 January 1996.

Commentary

This was a very complicated area of the law where there were a number of cases defining the limits of liability of assignees of the original landlord and of the original tenant.

Because the rules could operate very harshly on an original tenant and his guarantor, who could find themselves liable under privity of contract for rent on a lease many years after the tenant had assigned it, it was also an area of law where there was strong social pressure for reform. The insolvency of many business tenants during the recession of the late 1980s exacerbated and highlighted the unfairness of the law. The Law Commission Report No. 174 (1988) and draft Bill proposed measures for dealing with this. However, articles occasionally appeared pleading for the preservation of the value of a landlord's investment property, and nothing was done initially to implement the reforms, reflecting no doubt the strong 'landlord' lobby in Parliament. The Landlord and Tenant (Covenants) Act 1995 was therefore originally introduced as a private member's Bill although subsequently adopted by the (then) government. Its main aim is to limit the possible liability of an assigning tenant to the default of his immediate assignee only in leases made on or after 1 January 1996, and this provision cannot be contracted out of. There are some sections of the Act which apply also to pre-1996 leases, however, so affording some relief to tenants and guarantors of these earlier leases.

There are two preliminary points which the student should bear in mind when approaching this topic, whether in relation to pre-1996 or post-1995 leases.

First, privity of estate, which is still relevant to pre-1996 leases, exists only between the landlord for the time being and the tenant for the time being. Therefore, if the tenant, instead of assigning the original term, subleases it, then, even if the sublease is for only one day less than the whole of the remainder of the term, there will be no privity of estate between the head-landlord (or his assignee) and the subtenant (or his assignee).

Secondly, the assignment of the lease is the disposition of a legal estate and must therefore be effected by deed, even if the lease itself is within the Law of Property Act 1925, s. 54(2) and so capable of being created by word of mouth (*Crago* v *Julian* [1992] 1 WLR 372). The rules do not apply on the assignment of an equitable lease.

Suggested Answer

(a) A lease is essentially a contract, albeit one which creates an interest in land, and privity of contract between the original landlord and the original tenant means that all the covenants contained in a pre-1996 lease should be enforceable by and against each of them throughout the term of the lease.

As regards these leases, after assignment of the reversion the original landlord's right to sue the original tenant is limited to personal covenants. This is the result of the interpretation in *Re King* [1963] Ch 459 of the Law of Property Act 1925, s. 141(1), which provides that the benefit of all those tenant covenants 'having reference to the subject-matter' of the lease pass with the reversion to the landlord's assignee. Therefore the original landlord has no right to sue on such covenants after assignment of the reversion, even if the breach occurred before such assignment (*Arlesford Trading Co. Ltd* v *Servansingh* [1971] 1 WLR 1080, where the assignee of the landlord's reversion was able to recover arrears of rent which became due before the assignment). Conversely, the original tenant, after assignment of the lease, may still sue the original landlord for a breach of the landlord's covenant occurring before the tenant assigned (*City and Metropolitan Properties Ltd* v *Greycroft Ltd* [1987] 1 WLR 1085). In *Greycroft* the tenant recovered damages for breach of a repairing covenant from the original landlord after assignment where the breach had caused him to lose a purchaser of a term under a long lease. These rules are, to say the least, quite complex.

The real harshness of the privity of contract rule is in the continuing liability of the tenant and any surety of his on all the covenants in the lease throughout the term of the lease. An assignee who enters into a direct covenant with the landlord (which the terms of a lease often require him to do) may also remain liable under privity of contract. Many tenants of pre-1996 leases are under the delusion that once they have parted with the term of their lease, they are no longer liable on its covenants. This is, unfortunately for them, not generally true. Privity of contract means that if an assignee of the lease defaults on payment of rent, the landlord (even by assignment of the reversion) may sue the original tenant and his surety for arrears on a covenant to pay rent. He may also sue a previous assignee of the lease if he had entered into a covenant directly with the landlord. Moreover, the original tenant may be liable too for any increases in the rent agreed between the landlord and an assignee of the lease (*Centrovincial Estates plc* v *Bulk Storage Ltd* (1983) 46 P & CR 393), assuming that a rent increase was contemplated by a rent-review clause in the original lease (*Friends Provident Life Office* v *British Railways Board* [1996] 1 All ER 336). This Court of Appeal decision ameliorated the position of original tenants and earlier assignees to some extent in that it held they are liable only to the extent of the contractual obligations they have undertaken, and not for additional obligations due to an unauthorised variation of the lease, such as improvements contrary to the terms of the lease by a subsequent assignee.

The result of this rule during the recession meant that, on the insolvency of an assignee, many original tenants were sued by landlords for rent on leases which they had assigned many years before and had forgotten all about! An original tenant who is made to pay may be able to recover an indemnity from assignees of the lease and their guarantors, under an express or statutory indemnity covenant, or under the rule in *Moule* v *Garrett* (1872) LR 7 Ex 101. However, an indemnity against an insolvent assignee is of little value; and even if there is a solvent assignee further down the chain, it was decided in *RPH Ltd* v *Mirror Group (Holdings) Ltd* [1993] 1 EGLR 74, that a tenant cannot insist that an insolvent assignee should sue such a solvent assignee.

Under a pre-1996 lease, once the original parties have assigned the lease or the reversion, or both, there will be privity of estate only between the landlord for the time being and the tenant for the time being, and not privity of contract. The new landlord by assignment will of course have the benefit of the tenant's covenants having reference to the subject-matter of the lease by the operation of the Law of Property Act 1925, s. 141(1); and s. 142(1) of the same Act provides that he is subject to the burden of the original landlord's covenants. He will not be liable, however, for breaches of covenant which occur before the assignment to him (*Duncliffe* v *Caerfelin Properties Ltd* [1989] 2 EGLR 38).

The tenant for the time being will have the benefit and the burden of covenants which 'touch and concern the land'. This principle is known as the rule in *Spencer's Case* (1583) 5 Co Rep 16a, and it has been held that such covenants are effectively the same as the covenants defined in the Law of Property Act 1925, ss. 141 and 142, as 'having reference to the subject-matter' of the lease.

The effect of *Greycroft (supra)* would appear to be, however, that the tenant for the time being cannot sue for breaches of covenant which occur before the assignment to him.

The covenants which pass under ss. 141 and 142 and the rule in *Spencer's Case* are those which affect the landlord *qua* landlord and the tenant *qua* tenant (*Cheshire and Burn's Modern Law of Real Property*, 15th edn, ed. E. H. Burn, 1994). It was held by the House of Lords in *P & A Swift Investments* v *Combined English Stores Group plc* [1989] AC 643, that a surety's covenant to pay rent on the default of a tenant is such a covenant, so that the benefit of it will pass to an assignee of the reversion. In *Hua Chiao Commercial Bank Ltd* v *Chiaphua Industries Ltd* [1987] AC 99, however, the Privy Council held that a landlord's covenant to repay a security deposit made by the original tenant was a purely personal one, the burden of which did not pass under s. 142(1) to an assignee of the reversion.

(b)(i)   As regards new leases made on or after 1 January 1996, the Landlord and Tenant (Covenants) Act 1995 institutes a new regime which considerably limits a tenant's liability for the default of a future assignee.

Section 3 provides that the benefit and burden of *all* landlord and tenant covenants shall pass on assignment of the lease or the reversion. Sections 141 and 142, Law of Property Act 1925 and the rule in *Spencer's Case* are therefore abolished. This means that an assignee of a landlord or a tenant has no rights relating to the time before the assignment, and reverses the old law in *Re King* for the landlord, so that a previous landlord and not a new landlord has a right to sue for arrears of rent. The law for a tenant is unchanged and remains as in *City & Metropolitan Properties* v *Greycroft*.

It is not clear what will now be regarded as a purely personal covenant which will not pass with the lease or reversion. Presumably one where the tenant or the landlord enters into a covenant in their own name which does not in any way concern their relationship as landlord and tenant might qualify, but what about a covenant to repay a tenant's rent deposit which was held to be personal and unenforceable by the tenant's assignee against the landlord's assignee in *Hua Chiao Commercial Bank Ltd* v *Chiaphua Industries Ltd* [1987] AC 99)?

The main provision of the new Act is that a tenant is *automatically* released from liability on covenants in the lease after assignment. There can be no contracting out of this provision, and it applies *except* for:

(a)   existing breaches of covenant;

(b)   where it is not an authorised assignment, i.e., where assignment is in breach of covenant, or by operation of law (on death or bankruptcy of the tenant).

An authorised guarantee agreement (AGA) can be required by the landlord as a reasonable condition precedent for granting consent to assign. Under it, the tenant guarantees the performance of the covenants by his immediate assignee, but not for any other later assignees. Where (a) or (b) above applies, the tenant's liablity will continue until the next authorised assignment takes place.

The requirement for an AGA as a condition for consent to assign has resulted in a corresponding amendment to s. 19(1), Landlord and Tenant Act 1927 as regards commercial leases, and a new s. 19(1A) has been inserted by s. 23. Whereas it has hitherto not been possible for a landlord to specify what would be reasonable reasons for his refusal of consent to an assignment (*Re Smith's Lease* [1951] 1 All ER 146), it will now be possible for a landlord to specify this. There would therefore now appear to be two types of reasons for which a landlord may refuse his consent — factual ones (rent deposit, an assignee to have certain net profits, the outgoing tenant to give an AGA), and discretionary ones (that the assignee is not financially viable, or would be in competition with another tenant of the landlord's) — to which the 'reasonable' test of s. 19(1) will still apply.

A tenant who gives an AGA is liable as a guarantor and the general law as to guarantees applies to him. This means that his liability as guarantor would end if it was varied even slightly without his consent. Section 18, which applies also to old leases created before 1 January 1996, provides that in any event a tenant will not be liable for any substantial variation in the lease not contemplated by its terms. (This had of course already been judicially decided by the Court of Appeal in *Friends Provident Life Office* v *British Railways Board*).

Under the general law of guarantees, a guarantor who pays out on the default of the debtor whom he has guaranteed has a right of recovery against him. The indemnities implied on an assignment for value under s. 77, Law of Property Act 1925 and s. 24, Land Registration Act 1925 (whether for value or not) are therefore no longer necessary, and these sections have been repealed as regards post-1995 leases. The repeal of these sections presumably also protects any intermediate assignee from a claim, and the rule in *Moule* v *Garrett* (1872) LR 7 EX 101 would also appear to become otiose.

The Act does not provide for an automatic release of the landlord from his liabilities on assignment of the reversion. He may, however, serve a notice on each tenant within four weeks of the assignment requesting a release. If the tenant objects, the landlord can apply to the court for a release, which the court may grant if it considers it reasonable to do so. If the landlord does not serve a notice, or is not released, he remains liable on the landlord's covenants in the lease along with the new landlord, and could be liable if the new landlord defaults on repairs or services. He may apply again for release on the occasion of the next assignment of the reversion.

The effects of the Act will be felt mainly in the area of commercial leases; it was commercial tenants who suffered most from the harshness of the privity of contract rule. Some commentators have predicted that it will result in more subleases rather than assignments, but it is obviously too early to assess its full impact as yet.

(b)(ii)   Certain sections of the new Act apply to older pre-1996 leases as well as to new ones. Section 18, which applies to both, has already been mentioned above.

After 1 January 1996, a landlord who wishes to proceed against a former tenant or guarantor must first serve a default notice within six months of the default for which he is seeking to recover. The default must be for a fixed sum such as rent, service charges or liquidated damages, such as a debt for repairs carried out by the landlord.

Any person who then pays on a default notice may, within 12 months, require the landlord to grant to him an overriding lease. This is a reversionary lease of up to three days longer than the term of the lease on which the tenant has defaulted. He thereby becomes the landlord of the defaulting tenant and has a power of forfeiture so that he may obtain possession and so seek to recover some of his losses.

The landlord must grant the reversionary lease within a reasonable time. If more than one person requests an overriding lease, it should be granted to the first person to make the request. If the landlord receives more than one request on the same day, previous tenants have priority over previous guarantors and earlier tenants over later tenants.

12 Easements and Profits

INTRODUCTION

The law of easements is a relatively discrete topic, so that questions which mix this with other areas of land law are somewhat uncommon. Lectures on easements generally work through the subject in a systematic way, starting with the nature of and requirements for an easement, then the methods by which an easement can be created (distinguishing between legal and equitable easements), followed by fluctuations in user, and finishing with the means by which an easement may be discharged. You should not, however, imagine that every answer you give to a question on easements needs to work through all aspects of the subject, nor in the same sequence. You must answer the question asked, not write everything that you know. You will need to identify the particular areas of the law of easements which give rise to difficulties, and apply the law to the facts. You should not spend time considering points of law which, on the facts, do not cause problems.

Take, for instance, the requirements for an easement as laid down in *Re Ellenborough Park* [1956] Ch 131, where it was held that:

(a)   there must be a dominant and a servient tenement;

(b)   the easement must accommodate the dominant tenement;

(c)   the dominant and servient owners must be different persons; and

(d)   the right must be capable of forming the subject-matter of a grant.

A question on easements on your examination paper may require you to deal with all, some, or indeed none, of these requirements — it may after all be a question largely or exclusively on some other aspects of easements. If the question does involve one or more of the requirements in *Re Ellenborough Park*, you should deal with those that are relevant to the problem only. Question 1 in this chapter, for instance, deals (amongst other things) with (b) and (d). Question 2 also deals with them (more briefly); and Questions 3 and 4 merely touch on (d) only (in regard to the point on *Phipps* v *Pears* [1965] 1 QB 76 and *Copeland* v *Greenhalf* [1952] Ch 488 respectively). In each case it is unnecessary and, indeed, a waste of time and effort, to state all the requirements laid down in *Re Ellenborough Park* and then to consider whether these are met. A right of way is clearly capable of comprising an easement: it would have been a waste to have discussed this matter in Question 3.

Keep your powder dry for the issues which really do matter in a question. All of the problems in this chapter also involve, in varying degrees, other aspects of the law of easements. It is important to identify the areas which would in practice give rise to legal argument, so that your answer gives sufficient attention to each. Writing 'out of time' at the end of an answer does not secure any extra marks: it merely draws attention to the fact that you fell down on time management.

QUESTION 1

In 1981, Miranda was the owner of a plot of freehold land. At one end of the plot, and adjoining the main road, stood a house and garden. In the middle of the plot there were tennis courts and a shed, and beyond that was a muddy wood which adjoined a lane. Miranda and her tennis partners often searched the wood for their lost balls.

In 1982, Miranda contracted to sell the house and garden to Silvia, and permitted Silvia to go into immediate possession. Miranda (who had herself never used the shed) also allowed Silvia to store her diesel lawnmower in the shed. The subsequent conveyance to Silvia contained a reservation of a right of way from the main road across the garden to the tennis courts. *deed*

legal.

legal

In 1983, Miranda conveyed the middle part of the plot (containing the tennis courts and the shed) to Ophelia, who began hiring out the tennis courts for club matches. Over the years, the frequency of such hirings out has increased steadily. Miranda is concerned that the increased foraging for lost balls in the wood is damaging the rare plant species which grow there. Furthermore, whilst in the past visitors to the tennis courts have crossed the garden on foot, they have recently started to traverse it in minibuses and coaches. When Silvia complained to Ophelia last week, Ophelia demanded that Silvia remove her lawnmower from the hut.

Advise Miranda and Silvia.

Commentary

The problem involves three separate aspects of the law of easements: whether certain rights can exist as easements; implied easements; whether the burden of an easement affects a person who takes a conveyance of the burdened land; and increase in intensity. The suggested answer tackles these matters as follows:

(a)   whether there can exist an easement to forage for balls; and, if so, whether, and by what means such an easement was created;

(b)   whether there can exist an easement to store a lawnmower in a shed; and, if so, whether, and by what means, such an easement was created; and

(c)   the scope of an easement by reservation, and increase in the intensity of its user.

You will find it helpful to draw a diagram in your rough notes, which should look something like this:

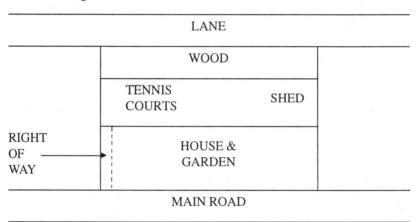

LANE

WOOD

TENNIS COURTS   SHED

RIGHT OF WAY

HOUSE & GARDEN

MAIN ROAD

Suggested Answer

Miranda, as the owner of the wood, will be able to prevent the foraging for balls unless Ophelia and her visitors have a legal right to forage. As Miranda does not appear to have given a contractual licence for such purpose, such right, if one it be, can exist only as an easement. To be valid, an easement must accommodate the dominant tenement, i.e., it must benefit it as a piece of land. The right claimed must not be merely a personal benefit to the owner; *Hill* v *Tupper* (1863) 2 H & C 121. As the benefited land comprises tennis courts, this will probably be satisfied. More difficult to surmount, however, is the requirement that the right claimed be of definite scope, which thus excludes a mere right to wander at will over another's land (*ius spatiandi*). In *Re Ellenborough Park* [1956] Ch 131, the right to walk at will in a garden qualified as an easement because there were defined pathways: the visitors could not walk over the flower-beds. A right to forage for lost balls suggests no such restriction (since the balls could land anywhere). It is therefore unlikely that such a right could exist as an easement. If this is so, Miranda can sue the foragers in trespass, and she may be able to obtain injunctive relief to prevent future foraging.

If, however, such a right is held capable of existing as an easement, it is necessary to determine if such easement was acquired in any of the ways recognised by the law. It might have been created impliedly. When Miranda owned the tennis courts, her foraging for lost balls may be considered to be the exercise of a quasi-easement over the wood for the benefit of the tennis courts. Unless Miranda excluded implied easements from the conveyance to Ophelia, the grant would have been effective to vest in Ophelia all those quasi-easements over the retained land which are continuous and apparent, necessary to the reasonable enjoyment of the land granted, and which were, at the time of the grant, used by the grantor for the benefit of the part granted (*Wheeldon* v *Burrows* (1879) 12 ChD 31). These are cumulative, not alternative, requirements: *Wheeler* v *J.J. Saunders Ltd* [1996] Ch 19 (CA). 'Continuous' means a right which does not require personal activity for its enjoyment. Strictly, this excluded a right of way, but such a right has been held to pass under this doctrine (*Borman* v *Griffith* [1930] 1 Ch 493). 'Apparent' means a right which is discoverable by inspection of the land. Since the wood is muddy, there may be evidence of the foragers' footprints, which would meet this requirement. The quasi-easement could not, however, pass to Ophelia under the Law of Property Act 1925, s. 62, because, when Miranda herself foraged, she did so as owner of the wood, not through the exercise of a 'liberty' or 'privilege' (*Long* v *Gowlett* [1923] 2 Ch 177).

Ophelia will not be able to prevent Silvia from continuing to store her lawnmower in the shed if Silvia has an easement to do so. The right claimed as an easement must not be so extensive as to amount to possession of any part of the servient tenement (*Copeland* v *Greenhalf* [1952] Ch 488). In *Grigsby* v *Melville* [1972] 1 WLR 1355 (affirmed [1974] 1 WLR 80) a claim to store bottles in a cellar failed because, on the facts, it amounted to a claim to exclusive user. If the owner is excluded from possession for short periods only, however, a right can be an easement (*Miller* v *Emcer Products Ltd* [1956] Ch 304 (use of a lavatory); *London & Blenheim Estates Ltd* v *Ladbroke Retail Parks Ltd* [1994] 1 WLR 31 (limited right to park a car)). Similarly, provided it is limited in extent, a right of storage can also qualify (*Wright* v *Macadam* [1949] 2 KB 744 (storage of coal in a shed)). Whether Silvia's claim to store her lawnmower can comprise an easement will therefore depend upon the comparative sizes of the mower and the shed, and the manner of storage. If the mower fills the shed or otherwise prevents reasonable user by Ophelia, the claim will probably fail. If it succeeds, it will include the ancillary right of way across Ophelia's land in order to fetch and return the mower.

Even if the storage of the mower can comprise an easement, Silvia must still establish that such an easement was acquired. When she went into possession of the house and garden between contract and completion, she had merely a licence from Miranda to use the shed for storing the mower, and such licence could have been withdrawn at any time. However, unless it provided otherwise, the conveyance would have passed to Silvia, as legal easements, all 'liberties' and 'privileges' at the time of the conveyance enjoyed with the land (Law of Property Act 1925, s. 62). Diversity of ownership or occupation is required at the time of the conveyance (*Long* v *Gowlett* [1923] 2 Ch 177; approved in *Sovmots* v *Secretary of State for the Environment* [1979] AC 144 (HL)), and that is satisfied because Silvia was in possession prior to completion. The permission to store could thus be transformed, on the conveyance, into a legal easement (cf. *Goldberg* v *Edward* [1950] Ch 247).

An alternative claim to an easement of storage based on the doctrine of *Wheeldon* v *Burrows* is less likely to succeed. Although Miranda may be considered, before completion, to be exercising, through Silvia, a quasi-easement, the requirement that the right claimed be necessary for the reasonable enjoyment of the dominant tenement is unlikely to be satisfied: there are many other places where the mower could be stored, and Miranda herself never found it necessary to use the shed for this purpose.

The burden of any easement of storage will bind Ophelia, the present owner of the servient tenement: in land with unregistered title, because it is a legal right; in land with registered title, because it is an overriding interest (Land Registration Act 1925, s. 70(1)(a)).

By virtue of the Law of Property Act 1925, s. 62, Ophelia will take the benefit of the right of way over the garden expressly reserved out of the grant to Silvia. Therefore, whether Silvia can prevent large numbers of Ophelia's guests crossing her garden in motor vehicles depends upon the scope of such reservation. If the reservation does not specify whether the right is one to cross on foot only, or by some other means, it will be construed against the grantor. Before 1926, a reservation took effect by way of a re-grant and was thus construed against the purchaser. After 1925, a reservation operates without any re-grant (Law of Property Act 1925, s. 65). Nevertheless, there are dicta of the Court of Appeal to the effect that a post-1925 reservation is also to be construed against the purchaser (*St. Edmundsbury and Ipswich Diocesan Board* v *Clark (No. 2)* [1975] 1 WLR 468). Evidence relating to the physical nature of the access may give some indication of the easement's scope. In the absence of any evidence, however, the reservation will be construed in favour of Ophelia, i.e., to include the use of motor vehicles.

Although there does not appear to have been any change in user of the right of way, it seems that there has been increased intensity of user. In contrast to an easement acquired prescriptively (*British Railways Board* v *Glass* [1965] 1 Ch 538) the scope of an express easement is determined at the time of the grant (*Jelbert* v *Davis* [1968] 1 WLR 589). Silvia can therefore restrain any increase in intensity beyond what could have been contemplated in 1982. Excessive user does not itself, however, cause the easement to be lost (*Graham* v *Philcox* [1984] 1 QB 747).

QUESTION 2

In 1953 Joe, the fee simple owner of Greenacre, agreed with one of his neighbours, Celia, that she might park her car from time to time on a corner of one of his fields near to her house.

In 1970 Joe erected a large greenhouse on the boundary of one of his fields and started to grow in it tomatoes for sale. In connection with this, and at about the same time, he put up a sign on the wall of a neighbouring cottage, which belonged to Harry, advertising the sale of fresh eggs and produce. Also in 1970, Joe installed a water butt to catch the rain from the greenhouse roof. When Joe was not about, Celia used to cross onto Joe's land to draw water from the butt in order to wash her car when it was parked on her own land.

In 1973 Harry leased his cottage to Tommy for a term of years which expired nine months ago. After the termination of this lease, Harry conveyed his cottage to William, who has now obtained planning permission to erect a house that, when built, will block direct sunlight to Joe's greenhouse. William is also objecting to the presence of Joe's sign on his cottage wall.

Celia has now concreted over the area of the field where she parks her car. Joe wishes to prevent any further user of this area for parking, and to stop Celia drawing water from his butt.

Advise Joe.

Commentary

The question raises (*inter alia*) the issue considered in *Pugh* v *Savage* [1970] 2 QB 373, of prescription under the statute where the servient tenement has been subject to a lease during the 20 years next before action. The question does not, however, deal with the same issue in relation to user for a period of 40 years. This is considered in the answer to Question 3 of this chapter.

In studying the law of easements you may also deal with profits, and the extent of the knowledge you need about profits for the purpose of your examinations may be gauged from how extensively they are treated in your course. If the treatment is fairly extensive, you may be asked detailed questions about profits, and you might be asked to compare them with easements. The answer to the present question touches on profits only briefly.

Suggested Answer

Joe will be unable to prevent Celia from parking her car in the corner of his field if she has acquired an easement to do so. A right to park a car anywhere within a specified area is capable of being an easement (*Newman* v *Jones* (22 March 1982, unreported, Megarry V-C), *Handel* v *St Stephens Close Ltd* [1994] 5 EG 159), and of accommodating the dominant tenement (*Re Ellenborough Park* [1956] Ch 131). More evidence is therefore needed in the problem to ascertain whether Celia has been parking anywhere within a larger defined area in the corner of Joe's field, or merely in a particular space; the concreting suggests the latter. The right to park in a particular space probably cannot exist as an easement, since it amounts to a claim to exclusive possession, and would thus deprive the servient owner of the reasonable use of that part of his land (*London & Blenheim Estates Ltd* v *Ladbroke Retail Parks Ltd* [1994] 1 WLR 31). In any event, a mandatory injunction will be available to compel Celia to remove the concreting.

If Celia's right were to park anywhere within a defined area and were thus considered capable of existing as an easement, she would still need to establish that such easement had been created. As there was no express grant, any such right could arise only by prescription or by presumed grant. Like all the other possible easements in the problem, it could not arise by prescription at common law, since it is easy to establish that it could not have been enjoyed since 1189 (*Bury* v *Pope* (1588) Cro Eliz 118).

Under the Prescription Act 1832, s. 2, where the claim to an easement (other than an easement of light) has been actually enjoyed without interruption for 40 years, the right is deemed absolute and indefeasible unless it was enjoyed by written consent or agreement. The user must still, however, have been *nec vi* (not by force) and *nec clam* (nor by stealth) (*Gardner* v *Hodgson's Kingston Brewery Co. Ltd* [1903] AC 229), which appears to have been the case here. Even where there is written consent, it will not prevent an easement from being acquired if there is 40 years' user thereafter, i.e., only written permission given *during* the 40 years will defeat the claim (*Gardner* v *Hodgson's Kingston Brewery Co. Ltd*). There is no evidence of such consent here.

The user that Celia must establish is user 'next before action'. Thus any rights she has under the statute are inchoate until recognised in court proceedings. If, therefore, Joe interrupts the user, and Celia acquiesces in it for a period of at least one year, Celia's inchoate rights will be lost (Prescription Act 1832, s. 4).

If Joe were able so to destroy a claim under the statute, Celia might, as a last expedient, claim a presumed easement of parking under the doctrine of lost modern grant. Twenty years' enjoyment *nec vi, nec clam, nec precario* (not by force, nor by stealth, nor by permission), which does not need to be next before action, raises a presumption that in the past there was a grant (since lost) (*Bryant* v *Foot* (1867) LR 2 QB 161). Even evidence that no such grant was made is ineffective to rebut the presumption (*Tehidy Minerals Ltd* v *Norman* [1971] 2 QB 528). In practice, Celia would probably claim an easement under both the Prescription Act 1832 and the doctrine of lost modern grant.

Although a right to remove something from the land of another must generally fall within the category of *profits à prendre*, a right to draw water cannot be a profit because, even though water collected in a butt is capable of ownership, water is not part of the soil or the produce of the soil (*Alfred F. Beckett Ltd* v *Lyons* [1967] Ch 449). If the claim is therefore to rank as an incorporeal hereditament, it must be capable of comprising an easement. A right to take water to wash one's car would not appear to satisfy the requirements of *Re Ellenborough Park* [1956] Ch 131, since it seems not to accommodate the alleged dominant tenement, but merely to be a personal benefit to the owner of the car (cf *Hill* v *Tupper* (1863) 2 H & C 121). In any event, Celia's apparent secrecy (*clam*) in drawing the water will preclude her from claiming that any such alleged easement was acquired by prescription.

Joe will be able to prevent the construction of the house in the way proposed if he can establish an easement of light to his greenhouse. A right to receive a specially high degree of light for growing plants in a greenhouse was held to comprise an easement in *Allen* v *Greenwood* [1980] Ch 119. Under the Prescription Act 1832, s. 2, an easement of light can be acquired by 20 years' uninterrupted actual enjoyment (next before action) unless with written consent or agreement. In this instance, therefore, the user does not have to be as of right. For the same reason, the general requirement that acquisition be by a fee simple owner against a fee simple owner does not apply to the acquisition of an easement of light under the statute. Thus, the time during which Harry's cottage is let to Tommy does not stop the period of 20 years from running (*Simper* v *Foley* (1862) 2 J & H 555). It would therefore appear that Joe could, by action, both establish the acquisition of an easement of light and also obtain an injunction to prevent William's building on his land so as to interfere with such easement.

A right to have a signboard affixed to the wall of another's house is capable of being an easement (*Moody* v *Steggles* (1879) 12 ChD 261 (sign advertising a public house). Although Joe's sign relates to his business, it will probably be held (as in *Moody* v *Steggles*) to accommodate the dominant tenement, in this case, Greenacre. Twenty years ago, Harry's cottage was leased to Tommy. This will not, however, prevent the period of 20 years next before action required under the Prescription Act 1832, s. 2, from running, since Joe's sign had been affixed at a time when the fee simple owner (Harry) was in possession (*Pugh* v *Savage* [1970] 2 QB 373).

Joe may alternatively plead that he has acquired either or both the easement of light and the easement relating to his sign under the doctrine of lost modern grant. This is possible since the period of 20 years' user that gives rise to the presumption may include a period during which the servient land was tenanted where (as here) there was initial user against a fee simple owner (*Pugh* v *Savage*).

QUESTION 3

In 1950, Abbey was the fee simple owner of Fox's Farm, which comprised two adjacent plots: Greenacre to the east and Redacre to the west. Two semi-detached cottages stood on Fox's Farm: one on each plot. Access to Redacre was via a public lane which abutted the western boundary of Redacre. Adjacent to Greenacre, and lying between it and the main road to the east, was Pinkacre. From 1951, with the oral consent of Ben, the fee simple owner of Pinkacre, Abbey began using the footpath on Pinkacre in order to gain access from Greenacre to the main road.

In 1982, Ben leased Pinkacre to Colin for a term which expired two years ago. Immediately at the termination of the lease, Ben orally assured Abbey that he could continue to use the footpath.

In 1984, Abbey conveyed Redacre to Derek, who had been a tenant of Redacre for the preceding year. The conveyance did not reserve for Abbey a right of way over Redacre to reach the lane. While a tenant, Derek had kept sheep on Redacre, and Abbey had allowed him to graze them on Greenacre.

Ben is now refusing Abbey the use of the footpath. Without access through either Pinkacre or Redacre, Greenacre is landlocked. To add to Abbey's problems, Derek has demolished the cottage on Redacre and has refused to provide shoring to support the exposed wall of Abbey's formerly adjoining cottage, which is now suffering from instability and exposure to the weather. Derek is also claiming the right to graze his sheep on Greenacre.

(a) Advise Abbey.

(b) How (if at all) would your advice differ if, in 1951, Ben had executed a deed by which he conferred on Abbey what was described as a 'licence' to use the footpath over Pinkacre in order to reach the main road from Fox's Farm?

Commentary

This question covers a lot of different points, which means you are not expected to linger very long over any one of them. Those candidates who insist on writing 'all they know' type answers will fare very badly.

You will find it useful to draw a sketch:

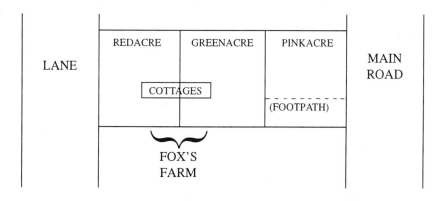

A plan of the answer might be as follows:

Part (**a**):

    (a)   Acquisition of an easement to use Pinkacre footpath (Prescription Act 1832)

        (i)   20-year period: defeated by oral consent;

        (ii)   40-year period: not so defeated;

            (aa)   acquisition against fee simple owner: lease to Colin;

            (bb)   deduction under Prescription Act 1832, s. 8.

    (b)   Implied easements: reservations:

        (i)   necessity: Greenacre landlocked:

        (ii)   mutual: easement of support, but not against weathering.

    (c)   Ben's access to Pinkacre to effect works (Access to Neighbouring Land Act 1992).

    (d)   Derek's sheep-grazing: acquisition of profit — implied grant:

        (i)   not *Wheeldon* v *Burrows*;

        (ii)   Law of Property Act 1925, s. 62: diversity of occupation.

Part (**b**):

Ben's 'licence':

        (i)   despite deed, probably merely permissive;

        (ii)   permission by deed destroys claim to easement by prescription even under 40-year period of Prescription Act 1832.

Although the question is in two parts, it should be apparent that the larger share of the answer (perhaps 80 per cent or more) needs to be devoted to the first part.

In part **(b)** the questioner is testing your knowledge and understanding of specific points, i.e., that arising in *IDC Group Ltd* v *Clark* [1992] 2 EGLR 184, and the impact of written permission on the acquisition of an easement by prescription under the Prescription Act 1832. The variation of facts indicated in part **(b)** does indeed suggest that the advice would differ in some respects from that in part **(a)**. Do not, however, assume that the answer to: 'Would your advice be different if . . .?' is always yes.

The only difficult aspect in the problem is that involving the lease to Colin. This involves not merely (as in Question 2), an appreciation of the issues raised in *Pugh* v *Savage* [1970] 2 QB 373; but, because the 40-year period is relevant here, also a knowledge of the effect of the Prescription Act 1832, s. 8. The law on this would appear to be as follows:

(a)   if the user begins at a time when the servient tenement is leased, the period of 40 years cannot begin to run until the lease comes to an end (as in *Pugh* v *Savage*);

(b)   if the user begins at a time when the fee simple owner is in possession of the servient tenement, a claim under the 40-year period will not be defeated merely because, 40 years next before action, the servient tenement was subject to a lease (also as in *Pugh* v *Savage*);

(c)   however, where the lease was one for a term of at least three years, even if user began as in (b), if the fee simple owner brings an action within three years of the expiration of the lease, the time during which the land was leased is to be discounted from the period of 40 years (Prescription Act 1832, s. 8). Thus the time during which the land was leased is counted only if no such action is brought within three years of its termination.

It is (c) which is relevant to the present problem.

Suggested Answer

(a)   Abbey will have a right to use the footpath over Pinkacre if he has acquired an easement by prescription. A claim that an easement was acquired under the Prescription Act 1832, s. 2, by virtue of 20 years' user will be defeated by the oral permission that Ben gave Abbey two years ago since this falls within the period of 20 years 'next before action' (s. 4). Abbey cannot therefore show that the relevant period of user was *nec precario* (*Healey* v *Hawkins* [1968] 1 WLR 1967). This will also defeat a claim based on lost modern grant (*Bryant* v *Foot* (1867) LR 2 QB 161). By contrast, oral consent will not defeat a prescriptive claim based on the 40-year period, whether such consent is given at the commencement of the user or within the 40 years 'next before action'. Only a written consent will have this effect (Prescription Act 1832, s. 2).

An easement can be acquired prescriptively only by and against a fee simple owner. In the problem, the user of the footpath over Pinkacre began while Ben was in possession. The mere fact that for some of the period comprising the 40 years 'next before action' Pinkacre was leased to Colin will not, therefore, itself prevent Abbey from claiming under the 40-year period in s. 2 (*Pugh* v *Savage* [1970] 2 QB 373). However, if Abbey claims under the 40-year period, Ben will (provided he resists Abbey's claim within three years of the termination of Colin's lease) be able to deduct the period during which Pinkacre was leased to Colin from the computation of the period of 40 years (Prescription Act 1832, s. 8). Since Colin's lease ended two years ago, Ben will have one year in which to resist. If he does so, Abbey's claim will fail, since he will be able to establish user for merely 33 years, i.e., 31 years before the grant of the lease, and two years after its termination. If Ben fails to resist within one year, however, Abbey will be able to include the period of the lease, and therefore should be able to establish 40 years' user 'next before action'.

It is unclear whether anything short of legal proceedings (such as blocking the right of way) suffices for a claim to be 'resisted' within s. 8. However, if Ben were to prevent Abbey's user of the path, and Abbey were to submit to it or acquiesce in it for a year, there would be an interruption which would destroy Abbey's claim (s. 4).

Because of the general rule that a grant is construed in favour of the grantee, the reservation of an easement to a grantor will not be readily implied: it will usually need to be express. One exception, however, is where the conveyance by the grantor would leave his retained land landlocked. In such circumstances, a reservation of a right of way will be implied in favour of the grantor, unless the conveyance contains a contrary intention (*Nickerson* v *Barraclough* [1981] Ch 426). No such contrary intention appears from the problem. Such an easement of necessity can arise even where (as in the problem) some of the surrounding land (Pinkacre) belongs to a third party (Ben) (*Barry* v *Hasseldine* [1952] Ch 835). The necessity must exist at the time of the grant. In 1984, when Abbey conveyed Redacre, his use of the footpath over Pinkacre was merely permissive: such precarious user will not preclude the implication in the conveyance to Derek of an easement of necessity over Redacre (*Barry* v

Hasseldine). Similarly, once acquired, the easement of necessity will not be destroyed by Abbey's subsequent acquisition of a right of way over Pinkacre.

Abbey's non-exercise of his right of way over Redacre since 1984 will not cause it to be lost: being less than 20 years, the period of non-user is too short to evidence abandonment. In any event, there has been no reason for Abbey to exercise such right until now (cf. *Benn* v *Hardinge* (1992) 66 P & CR 246). Abbey may select any convenient route over Redacre to reach the lane (*Bolton* v *Bolton* (1879) 11 ChD 968). Once selected, the route cannot be changed (*Deacon* v *South Eastern Railway* (1889) 61 LT 377).

Another exception to the rule against implied reservation is where a grantor conveys one of two houses supported by one another. From such circumstances, the mutual grant and reservation of easements of support are readily implied (*Richards* v *Rose* (1853) 9 Exch 218). Therefore Abbey will be able to compel Derek to provide the necessary shoring to stabilise the remaining cottage. A right to have a wall protected from weathering, however, is incapable of existing as an easement (*Phipps* v *Pears* [1965] 1 QB 76). Abbey cannot therefore compel Derek to provide weatherproofing for the exposed wall or sue Derek for damages for his loss. Abbey will need to execute and pay for such works himself.

If Abbey needs to enter upon Redacre to carry out such works, and Derek refuses to allow access, Abbey may apply for an access order under the Access to Neighbouring Land Act 1992, s. 1. The court must be satisfied that such works are reasonably necessary for the preservation of Greenacre, and that they cannot be carried out (or would be substantially more difficult to carry out) without access to Redacre. Since these works comprise the maintenance, repair and (perhaps) renewal of a building, they rank as 'basic preservation works' (s. 1(4)), and are therefore treated as reasonably necessary for the preservation of Greenacre.

Derek will have a right to graze his sheep on Greenacre if he has acquired a *profit à prendre* to do so. He may have acquired such a profit by implied grant. A profit probably cannot be acquired under the rule in *Wheeldon* v *Burrows* (1879) 12 ChD 31 since it lacks the qualities of continuity and apparency, and of being reasonably necessary for the enjoyment of the land. It can, however, be acquired under the Law of Property Act 1925, s. 62(1), which, on a conveyance, converts into a legal right that which, prior to the conveyance, was merely a 'liberty' or a 'privilege' enjoyed with the land. The requirement that there be prior diversity of occupation (*Long* v *Gowlett* [1923] 2 Ch 177) is satisfied, because Derek had, until the conveyance, been grazing the sheep permissively on Greenacre while tenant of Redacre. Unless, therefore, the conveyance contains a contrary intention, it will convert Derek's quasi-profit of grazing into a legal profit, which Abbey will be unable to restrain.

(b) Although the document executed by Ben in 1951 was in the form of a deed, the use of the term 'licence' suggests that, rather than granting an easement, the document merely gave a permissive user. Whereas in the context of residential accommodation the use of the term 'licence' is not decisive against the grant of a lease (*Street* v *Mountford* [1985] AC 809), in the case of commercial interests over land (such as the right to pass over it) the courts are more willing to accept the parties' own description of the right conferred as decisive. This is particularly the case where the parties both had legal advice (*IDC Group Ltd* v *Clark* [1992] 2 EGLR 184). Furthermore, if he has not provided consideration for the licence, Abbey will not be able to sue for damages for its revocation. A written consent, moreover, even if given only at the beginning of the period of user, will defeat a claim to the acquisition of an easement under the 40-year period (Prescription Act 1832, s. 2). Abbey will therefore be unable to establish an easement to use the footpath, and Ben may lawfully revoke his licence to do so.

QUESTION 4

In 1992 Clements and Bailey were the adjoining freehold owners of Nos. 3 and 5 Shoreditch Lane respectively. Clements had difficulty parking his car in the garage of No. 3 without using the driveway of No. 5. Following discussions between them, Clement and Bailey in 1993 entered into a written contract (signed by each of them) whereby, in consideration for the sum of £1,000, Bailey agreed to grant to Clements and his successors in title a right to use the driveway of No. 5 for the purpose of parking a motor vehicle in the garage of No. 3.

In 1998, Bailey sold and conveyed the freehold of No. 5 to Stepney, who knew nothing of the contract between Clements and Bailey. Stepney has now objected to Clement's use of the driveway of No. 5.

(a) Advise Clements, explaining how your advice would differ according to whether the title to No. 5 were registered or unregistered.

(b) To what extent would your advice differ if, shortly after the conveyance to Stepney, Clements demolished the garage to No. 3 and only last week expressed an intention of building a new garage in the same place?

Commentary

Easements can be either legal or equitable. It is surprising how many students seem to find an equitable easement where none exists. Equitable easements arise in somewhat narrow circumstances only. First, a legal easement can exist only if it is held for a period equivalent to an estate in fee simple absolute in possession, or for a term of years absolute (Law of Property Act 1925, s. 1(2)(a)). An easement for any other period (such as an easement for life) can exist as an equitable easement only. Secondly, a contract to grant a legal easement, it appears, does give rise to an equitable easement; this is dealt with in part (a) of the answer. It should be remembered that, whereas the rule in *Wheeldon* v *Burrows* (1879) 12 ChD 31 can apply on a contract to convey a legal estate (in which event it will give rise to an equitable easement), the Law of Property Act 1925, s. 62, can create an easement only upon a conveyance — which means that any such easement will be a legal one.

Suggested Answer

(a)   Assuming that the written agreement satisfies the requirements of the Law of Property (Miscellaneous Provisions) Act 1989, s. 2, it is a valid contract to create a legal easement. In *E.R. Ives Investment Ltd* v *High* [1967] 2 QB 379, Lord Denning MR considered that an interest could rank as an equitable easement only if it could have existed as a legal easement before 1926: applying this test (which was followed in *Poster* v *Slough Estates Ltd* [1969] 1 Ch 495), the contract between Clements and Bailey does not create an equitable easement. The majority of the Court of Appeal in the *Ives* case, however, held that an enforceable agreement to create a legal easement itself creates an equitable easement, and Scott J followed this in *Celsteel Ltd* v *Alton House Holdings Ltd* [1985] 1 WLR 204. This broader approach is more consistent with the principle that a valid contract to grant a legal easement itself creates an equitable easement according to the maxim that equity looks upon as done that which ought to be done (cf. *McManus* v *Cooke* (1887) 35 ChD 681). It would therefore seem that, from the agreement made in 1993, Clements acquired an equitable easement to use the driveway for the purpose of parking his car in his own garage.

The difficulty for Clements, however, is that the servient land has since been conveyed to a third party, Stepney. The issue is therefore whether Clements' equitable easement is binding on Stepney. If it is, Clements will be able, if necessary, to obtain an injunction to prevent Stepney from interfering with the exercise of such right.

If the title to No. 5 was unregistered when it was conveyed to Stepney, it is important to ascertain whether the equitable easement was protected by registration as a Class D(iii) land charge under the Land Charges Act 1972, s. 2(5), before the completion of Stepney's purchase. If it was so protected, the easement is binding on Stepney. If it was not, it is void against Stepney if he was a purchaser of the legal estate for money or money's worth (s. 4(6)).

If the title to No. 5 was already registered upon the transfer to Stepney, Stepney would have taken free of the equitable easement unless it was either protected by a notice on the register at the time of the transfer, or, in the absence of such protection, if, upon the transfer to Stepney, it ranked as an overriding interest within the Land Registration Act 1925, s. 70(1). Section 70(1)(a) includes in a list of overriding interests 'rights of way, watercourses, rights of water, and other easements not being equitable easements required to be protected by notice on the register'. In the *Celsteel* case, it was argued that, since no equitable easements are positively required to be protected by notice, all equitable easements are overriding interests. This argument was, however, rejected by Scott J. His Lordship construed 'required to be registered' to mean 'need to be protected', so that the exception in the paragraph covered all equitable easements save those which under some other statutory provision or legal principle could obtain protection otherwise than by notice on the register. Scott J considered the most obvious example to be an equitable easement protected under s. 70(1)(g) as part of the rights of a person in actual occupation. The problem with this view is that a right which involves actual occupation of the servient land appears to confer a right of at least joint user, and this is generally considered too extensive a right to qualify as an easement (*Copeland v Greenhalf* [1952] Ch 488: see Thompson [1986] *Conv* 31). In any event, however, it is unlikely that a right of way can be considered to confer a right of actual occupation.

In the *Celsteel* case, Scott J held that an equitable easement that was at the relevant time openly exercised and enjoyed by the owner of the benefited land was an overriding interest by virtue of the Land Registration Rules 1925, r. 258. This rule deems 'rights, privileges, and appurtenances appertaining or reputed to appertain to land or demised, occupied or enjoyed therewith,' which adversely affect registered land, to be overriding interests within the Land Registration Act 1925, s. 70. If, therefore, the evidence reveals that Clements' equitable right of way over the driveway of No. 5 was enjoyed with No. 3 and for its benefit, such right will comprise an overriding interest and will be binding upon Stepney.

If, however, it were to be held that Lord Denning MR's view in the *Ives* case is the correct one, and that an agreement for an easement does not create an equitable easement, then the interest so created would be binding upon Stepney only if it had been registered at the appropriate time as an estate contract, either as a minor interest (where the title to No. 5 was registered) or as a Class C(iv) land charge (Land Charges Act 1972, ss. 2(4) and 4(6)). In registered land, however, the estate contract might be protected as an overriding interest within the Land Registration Rules 1925, r. 258, in the same way as an equitable easement.

(b) An easement will *prima facie* be extinguished by abandonment if the dominant owner destroys the thing in respect of which the right was enjoyed. Although this doctrine of implied release has been developed in regard to legal easements, the same principle would appear to be applicable to equitable easements. Clements' demolition of his garage would therefore *prima facie* cause his easement to be lost. If Clements were to rebuild a new garage, access to which could be obtained without the need to pass over the driveway of No. 5, the evidence of abandonment would be strong. Thus in *Moore* v *Rawson* (1824) 3 B&C 332, the right to light in respect of certain windows was lost when the wall containing them was pulled down and replaced by another wall without any windows. By contrast, in *Cook* v *Bath Corporation* (1868) LR 6 Eq 177, the bricking-up of a door for 30 years was held not to be an abandonment of a right of way.

The mere demolition of the old garage will not, however, cause the easement to be lost if, at the time he pulls the old garage down, Clements either intimates his intention to build a new one, or does some act to show that he has such an intention, or if he in fact builds a new garage within a reasonable period of time (see Holroyd J in *Moore* v *Rawson*). The easement will be lost if Clements, having demolished the old garage without any indication of intention to build a new one, allows a long period of time to elapse before building a replacement (*Moore* v *Rawson*). A long period of time probably means a period of many years, since the courts are not prepared to hold that an easement has been abandoned unless the person entitled to it has demonstrated a fixed intention never thereafter to assert the right (*Tehidy Minerals Ltd* v *Norman* [1971] 2 QB 528). The presumption of abandonment is, however, stronger if the dominant owner, without protest, allows the servient owner to incur expense in the belief that the easement no longer exists (*Cook* v *Bath Corporation*). Alternatively, such circumstances might give rise to an estoppel (cf. *Crabb* v *Arun District Council* [1976] Ch 179).

Therefore, even if Clements did not express any intention to rebuild the garage when he demolished it, unless he has allowed Stepney to spend money in the belief that the easement has been abandoned or never existed, it is most unlikely that Clements would as yet be held to have abandoned his right of way.

13 Covenants Affecting Freehold Land

Before you start to write your answer to a problem question involving the running of the benefits and burdens of freehold covenants, you might find it useful to clarify the legal position by drawing a diagram showing the various legal relationships amongst the parties. This is best done in your rough notes rather than in the answer itself, as many examiners prefer to read words than to look at pictures. You could adapt (as appropriate) the following basic diagram, which represents the following transactions: A sells and conveys part of his land to B, taking a covenant from B. A disposes of his remaining land to C, and B sells and conveys his land to D.

A (covenantee)------------------------------C (successor in title to A)

B (covenantor)------------------------------D (successor in title to B)

Having drawn such a diagram, you should ask yourself three things:

(a) Who is suing (or might be advised to sue) whom?

(b) Are these the original parties or successors in title or others, e.g., persons with a derivative title, such as lessees, or adverse possessors?

(c) What remedies are (or ought to be) sought?

The basic diagram indicates four possible actions involving the original parties to the covenant and their successors in title: A against B, A against D, C against B, and C against D.

(a)   If A retains the benefited land, he can always sue B at common law for damages for breach of covenant. If B still retains the land, A may also be able to obtain against B either an injunction (if the covenant is negative) to prevent B from breaching it; or an order for specific performance (if the covenant is positive) to compel him to perform what he covenanted to perform.

The person identified as 'A' in the diagram means an original covenantee. This may be more than one person, and it may include someone who is not specifically named in the covenant. This is the effect of the Law of Property Act 1925, s. 56, which enables a person to take the benefit of a covenant affecting land even though he is not named as a party to the conveyance. If such a person still retains the benefited land, he can enforce the covenant (if at all) as an original covenantee: annexation or assignment is irrelevant. This situation arises in Question 2 in this chapter.

(b)   If A has sold and conveyed the benefited land to C but B retains the burdened land, C can sue B at common law for damages for breach of covenant if C has acquired the benefit of the covenant at common law. C will acquire the benefit of the covenant at common law if it is either expressly assigned to him (which can be effected under the Law of Property Act 1925, s. 136), or if, at the time it was entered into, it was annexed to the land. Annexation is possible only if the covenant touches and concerns the benefited land. If, however, C wishes to obtain an injunction against B, C will need to show that he has acquired the benefit of the covenant in equity. Again, this is possible only if the covenant touches and concerns the benefited land, is negative in substance, and if it has been either annexed to the land or assigned to C. In the case of assignment in equity, the conveyance of the land and the assignment of the benefit of the covenant must be simultaneous. This is in contrast to the position at common law. This issue is dealt with in Question 2 in this chapter.

(c)   If A retains the benefited land, but B has sold and conveyed the burdened land to D, A can never sue D at common law for damages for breach of covenant, since the burden of the covenant does not run at common law. A can, however, still sue B at common law for damages for breach of covenant. A may nevertheless be able to obtain an injunction against D to prevent him from breaching the covenant. This is possible only if the requirements of *Tulk* v *Moxhay* (1848) 2 Ph 774 for the running of the burden of a covenant in equity are satisfied, i.e., if the covenant touches and concerns the benefited land, is negative in substance, and is binding upon D (which may not be the case if it was not protected by registration as a land charge or a minor interest).

(d)   If both A and B have sold and conveyed their respective pieces of land, C can again sue B for damages at common law if the requirements specified in (b) above are met. If C wishes to obtain an injunction against D, he must show that he (C) has obtained the benefit of the covenant in equity (either by annexation or assignment), and also that D acquired the property subject to the burden of the covenant, as in (c). Whenever it is necessary to show the passing of the burden of a covenant, the common law rules are of no assistance, and it is necessary to consider the rules of equity.

Since the Chancery Amendment Act 1858 it has been possible for equitable damages to be awarded in lieu of, or in addition to, an equitable remedy. This power, now contained in the Supreme Court Act 1981, s. 50, is discussed in Question 4 in this chapter. Since the burden of a restrictive covenant in equity binds the land rather than the covenantee's estate in the land, the burden of such a covenant is enforceable in equity against anyone who comes to the land (other than a *bona fide* purchaser). This includes a person who does not have the same estate in the land as the covenantor, including, therefore, an adverse possessor. An injunction may therefore be sought against an adverse possessor whose actions are in breach of a restrictive covenant. In such a case, the plaintiff may seek damages against the adverse possessor in addition to an injunction (or as an alternative should the court refuse to make an order for injunctive relief). The result is that damages in equity may be awarded against a person who could not have been liable in damages for breach of covenant at common law.

If the benefit has not been annexed to the land, it may nevertheless have passed to the plaintiff by assignment, or by operation of law. Both of these methods are considered in Question 2 in this chapter.

A building scheme is a further means by which the benefits and burdens of restrictive covenants can pass in equity. These are considered in Question 3 in this chapter.

Question 4 in this chapter is a problem involving the possible discharge of a restrictive covenant.

QUESTION 1

In 1990 Pip was the fee simple owner of a plot of some 5,000 acres, the title to which was unregistered. The plot slopes gently from north to south. The northern half of the plot (called Fruitlands) comprises orchards; the southern half (called Homestead) comprises a dwelling-house and extensive gardens. In 1991, Pip conveyed Fruitlands to Squeak. In the conveyance to him, Squeak covenanted with Pip:

    (a)   to maintain the drainage ditches on Fruitlands in order to prevent the flooding of Homestead; and

    (b)   to use Fruitlands for agricultural purposes only.

The second of these covenants was immediately registered against Squeak's name as a land charge, Class D(ii).

In 1992, Pip conveyed Homestead to Cherry. The following year, Squeak conveyed Fruitlands to Wilfred.

Wilfred has neglected to repair the drainage ditches on Fruitlands, with the result that Cherry's land is periodically flooded. Wilfred also intends to build a block of flats on part of Fruitlands.

Advise Cherry.

Commentary

This question raises the issue of the extent to which the benefit and burden of both positive and negative covenants run with the land of the covenantee and the covenantor respectively. A sketch of the legal position is as follows:

A (Pip)- -(1992)- -**C** (Cherry)

↑

(1991)

|

B (Squeak)- - - - - - - - - - - - - - - - - -(1993)- -**D** (Wilfred)

You will find it useful to consider the benefit and burden separately. In the absence of any evidence in the problem of any assignment of the benefit, the only issue to consider on the benefit side is whether the benefit has been effectively annexed. Annexation has caused much difficulty in recent years. It would have been simpler if equity had simply followed the law, and treated the benefit as being annexed to the land in those cases in which it can pass at common law. However, at least in the past, it appeared that the equitable rules relating to annexation were different from, and (unfortunately) more technical than, the rules relating to annexation at common law (see *Rogers* v *Hosegood* [1900] 2 Ch 388, and *Re Ballard's Conveyance* [1937] 1 Ch 473). *Federated Homes Ltd* v *Mill Lodge Properties Ltd* [1980] 1 WLR 594 may have changed this, both by extending the scope of implied annexation in the Law of Property Act 1925, s. 78, and by casting doubt upon the correctness of *Re Ballard's Conveyance*. The decision in *Federated Homes* has also considerably reduced the importance of assignment.

Most candidates will be able to point out that the burden of covenants cannot run at common law, whereas the burden of negative covenants is enforceable in equity against most persons coming to the land, provided equity's other requirements are met. The student should not, however, forget that the effect of the common law rule is that the original covenantor remains liable in damages for breaches of covenant which occur even after he has conveyed the burdened land. Although Cherry's bringing an action for damages against Squeak for breach of the covenant to maintain the drainage ditches does not itself ensure that those ditches are repaired, it may indirectly (through a chain of covenants) have this effect.

The present question does not involve covenants entered into before 1926. These are subject to the Conveyancing Act 1881, s. 58, which deems (pre-1926) covenants relating to land to be made with the covenantee and his *assigns*. This was assumed to mean assigns of the *covenant*, rather than of the land — a view confirmed in *J. Sainsbury plc* v *Enfield LBC* [1989] 1 WLR 590. For annexation to occur, it was therefore still considered necessary that the covenant itself used words indicating an intention that the benefit was to run with the land. Such intention was evinced by words indicating that the covenant was to enure for the benefit the covenantees, their assigns and others claiming under them as owners of the lands for the benefit of which the covenant was taken (*Rogers* v *Hosegood* [1900] 2 Ch 388).

Post-1925 covenants, such as the one in the present problem, are governed by the Law of Property Act 1925, s. 78. This deems a covenant relating to land of the covenantee to be made with the covenantee and (*inter alia*) his successors in title. This expression is deemed to include the owners and occupiers for the time being of the *land* of the covenantee intended to be benefited. Given the clear difference in wording between this section and that of its predecessor of 1881, it is hardly surprising that the Court of Appeal in *Federated Homes* considered that the law relating to annexation had been changed by s. 78.

Suggested Answer

Neither Cherry nor Wilfred were the original parties to the covenants contained in the conveyance of 1991. If, therefore, Cherry is to obtain injunctive relief against Wilfred for breach of either covenant, he must establish both that he is entitled to the benefit of each covenant and that Wilfred is subject to the burden of each.

The initial problem for Cherry is that, at common law, the burden of a covenant does not run with the burdened land (*Austerberry* v *Corporation of Oldham* (1885) 29 ChD 750 (CA), recently affirmed by the House of Lords in *Rhone* v *Stephens* [1994] 2 WLR 429). Neither covenant therefore binds Wilfred at common law. In equity, the burden of a covenant can bind (*inter alia*) the covenantor's successor in title, but only if the covenant is negative in substance and the other requirements of the rule in *Tulk* v *Moxhay* (1848) 2 Ph 774 are satisfied. A positive covenant (i.e., one which requires the expenditure of money to prevent its being breached) cannot be enforced against such successor in equity. The covenant to maintain the drainage ditches is clearly a positive covenant as it requires expenditure of money. Thus, regardless of whether he can show that the benefit of the covenant has passed to him, Cherry will not be able to compel Wilfred to maintain the ditches.

The corollary of the principle of *Austerberry* v *Corporation of Oldham* is that the original covenantor remains liable on a covenant at common law even after he has parted with the land. Cherry will therefore be able to sue Squeak for damages for breach of covenant (a) if he can show that he has acquired the benefit of such covenant at common law.

In order for the benefit of a covenant (whether positive or negative) to run with the land at common law (i.e., to be annexed to the land), the covenant must satisfy several requirements. First, it must touch and concern the covenantee's land; evidence that the value or occupation of Homestead is improved by the restriction upon the user of Fruitlands will suffice. Secondly, both the covenantee and his successor in title must have a legal estate in such land; this is clearly the case here. Thirdly, there must be an intention when the covenant is made that the benefit is to run with the land.

This third requirement gives rise to difficulties. The Law of Property Act 1925, s. 78, deems a covenant relating to land of the covenantee to be made with the covenantee and (*inter alia*) his successors in title, which expression is deemed to include the owners and occupiers for the time being of the land of the covenantee intended to be benefited. Clearly, therefore, it does not matter that Squeak expressly covenanted with Pip alone because Pip's successors in title are statutorily included. It was, nevertheless, for many years thought that the section had not done away with the need for the covenant to indicate that it was taken for the benefit of the covenantees' land (*Rogers v Hosegood* [1900] 2 Ch 388). Were this interpretation correct, the covenants in the problem would not have been annexed to the land and would not therefore have passed to Cherry unless assigned to him.

However, in *Federated Homes Ltd v Mill Lodge Properties Ltd* [1980] 1 WLR 594, the Court of Appeal held that s. 78 effects an automatic annexation of the benefit of any covenant that is shown to benefit land of the covenantee, even if the covenant does not itself state this expressly. The decision in *Federated Homes* has been criticised as giving the section an effect it was not intended to have (see Newsom (1982) 98 *LQR* 202), for effectively reviving covenants thought to have become unenforceable, and for undermining the law relating to the passing of the benefit by assignment. Furthermore, the section has subsequently been held not to apply where the covenant makes it clear that the benefit is not annexed (*Roake v Chadha* [1984] 1 WLR 40). No such exclusion is apparent here. Therefore, on the authority of *Federated Homes*, it would seem that the benefit of each covenant was annexed to the land.

Cherry can, therefore sue Squeak, the original covenantor, for damages for breach of the covenant. If, as would be usual, Squeak obtained an indemnity covenant from Wilfred when he conveyed Fruitlands to Wilfred, Cherry's threat to sue Squeak for damages, which would in turn induce Squeak to sue Wilfred for damages, might be sufficient to induce Wilfred to repair the ditches. No such indirect method of enforcement will avail Cherry, however, if Squeak did not take an indemnity covenant, or if he is untraceable or bankrupt, or if he has died and his estate has been wound up.

Covenant (b), by contrast, is negative in substance, so Cherry may be able to obtain an injunction against Wilfred to prevent the building under the doctrine of *Tulk v Moxhay* (1848) 2 Ph 774. For this to occur, it must be shown that the original parties to the covenant intended that the burden of the covenant should run with the land of the covenantor. Although Squeak appears to have expressly covenanted on his own behalf only, the effect of the Law of Property Act 1925, s. 79, is (subject to a contrary intention) to treat the covenant as being made by the covenantor on behalf of himself and (*inter alia*) his successors in title. This requirement is therefore also met. If covenant (b) satisfies these and the other requirements for *Tulk* v *Moxhay* (1848) 2 Ph 774 (i.e., that it touches and concerns the land, and was taken for the benefit of the covenantee's land), it will be binding upon Wilfred since it was protected by registration as a land charge.

Cherry will also have to establish that the benefit of covenant (b) has been passed to him in equity. Broadly, the requirements for equitable annexation are the same as those for annexation at common law, discussed above, except that in equity it suffices if the plaintiff has merely an equitable interest in the benefited land. In *Federated Homes*, the burdened land remained in the ownership of the covenantor. Nevertheless, because the plaintiff sought an injunction, an equitable remedy, the case appears to have concerned annexation in equity. In any event, in *Roake* v *Chadha*, where there had been a change in the ownership of the burdened land, the judge proceeded on the basis that the principle in *Federated Homes* was equally applicable to annexation in equity (see Todd, [1984] *Conv* 68). It is therefore likely that the benefit of covenant (b) has been annexed in equity.

An additional complexity in relation to equitable annexation was, however, added in *Re Ballard's Conveyance* [1937] 1 Ch 473, in which Clauson J held that if the benefit of the covenant were expressed to be for the benefit of the vendor's retained land, it would not be annexed to each part of it. Therefore, unless the covenant touched and concerned the whole land, there would be no annexation at all. Since Homestead presumably comprises some 2,500 acres, the absence of appropriate words of annexation to each and every part would appear to be fatal to Cherry.

However, Brightman LJ in *Federated Homes* cast doubt on the soundness of the reasoning in *Ballard*, and considered it inconsistent with both *Williams* v *Unit Construction Co. Ltd* (1951) 19 *Conv* 262 and *Smith and Snipe's Hall Farm* v *River Douglas Catchment Board* [1949] 2 KB 500 (although these both concerned annexation at common law). Brightman LJ's dicta are more sensible, and will probably be followed. It would therefore seem that the benefit of covenant (b) has been annexed in equity to Homestead, and is enforceable by Cherry, who will be able to prevent Wilfred from building.

QUESTION 2

In 1974 Clifford, the fee simple owner of Whiteacre, the title to which was unregistered, conveyed part of it to Arlington. In the conveyance, Arlington covenanted on behalf of himself and his successors in title with Clifford and with the other owners for the time being of land adjoining Whiteacre not to use the land thereby conveyed to him (*inter alia*) as a fish-and-chip shop. The conveyance expressly stated that the benefit of the covenant was not to pass to any subsequent owner of the benefited land except by assignment.

At the time of the conveyance from Clifford to Arlington, Buckingham was the fee simple owner of an adjacent plot, Blackacre. In 1980, Buckingham conveyed Blackacre to Ashley. This conveyance did not contain an express assignment of the benefit of Arlington's covenant; but in the negotiations preceding the conveyance to Ashley, Buckingham represented to Ashley that he would have the right to enforce the covenant.

In 1985, Arlington conveyed his part of Whiteacre to Lauderdale, who has recently expressed the intention of opening a fish-and-chip shop on that land. Ashley died last month. By his will, he gave all his property to Godolphin, whom he also appointed his executor.

Advise Godolphin if he can prevent Lauderdale from opening the fish-and-chip shop.

Commentary

As in the previous question, both the benefited and the burdened land have been assigned. Since the covenant is negative in substance, the answer needs to state that the burden can be enforced against Lauderdale, the successor in title to the original covenantor, provided it was protected by registration. This question is, however, primarily concerned with the passing of the benefit and whether the benefit of the covenant has passed to, and is enforceable by, Godolphin. This requires showing that the benefit of the covenant was acquired by Buckingham in the first place (explaining the impact of the Law of Property Act 1925, s. 56), and was then passed on from him to Ashley (by assignment), and then from Ashley to Godolphin (through operation of law). Annexation, it should be noted, is expressly excluded by the wording of the covenant, as it was in *Roake* v *Chadha* [1984] 1 WLR 40. Too long should not therefore be spent on annexation: it is sufficient to show why it is that annexation cannot be relied upon in this question.

Suggested Answer

If Godolphin is to succeed, he must establish both that Lauderdale is subject to the burden of the covenant, and that he has himself acquired, and is entitled to enforce in equity, the benefit of the covenant.

First, the burden. Since the covenant in the problem is negative in substance, it may bind Lauderdale, as successor in title to the original covenantor, under the doctrine of *Tulk* v *Moxhay* (1848) 2 Ph 774. For this doctrine to operate, the covenantee (or his successors) must, both at the time of the covenant and subsequently, own nearby land for the protection of which the covenant was entered into — which is the case here. The restrictive covenant must also 'touch and concern' the dominant land, i.e., affect its mode of occupation or value. This requirement may also be satisfied, if, for example, it may be inferred that the covenant was taken in order to benefit Whiteacre and adjoining plots from the smells emanating from a fish-and-chip shop. Evidence may therefore be needed to show whether Blackacre is in fact capable of benefiting from such covenant. It must also be shown that the burden was intended to run with the land: this is satisfied by Arlington's having covenanted on behalf of himself and his successors in title.

Even if these requirements are met, however, if Lauderdale was a purchaser of the legal estate for money or money's worth, he will still take free of the covenant unless it was registered, before the completion of his purchase, as a land charge, Class D(ii). This is the case even if, at that time, he knew of the covenant's existence (*Midland Bank Trust Co.* v *Green* [1981] AC 513).

Secondly, the benefit. If Godolphin is to enforce the covenant by means of an injunction against Lauderdale, he must show that he has acquired the benefit of the covenant in equity. This requires him to establish that he acquired it as Ashley's executor, and that Ashley had in turn himself acquired it from Buckingham.

Buckingham was not named as a party to the 1974 conveyance, i.e., he was not an express covenantee. Nevertheless, by virtue of the Law of Property Act 1925, s. 56, a person may take (*inter alia*) the benefit of any covenant respecting land, although he be not named as a party to the conveyance. In effect, the section enables a person who could have been a party to the conveyance to be an original covenantee, provided that he can be identified. In *Re Ecclesiastical Commissioners for England's Conveyance* [1936] Ch 430, where the covenant was made (*inter alia*) for the benefit of the owners for the time being of land adjacent to that conveyed, it was held that such owners, being identifiable, could have enforced the covenant. It would therefore seem that, since he can be similarly identified from the wording of the covenant, Buckingham, as owner for the time being of land adjoining Whiteacre, could likewise have enforced the covenant made by Arlington.

Only owners for the time being can take the benefit of the Law of Property Act 1925, s. 56, and this therefore excludes Ashley, who acquired Blackacre only subsequently. It is also unlikely that the benefit of the covenant passed to Ashley by reason of its annexation to Blackacre. The Law of Property Act 1925, s. 78(1), deems a covenant relating to any land of the covenantee to be made with the covenantee and (*inter alia*) his successors in title. In *Federated Homes Ltd* v *Mill Lodge Properties Ltd* [1980] 1 WLR 594 the Court of Appeal held that this section caused the benefit of a covenant relating to land of the covenantee to be automatically annexed to the land. It was held to have this effect in that case, even though the particular covenant (like the one in the problem, and unlike that considered in *Rogers* v *Hosegood* [1900] 2 Ch 388) did not expressly state that it was for the benefit of the covenantee's land.

Despite *Federated Homes*, however, it is now clear that annexation is not automatic, and that it can be excluded. Thus, in *Roake* v *Chadha* [1984] 1 WLR 40, the covenant provided that it was not to enure for the benefit of any subsequent owner of the vendor's retained land unless expressly assigned. While accepting that the Law of Property Act 1925, s. 78, meant that the range of persons with whom the covenant was made could not be reduced, it was held that annexation could still be excluded, and in that case was, by the words of the covenant itself. The wording of the covenant in the problem, expressly limiting the passing of the benefit to assignment, has a similar effect. Annexation is thus excluded.

If, therefore, the benefit of the covenant passed to Ashley, this can only have been through assignment. The requirements for a valid assignment in equity are five-fold, and were laid down by Romer LJ in *Miles* v *Easter* [1933] Ch 611, thus:

(a)   the covenant must have been taken for the benefit of land of the covenantee;

(b)   the land must be indicated with reasonable certainty;

(c)   the dominant land must be retained in whole or in part by the plaintiff; and

(d)   be capable of benefiting from the covenant; and

(e)   the assignment of the covenant and the conveyance of the land to which it relates must be contemporaneous.

In the question the first three requirements of *Miles* v *Easter* appear to be satisfied. The fourth requirement is satisfied if the covenantee is thereby enabled to dispose of his land to advantage, i.e., if it increases the value of his land (*Miles* v *Easter* at p. 631). Assuming therefore (as discussed earlier) that the covenant 'touches and concerns' the benefited land, the fourth requirement is satisfied also.

Unless the assignment is contemporaneous with the conveyance — the fifth requirement — the benefit of the covenant is lost in equity. Thus, in the absence of an express assignment to Ashley, the fifth requirement is met only if a contemporaneous assignment can implied. In *Miles* v *Easter* itself, there are conflicting dicta, both at first instance and in the Court of Appeal, regarding the need for the assignment to be (as in that case) express. Other authorities, however, suggest that the assignment may be implied, i.e., that it is enough that the vendor stated in the contract for the sale of the land, or represented to the purchaser in the negotiations preceding the sale, that the latter would have the right to enforce the covenant (*Renals* v *Cowlishaw* (1878) 9 ChD 125, at pp. 129–131, and *White* v *Bijou Mansions* [1937] Ch 610, at p. 622. It would therefore appear from the facts of the problem that Ashley acquired the benefit of the covenant by implied assignment effected at the same time as the conveyance to Ashley.

The final issue is therefore whether the benefit of the covenant has passed from Ashley to Godolphin. An express assignment by Ashley to Godolphin as his personal representative is obviously unnecessary. The benefit of the covenant is personal property of the deceased, and will pass to his executor by operation of law (*Ives* v *Brown* [1919] 2 Ch 314; *Newton Abbot Cooperative Society Ltd* v *Williamson and Treadgold Ltd* [1952] Ch 286). After he has administered the estate, Godolphin will, in due course, no doubt execute a vesting assent of the retained portion of Whiteacre in favour of himself (*Re King's Will Trusts* [1964] Ch 542) together with an assignment of the benefit of the covenant. Even if not expressly assigned to himself as beneficiary, the benefit of the covenant would presumably be thereby assigned impliedly. Indeed, even in the absence of an assignment in the strict sense, the same result would ensue were he treated as retaining the benefit of the covenant as executor, since he would be holding it on a bare trust for himself as beneficiary (cf. *Earl of Leicester* v *Wells-next-to-*

the-Sea UDC [1973] Ch 110). Whatever his present capacity, therefore, Godolphin will be able to enforce the covenant.

QUESTION 3

'The requirements for a building scheme are merely indicia of an intention to create a community of interest with reciprocity of obligation. Where such intention is found, equity is willing to read the covenants in the light of the surrounding facts. A building scheme is therefore no more than a species of implied annexation, and the law relating to such schemes is purely evidential. The notion of reciprocity of rights and obligations is the only characteristic which a building scheme shares with the doctrine of mutual benefits and burdens laid down in *Halsall* v *Brizell* [1957] Ch 169.'

Discuss.

Commentary

One or two questions on your examination paper may ask you to discuss a quotation. The quotation may be a genuine one; but sometimes (as here) it will have been specially drafted (some might say 'concocted') for the purposes of the question. It is always important to address every matter with which the quotation deals; and you should be prepared to disagree with statements which you consider incorrect — and, of course, to explain why.

In the present question, the examiner is evidently trying to elicit from you a discussion of the juridical basis underlying building schemes and the quotation itself usefully provides a ready-made structure for your answer. The quotation comprises four sentences and it will be seen that each of them requires you to deal with a distinct point. The first invites you to consider whether the requirements for a building scheme are indeed no more than indications of an intention to create a community of interest. The second calls for a discussion of equity's approach to the construction of covenants once a building scheme has been found. The third effectively asks you to consider whether a building scheme is no more than a form of implied annexation. The last expects you to compare the principles underlying building schemes with the doctrine of mutual benefits and burdens.

You are probably unlikely to have a question involving these issues unless your lectures or tutorials have directed you to consider them. The present method of approach, however, may be taken to apply to all questions which take the form of lengthy quotations. The examiner will probably see many scripts written by candidates who choose to ignore the substance of the quotation, and treat the question as if it began 'Write all you know about ...'. Relatively few, in the writers' experience, will be the number of answers which really do seek to discuss the particular points raised in the light of the relevant law. For candidates prepared to apply and direct their knowledge, the higher marks are there just waiting to be earned.

Suggested Answer

The classic requirements for a building scheme (or scheme of development as it is sometimes known) were laid down by Parker J in *Elliston* v *Reacher* [1908] 2 Ch 374. The requirements are five-fold:

(a)   the plaintiff and the defendant should have derived their titles from a common vendor;

(b)   before the sale of the plots, the common vendor must have laid out his estate for sale in lots subject to restrictions intended to be imposed on all the lots;

(c)   the restrictions were intended by the common vendor to be and were for the benefits of all the lots sold;

(d)   the original purchasers must have bought their lots on the understanding that the restrictions were to enure for the benefit of the other lots; and

(e)   (added in *Reid* v *Bickerstaff* [1909] 2 Ch 305) the geographical area to which the scheme extends must be clear.

In *Elliston* v *Reacher* Parker J considered that, where all the points were established, 'the community of interest imports in equity the reciprocity of obligation which is in fact contemplated by each at the time of his own purchase'. In more recent years, the courts have tended to emphasise this broader element of reciprocity (see *Brunner* v *Greenslade* [1971] Ch 993, and *Jamaica Mutual Life Assurance Society* v *Hillsborough Ltd* [1989] 1 WLR 1101). They have therefore been less concerned to find that all five requirements have been met. In *Baxter* v *Four Oaks Properties Ltd* [1965] Ch 816, for instance, Parker J's second requirement was not satisfied, but the court found an intention to create mutually binding covenants and held that this sufficed to create a scheme. Further, in *Re Dolphin's Conveyance* [1970] Ch

654, the court considered that both the first and second requirements were unnecessary. Nevertheless, an intention to create a community of interest with reciprocity of obligation is not in itself sufficient; the fifth requirement must always be met (*Lund* v *Taylor* (1975) 31 P & CR 167; *Jamaica Mutual Life*). The vendor may, however, retain the right to exempt part of his retained land from the stipulations (*Allen* v *Veranne Builders Ltd* [1988] (unreported)).

Where the requirements of a building scheme are met, the court simply treats the covenants as being mutually enforceable amongst the owners of the lots. This suggests that the basis for enforceability is something other than annexation or assignment — that building schemes create their own rights and obligations through the principle of reciprocity. Extrinsic evidence is admissible in order to show that the requirements, and the element of reciprocity, are present; such evidence could be of the parties' acts and statements before conveyance (which might include, for instance, details of sales' advertisements), and even evidence from the common vendor's predecessor in title (*Kingsbury* v *LW Anderson Ltd* (1979) 40 P & CR 136).

It is sometimes contended that it is possible to achieve by a building scheme what cannot be achieved by annexation, i.e., the creation of reciprocal mutual rights amongst successive purchasers of lots. It is true that 'neither annexation nor assignment can enable the covenantee to distribute the benefits of later covenants to earlier purchasers' (Gray, *Elements of Land Law*, 2nd edn, London: Butterworths, 1993). Even outside a building scheme, however, earlier purchasers can take the benefit of the covenants entered into by later purchasers if the covenants are expressed to be made, not merely with the common vendor for the benefit of his retained land, but also with existing owners of previously sold plots for the benefit of such plots (Law of Property Act 1925, s. 56). By this means, the benefit of later purchasers' covenants are annexed to the land of earlier purchasers.

If, however, in the foregoing circumstances, a building scheme exists, earlier purchasers can enforce in equity the covenants entered into by later purchasers even if they are not made covenantees under the Law of Property Act 1925, s. 56. An earlier purchaser's equity could be treated as arising merely through the application of the principle of reciprocity. It could, alternatively, be treated as deriving from covenant. Under the latter analysis, where equity finds an intention to create mutually enforceable obligations, it will readily infer the intention to make earlier purchasers original covenantees of later purchasers' covenants and to annex the benefit to their land.

Implied annexation therefore means that, once there is sufficient evidence to show the existence of the scheme itself, extrinsic (or further extrinsic) evidence can be used to show that the covenants are annexed to the land. The older cases proceeded on this footing, and established that, where a building scheme exists, the court will construe the covenants with a view to ensuring that the benefit of each purchaser's covenant is annexed to the lots of all the others (*Spicer* v *Martin* (1889) 14 App Cas 12, HL). Similarly, in *Rogers* v *Hosegood* [1900] 2 Ch 388, both Farwell J (at first instance) and the Court of Appeal treated a building scheme as merely exemplifying the general rule that a deed is to be construed in the light of surrounding circumstances (see Bailey [1938] *CLJ* 339, at p. 364).

Although implied annexation appears to explain the earlier decisions on building schemes, the importance attached in modern times to the underlying principle of reciprocity of obligations has made it more difficult to reconcile some recent cases with any form of annexation. Thus, it has been held that, if two or more of the lots come into common ownership, the covenants are not destroyed, but will, upon severance, become once again enforceable amongst their owners *inter se* (*Brunner* v *Greenslade*; *Texaco Antilles Ltd* v *Kernochan* [1973] AC 609, PC). Furthermore, a Commonwealth court has expressed its preparedness to uphold a building scheme purely on the basis of intention, even if the conveyances contain not a single covenant (*Re Louis and the Conveyancing Act* [1971] 1 NSWLR 164).

The law relating to building schemes appears therefore to have outgrown its origins in the equitable rules pertaining to the construction of deeds. In this respect, its development is not unlike that of the doctrine of mutual benefits and burdens. This doctrine also developed from a principle relating to deeds, namely that if a person is named as a party to a deed and takes a benefit under it with knowledge of the facts, then he is bound by it, even though he does not execute it (*R* v *Houghton-le-Spring* (1819) 2 B & Ald 375). From this narrow basis, the law moved a long way so that, in *Tito* v *Waddell (No. 2)* [1977] Ch 106, at pp. 301–303, Megarry V-C was able to refer to the 'pure principle' of benefits and burdens, namely that a person who takes the benefit of a deed must also take it subject to the burdens it contains. In *Rhone* v *Stephens* [1994] 2 WLR 429, however, the House of Lords retreated from such wide formulation, and stated that the doctrine can apply only where the benefits and burdens are reciprocal and not independent of each other; the benefit cannot therefore be the whole benefit taken under the deed. Even within such confines, however, the doctrine can result in a subsequent purchaser of land being bound by a covenant made by a predecessor in title (*Hopgood* v *Brown* [1955] 1 WLR 213).

As the quotation states, the notion of reciprocity of obligations underpins both building schemes and the doctrine of mutual benefits and burdens, but there are considerable differences. First, a purchaser of a lot subject to a building scheme cannot escape from the obligations it imposes by choosing to forego the benefits it confers; whereas a purchaser who does not wish to take a benefit under a deed cannot be subjected to a reciprocal burden. Secondly, the only obligations that can be enforced in a building scheme are those which are negative or restrictive in nature; whereas, under the mutual benefits and burdens doctrine, even a positive obligation (such as the payment of a levy for the use of roads and sewers as in *Halsall* v *Brizell* itself) can be enforced. Thirdly, the obligations imposed by a building scheme are probably enforceable against subsequent purchasers only if protected by registration as a land charge or by notice; whereas the burdens imposed by the doctrine of *Halsall* v *Brizell* are not, as such, registrable as land charges (*Hopgood* v *Brown*).

QUESTION 4

Two years ago, Isabella purchased Udolpho, a large freehold property with extensive gardens in Gloucestershire. The property was subject to a restrictive covenant created in 1900 in favour of the owners of the adjoining properties and their successors in title. By the terms of the covenant, no further buildings were to be erected on Udolpho. Isabella, however, recently obtained planning permission to build a block of flats in the back garden of Udolpho.

The owners of adjoining properties, Catherine and Eleanor, have threatened to seek an injunction to prevent the building in breach of the covenant. Catherine is concerned that any building in the back garden of Udolpho would prevent her house receiving the benefit of evening sunshine. Although Eleanor's property does not itself enjoy a view over the valley, she is concerned that the building would obstruct the view of the valley from a lane one hundred yards from her property. This spot affords a prospect of Northanger Abbey surrounded by extensive oak woods. Isabella feels inclined to ignore her neighbours' objections and to begin the work of construction.

Advise Isabella.

Commentary

This question is concerned both with the remedies for a breach (or a threatened breach) of a restrictive covenant and also with the possible means by which such a covenant might be discharged. The latter aspect mostly involves going through the relevant grounds in the Law of Property Act 1925, s. 84 explaining how they have been interpreted by the courts, and applying them to the facts. The point of view, it should be noted, is that of the successor in title to the covenantor, rather than that of the objectors. Candidates who have worked at this area, particularly if they have their statute book (rather than a laundry list) in the examination room, should not find this question the Gothic horror that it might otherwise be.

A useful note on the benefit of a view in relation to an application to discharge or modify a restrictive covenant is Polden, 'Views in Perspective', [1984] *Conv* 429.

Suggested Answer

The proposed building would breach the restrictive covenant; so that, assuming the covenant is binding upon Isabella, and that the benefit of it has passed to Catherine and Eleanor (or to either of them), they could seek an injunction against Isabella to prevent her building. If Isabella were unwise enough to begin building in breach of the covenant, Catherine and Eleanor could seek a mandatory injunction requiring her to demolish any building put up in breach.

Where a restrictive covenant is breached, the court has had power (since the Chancery Amendment Act 1858) to award damages in lieu of an injunction. In a case of nuisance, it has been laid down that damages in lieu of an injunction will be awarded only if the injury to the plaintiff's legal rights is small, if it can be estimated in money, if it can be adequately compensated by a small money payment, and if it would be oppressive to the defendant to grant an injunction (*Shelfer* v *City of London Lighting Co. Ltd* [1895] 1 Ch 287). In *Wakeham* v *Wood* (1981) 43 P & CR 40, CA, these criteria were held to apply to determine whether damages should be granted in lieu of an injunction where there had been a breach of a restrictive covenant. In that case, the defendant had flagrantly breached a covenant against building in a way that would obstruct a view of the sea. The Court of Appeal granted the plaintiffs a mandatory injunction, and Waller LJ expressed the opinion that the value of a view could not be estimated in monetary terms, and therefore could not be compensated by a small money payment. Although Eleanor's property does not itself enjoy the view, the court might adopt a similar stance. The value of evening sunshine to Catherine's property would similarly appear to be inestimable. Isabella would therefore be running a considerable risk should she begin building in breach of covenant.

A restrictive covenant cannot be enforced if the character of the neighbourhood has been so altered since the covenant was entered into that it is now of no value to the plaintiff and it would be inequitable and senseless to enforce it (*Chatsworth Estates Co.* v *Fewell* [1931] 1 Ch 224). These criteria are unlikely to be satisfied in the problem, since the benefit of the evening sunshine and the protection of the view are of continuing value to Catherine and Eleanor respectively.

Isabella's best course of action, therefore, is to apply to the Lands Tribunal to have the covenant modified or discharged under the Law of Property Act 1925, s. 84, as amended by the Law of Property Act 1969. If it were to make an order discharging or modifying the restrictive covenant, the tribunal could also direct Isabella to pay such consideration as it thinks just to any persons entitled to the benefit of the covenant — which could clearly include Catherine and Eleanor.

Before making any order, however, the tribunal must be satisfied that one of several sets of circumstances is fulfilled, these being set out in the Law of Property Act 1925, s. 84(1) paras (a)–(c). The only paragraphs which might be relevant to the problem are (a) and (aa). The circumstances in para. (a) are that, by reason of the change in the character of the property or the neighbourhood or other material circumstances, the restriction ought to be deemed obsolete. Evidence of such changes in character would need to be produced; but, given that the covenant still protects the view over the valley and affords Catherine the benefit of evening sunshine, it is unlikely that Isabella will succeed under this paragraph.

Isabella might be able to make out a better case under para. (aa), which was added by the Law of Property Act 1969. This paragraph enables the tribunal to discharge or modify the covenant if its continued existence would (or unless modified would) impede some reasonable user of the land. The Lands Tribunal may not discharge or modify the covenant under this paragraph, however, unless it is satisfied that the restriction does not secure to persons entitled to the benefit of it any practical benefits of substantial value or advantage to them, or is contrary to the public interest. It must also be satisfied that, in either case, money will be an adequate compensation for any loss or disadvantage that any such persons will suffer from the discharged or modification: Law of Property Act 1925, s. 84(1A). In determining whether a case falls within s. 84(1A) and whether a restriction ought to be discharged or modified, the Lands Tribunal must take into account (*inter alia*) the development plan and any pattern for the grant or refusal of planning permission in the relevant areas.

The fact that Isabella has obtained planning permission to erect the block of flats is persuasive (but not decisive) evidence that the proposed user is reasonable (*Re Bass Ltd's Application* (1973) 26 P & CR 156). Assuming that the covenant impedes that user, the next matter to be determined (in accordance with *Re Bass*) is whether the proposed user secures practical benefits to the objectors. In *Re Bellamy's Application* (1977) JPL 456 the enjoyment of evening sunshine in a sun-lounge was held to be a practical benefit. A view can also be a practical benefit (*Gilbert* v *Spoor* [1983] Ch 27).

Although Eleanor does not have a view over the valley from her property, the view from the road near her property may enhance the enjoyment of her property. In *Gilbert* v *Spoor* [1983] Ch 27, a similar objection was made: namely, that the building would obscure a view enjoyed only from a road adjoining the objectors' property. The Court of Appeal rejected the argument that the benefit sought to be protected must be one that is capable of touching and concerning the benefited land; although, on the facts, it concluded that the covenant did touch and concern the objectors' land. In the problem, therefore, it would be open to the tribunal to find that the view from the road is a practical benefit to Eleanor.

If this requirement is met, the tribunal must then be satisfied that the benefits secured by the restrictive covenant are of substantial 'value or advantage' — a phrase which indicates that money value is not the only thing to be taken into account (*Re Bass*). In *Re Banks' Application* (1976) 33 P & CR 138 it was stated that a direct view of the sea was of immense value, and, in *Gilbert* v *Spoor* Eveleigh LJ considered that a power to preserve a magnificent view was of substantial value or advantage. If, as appears from the problem, the view over the valley is a particularly fine one, and the lane is easily accessible, this criterion might also be met. The enjoyment of evening sunshine is also capable of satisfying this criterion. It is essentially a matter of fact for the tribunal. Evidence that the objector has never personally admired the view, though relevant, is not fatal to the objection (*Gilbert* v *Spoor*).

It is very difficult to establish that the continued existence of the covenant is contrary to the public interest: in only two applications has such argument succeeded. In the first, *Re SJC Construction Co. Ltd's Application* (1974) 28 P & CR 200, there was a scarcity of building land, and unless the restriction were modified, £47,000 worth of building work would have to be destroyed. In the light of *Wakeham* v *Wood* (discussed above), the latter factor may now be of lesser significance. In the second, *Re Lloyd's and Lloyd's Application* (1993) 66 P & CR 112, a user covenant was modified to permit the premises to be used as a community care home. The restriction was considered contrary to the public interest because of the government's policy of care in the community and the acute need for such a home in the area. There is nothing in the problem, however, to suggest that a public interest argument could be made out there.

Finally, if the tribunal finds that the restriction does not secure practical benefits of substantial value or advantage, it must consider whether money will be an adequate compensation to the objector. In *Re Carter's Application* (1973) 25 P & CR 542 a covenant against erecting more than one dwelling-house on the plot was modified to permit infilling with a bungalow. The objectors' properties enjoyed merely glimpses of the sea, which was held not to be a substantial value or advantage. The objectors were awarded compensation of between £100 and £200. The applicant's offer to reduce the height of the bungalow by 2ft 6in was made a condition of the modification order.

If, therefore, the benefits of the view and evening sunshine are held not to comprise practical benefits of substantial value or advantage, it will be open to the tribunal to discharge or modify the covenant, and to require Isabella to pay consideration to Catherine and Eleanor. It might also assist Isabella's application in such circumstances if she is prepared to modify her building plans so that the view and the sunshine, whilst reduced, are not entirely lost. If, however, the restriction is considered to secure practical benefits of substantial value or advantage, the tribunal cannot permit discharge or modification of the covenant, even on payment of large amounts of compensation.

14 Mortgages

The law of mortgages is a topic usually dealt with towards the end of a land law course. This is because you need first to understand leases, land charges and the difference between legal and equitable interests which are all relevant to mortgages.

For a really sound understanding of the subject, some slight background knowledge of the nature of mortgages before 1926, and of how and why equity intervened to assist the oppressed mortgagor, will be an advantage. This is touched upon in Question 1(a), which also describes the relevant provisions of the Law of Property Act 1925 and the Land Registration Act 1925 for the creation of mortgages since then. The different ways in which an equitable mortgage may be created are dealt with in Question 4, which also considers the remedies available to an equitable mortgagee on default of the mortgagor.

The two main topics for questions on mortgages are probably restrictions on the equity of redemption ('clogs' on the equity), and the remedies of a mortgagee in the event of the mortgagor defaulting.

The first topic has been subject to a considerable change in the attitude of the courts since the early cases, where it was established that equity would intervene to mitigate the harshness of a bargain forced upon an oppressed mortgagor. Cases such as *Knightsbridge Estates Trust Ltd* v *Byrne* [1939] Ch 441 and *Kreglinger* v *New Patagonia Meat & Cold Storage Co. Ltd* [1914] AC 25, referred to in Question 2, reflect a readiness by the courts to perceive a mortgage as part of a wider commercial transaction where appropriate; they have been prepared to depart from the strict maxims of equity against clogs on the equity of redemption where they have felt that they operated unfairly.

A mortgagee's remedies on default of the mortgagor are to be found in both case law and statute law. The recession and hitherto unexperienced decline in property values, has led to some interesting adaptations of the power of sale in cases such as *Palk* v *Mortgage Services Funding plc* [1993] Ch 330 and *Target Home Loans Ltd* v *Clothier & Clothier* (1992) 25 HLR 48, referred to in Question 3. There have been cases on a mortgagee's or receiver's duties on a sale, and an entirely new interpretation of 'reasonable time' in s. 36, Administration of Justice Act 1970 (*Cheltenham & Gloucester Building Society* v *Norgan* [1996] 1 WLR 343).

Question 5 highlights a problem area for mortgagees which arises from co-ownership of, and sureties for, mortgaged property. There has been a steady stream of Court of Appeal cases in the wake of the House of Lords decision in *Barclays Bank plc* v *O'Brien* [1994] 1 AC 180. This is hardly surprising given that what is at stake is the co-mortgagor's or surety's home, and that the validity of the mortgage against a lender depends upon two factors which necessarily have to be determined on the particular facts of each case — that the co-mortgagor or surety was acting under the undue influence of the borrower (dispelled or not by the advice which they received), and that the lender had notice (constructive or imputed) of this. Some attempt has been made in the commentary to that question to extract a few principles which have emerged from these cases.

Lastly, Question 6 deals with the very difficult problem of priorities which could, in theory, arise between different mortgagees. The fact that there are so few modern cases on the statutory provisions relating to this may well be due to the era of rising property values in which (until the late 1980s) we have been living since the 1925 legislation. This meant that there was sufficient equity in a property to cover all the mortgagor's borrowing. The more recent falling market values, however, may yet produce some litigation on the conflicting provisions of the Law of Property Act 1925 and the Land Charges Act 1972, although the ever-increasing and accelerated registration of title, where these provisions do not apply, may save the courts from the difficult task of resolving the conflict.

Because this is a book on land law, we have not included a question on priorities of mortgages of equitable interests under a trust, which are governed by the rule in *Dearle* v *Hall* (1823) 3 Russ 1.

QUESTION 1

(a) Discuss the ways in which a legal mortgage may be created after 1925 in (i) unregistered land and (ii) registered land.

(b) David is the tenant of a 50-year lease of a shop. Five years ago, he borrowed £20,000 from Quickslip Bank plc in order to expand his business, and the sum was secured by a legal charge on the leasehold property. Quickslip Bank plc have recently discovered that David has had financial problems, as a result of which he had become in arrears with his rent, and the landlord has forfeited the lease. The landlord says that he had no notice of the mortgage to Quickslip Bank plc, and that the mortgage would, in any event, have been prohibited by the terms of the lease, which includes a covenant not to assign or sublet without first obtaining the landlord's consent in writing. Advise Quickslip Bank plc.

Commentary

This is a question on the nature of mortgages. In order to answer it well, you should be aware of the changes made by the Law of Property Act 1925, ss. 85–87 to the ways in which mortgages can be made. You also need to know the relevant provisions of the Land Registration Act 1925.

Part (a) is a straightforward account of the effect of the sections. Part (b) is an application of them. It also raises a problem which has beset mortgagees of leaseholds who may not have notice of forfeiture proceedings brought by a landlord until it is too late.

Suggested Answer

(a) Before 1926, a mortgage was made by an outright conveyance by the mortgagor of the fee simple estate in the mortgaged property to the mortgagee. On the date fixed for redemption, the mortgagee would re-convey the fee simple to the mortgagor on repayment of the loan. Early in the development of mortgages, a mortgagee was entitled to keep the mortgaged property if, for any reason, the mortgagor did not repay on the contractually agreed date. An unscrupulous mortgagee might therefore choose to disappear on the date fixed for redemption, thereby preventing repayment so as to be able to retain the property for himself. It was only with the assistance of equity, which recognised an equitable right to redeem even after the legal date for redemption had passed, that a mortgagor was able to recover his property on repayment, even after the contractual date for repayment.

Since the Law of Property Act 1925 came into force, it has not been possible to create a mortgage by a conveyance to the mortgagee of the full fee simple in the mortgaged property. The Law of Property Act 1925, s. 85(2) provides that any attempt to do so operates as a demise to the mortgagee for a term of 3,000 years.

After 1925 therefore, there are two ways in which a legal mortgage of a fee simple may be made — either by a demise of the property to the mortgagee with a proviso for cesser of the lease on redemption, or by a charge expressed to be by way of legal mortgage. The former gives the mortgagee a legal estate in the land and the rights incident to this, such as a right of possession (*Four-Maids Ltd* v *Dudley Marshall (Properties) Ltd* [1957] Ch 317). Thus both the mortgagor and the mortgagee have legal estates in the land — the mortgagor has the fee simple and the mortgagee has a legal lease.

A charge does not transfer any legal estate to the mortgagee, but merely designates certain property as security for the debt. However, the Law of Property Act 1925, s. 87(1) gives to a mortgagee by way of legal charge 'the same protection, powers and remedies' as if he were a mortgagee by way of demise. His position is further strengthened and equated with that of a mortgagee by way of demise by the inclusion of a charge by deed by way of legal mortgage as a legal interest in the Law of Property Act 1925, s. 1(2).

There are parallel provisions for the legal mortgage of leases in the Law of Property Act 1925, ss. 86(1) and (2). Section 86(1) provides that a legal mortgage of a lease may be made by subdemise or by charge by deed by way of legal mortgage. Section 86(2) provides that any attempt to mortgage a lease by an out-and-out assignment of the whole of the lessee's interest in the property takes effect as a subdemise for a term of ten days less than the term of the lease. The reason for the subdemise being for a shorter term is to allow for the creation of second and subsequent mortgages by the mortgagor granting leases for one day longer than the term of the first, or preceding, mortgage.

A mortgage by way of charge is a simpler form of mortgage than one by way of demise or subdemise. This will be particularly advantageous when mortgaging both freehold and leasehold properties, or leasehold properties of differing terms. A further advantage of a legal charge is that it will not constitute a breach of a covenant against assignment or subletting in a lease.

A mortgage of registered land is usually made by a charge by way of legal mortgage, although it may also be made by demise, or subdemise if it is a mortgage of a leasehold interest (Land Registration Act 1925, s. 27). In any event, to be legal, it must be created by deed and registered, and a chargee cannot exercise the remedies of a mortgagee until it is so registered. The legal charge must describe the land by reference to the register, or in such a way that the registrar can identify it, and must not refer to any other interest in the land which would have priority over it which is not registered or overriding (Land Registration Act 1925, s. 25).

Registered land may also be mortgaged in any way in which unregistered land may be mortgaged (Land Registration Act 1925, s. 106), or by deposit of the land certificate (s. 66), but such mortgages will be only equitable.

(b)   A legal charge of the leasehold property does not constitute a breach of a covenant against assignment or subletting as it is not a disposal of the leasehold term. Therefore, unless the covenant in the lease were more comprehensive and specifically mentioned charging, the execution of the legal charge to Quickslip Bank plc by David will not be a breach of this covenant.

The Law of Property Act 1925, s. 146(4), states that, where the lessor is proceeding by action or otherwise to forfeit a lease for breach of covenant or for non-payment of rent, an underlessee, including an underlessee by way of mortgage, may apply to the court to have the lessee's estate vested in him upon such conditions as the court thinks fit. If the court makes such an order, a new lease is created between the lessor and the underlessee or mortgagee. Although Quickslip has a mortgage by way of legal charge, it has a right to apply under this subsection, because the Law of Property Act 1925, s. 87(1), gives a mortgagee by way of legal charge the same 'protection, powers and remedies' as a mortgagee by way of demise or subdemise (*Grand Junction Ltd* v *Bates* [1954] 2 QB 160).

The problem does not state whether the landlord forfeited the lease pursuant to a court order or merely by taking peaceable re-entry. The method of forfeiture is, however, crucial to Quickslip, because it has a right to apply for relief under the Law of Property Act 1925, s. 146(4), only while the landlord is 'proceeding by action or otherwise' to forfeit the lease. Similar words are used in s. 146(2), which enables relief to be sought by the tenant. It has been held that, once a landlord has re-entered pursuant to a court order, he is no longer 'proceeding', so that the tenant's right to seek relief under s. 146(2) is lost (*Rogers* v *Rice* [1892] 2 Ch 170). However, if the landlord re-enters peaceably without a court order, he can still be considered to be 'proceeding' and the tenant is not precluded from applying for relief (*Billson* v *Residential Apartments Ltd* [1992] AC 494). Given the similarity of the wording of the two subsections, the same principles probably govern the right of a mortgagee to seek relief under s. 146(4).

Where the forfeiture is made for non-payment of rent, other forms of relief may be available to the mortgagee. If the landlord has re-entered pursuant to an order of the High Court under the Common Law Procedure Act 1852, s. 210, the mortgagee has six months after such entry to apply for relief. Such relief, if granted, takes the form of a new lease; but it will be granted only if the mortgagee pays all the arrears of rent, costs and damages. At the end of six months, the right to apply for relief is barred.

The Common Law Procedure Act 1852 applies, however, only if all the requirements of s. 210 are satisfied, and one such requirement is that the rent is six months or more in arrears. If, therefore, the arrears were less, the mortgagee's right to apply for relief derives from the equitable jurisdiction of the Court of Chancery, now exercisable by the High Court under the Supreme Court Act 1981, s. 38(1). Relief under this section will also be available if the landlord peaceably re-enters. The court will generally require an application to be made within six months of re-entry but it may accept an application made slightly after such period (*Thatcher* v *C.H. Pearce & Sons (Contractors) Ltd* [1968] 1 WLR 748, where the application was permitted even though made six months and four days after re-entry).

If the landlord has re-entered for non-payment of rent pursuant to an order of a county court, an underlessee (including a mortgagee) may apply for relief under the County Courts Act 1984, s. 138. The application for relief must be made within six months of the re-entry (County Courts Act 1984, s. 138(9A)). The High Court has no inherent jurisdiction to relieve a mortgagee whose application is made after the statutory period of six months (*United Dominion Trust Ltd* v *Shellpoint Trustees* [1993] 35 EG 121, CA).

The problem contains, however, one further twist, as it would appear that the Quickslip Bank plc did not receive any notification of the landlord's forfeiture proceedings. A landlord seeking an order of forfeiture from the High Court is obliged (under the Rules of the Supreme Court) to serve a copy of the writ upon any underlessee or mortgagee of whom it is aware. A parallel obligation applies (under the County Court Rules) if the landlord is proceeding in a county court. These rules do not help Quickslip if the landlord had not been notified of

Quickslip's legal charge. If, however, the landlord had been notified, and nevertheless failed to serve a copy of the proceedings upon Quickslip, the latter may be able to apply for relief in equity independently of statute (*Abbey National Building Society* v *Maybeech Ltd* [1985] Ch 190). Indeed, if the landlord deliberately refrained from notifying Quickslip, the latter might be able to claim relief even after six months of re-entry on the ground that the landlord should not be permitted to use the statutory time-limit as an engine of fraud. There is no direct authority to this effect, however, and the status of *Maybeech* is not entirely free from doubt (see *Smith* v *Metropolitan City Properties Ltd* [1986] 1 EGLR 52).

Subject to the foregoing caveat, therefore, if the landlord in the problem has re-entered pursuant to an order of the court, Quickslip will be able to seek relief only if it applies within six months of the re-entry. If the landlord has re-entered peaceably without a court order, Quickslip will need to apply for relief within a reasonable time. In any event, relief will not be granted which would prejudice the interests of a third party, e.g., a *bona fide* purchaser for value of a legal estate without notice of the right to apply for relief (*Fuller* v *Judy Properties Ltd* [1992] 1 EGLR 75).

QUESTION 2

Ten years ago, Quentin purchased a 50-year lease of a market garden with the aid of a mortgage for £100,000 from Sunnyveg plc. At that time, it was difficult to obtain finance and Quentin agreed to pay interest at 10 per cent above the bank base rate.

The mortgage deed provides that the capital outstanding should be recalculated annually to align with the retail price index, and that Quentin shall not redeem the mortgage for 25 years. Quentin further undertook in the mortgage deed that for the 25 years he would first offer to sell to Sunnyveg plc any asparagus produced by the market garden at the market price before selling it elsewhere.

Quentin has now obtained a more favourable offer of finance and would like to redeem the mortgage.

Advise him whether this might be possible, as to the terms of the mortgage generally, and whether the agreement relating to the asparagus crop is enforceable against him.

Commentary

The equity of redemption and 'clogs on the equity' is one of the favoured areas of mortgages for examination questions.

You should be aware of the different provisions which may be regarded as clogs on the equity. You should also be aware of the underlying principles which determine whether or not the court will be prepared to intervene — terms in the mortgage deed which are oppressive and unconscionable to the mortgagor.

There are a number of old cases which establish the principle. (Many of these should be of special interest to beer drinkers as they concern the 'tied house' provisions in the mortgages of public houses!)

As with so much of land law, the area reflects changing social circumstances, and illustrates the way in which equity is able to adapt broad principles to specific circumstances. There is a recognition that present-day mortgages may be part of wider agreements made between parties 'of equal bargaining power'. The down-trodden mortgagor of the last century, who was so frequently the object of equity's intervention, is very much less evident in the cases nowadays. The mortgagor has, of course, been given statutory protection too by the Consumer Credit Act 1974. This question does not cover the 1974 Act, but if your lecturer has given any prominence to it, then you should familiarise yourself with its provisions and the few cases there have been on it.

Suggested Answer

Equity has traditionally protected the mortgagor from the exploitation of his weaker position by an unscrupulous mortgagee. One of the ways in which this protection was effected was by the inviolability of the mortgagor's equity of redemption; this arises as soon as the legal date for redemption has passed.

Equity takes the view that the essential nature of a mortgage is a loan, and that on repayment of the loan, the mortgagor is entitled to have back his property freed from all obligations arising under the mortgage. This requirement of freedom from any encumbrances imposed in a mortgage deed is expressed in the equitable principle that 'equity will not allow a clog on the equity of redemption'.

One possible clog on the equity would be an undue postponement of the right to redeem the mortgage. Any such postponement which renders the right to redeem illusory will be void. Thus in *Fairclough* v *Swan Brewery Ltd* [1912] AC 565 a clause which provided that a mortgage was redeemable only one month before the expiration of the mortgagor's lease, leaving the mortgagor with no property worth redeeming, was held to be void.

Postponement, of itself, may not necessarily be bad however. In *Knightsbridge Estates Trust Ltd* v *Byrne* [1939] Ch 441, Greene MR said that a postponement would not be bad unless it was in some way oppressive or unconscionable. In that case, a postponement of the right to redeem for 40 years was upheld. The mortgagee had provided the mortgagor with finance at a time when credit was difficult to obtain. The parties were two large business associations and there was a reciprocal agreement that the mortgagee would not call in the loan for the period of postponement.

In this case, Quentin would still have 25 years of his lease left if he were to redeem after 25 years, so that the postponement would not appear to render the equity of redemption illusory as in *Fairclough*. However, Quentin does not appear to be a large commercial undertaking, as in *Knightsbridge Estates*, and there is no evidence of any reciprocal arrangement by Sunnyveg. It may therefore be possible for Quentin to obtain a declaration from the court that the postponement is oppressive and therefore void.

As part of its protection of the equity of redemption, equity has been anxious to ensure that a mortgagor should not have to pay an excessive rate of interest. Thus in *Cityland* v *Dabrah* [1968] Ch 166 a lump sum payment, which would have meant that the purchaser paid an interest rate of 57 per cent when spread over the period of the mortgage, was varied to give a rate of 7 per cent. This principle has been given statutory force with regard to certain qualifying mortgages within the Consumer Credit Act 1974 if the terms of the mortgage are 'oppressive and unreasonable'. A rate of 10 per cent above the base rate might well be oppressive and it might be possible to obtain an order varying it.

However, it will not necessarily be oppressive or unconscionable to link both capital and interest to a particular index. In *Multiservice Bookbinding Ltd* v *Marden* [1979] Ch 84 outstanding capital was recalculated according to the exchange rate with the Swiss franc which, after inflation and devaluation of sterling, more than doubled the original loan! As the provision was made to protect the mortgagee and was not intended to take advantage of the mortgagor, it was upheld. It is probable therefore that the recalculation of capital outstanding on Quentin's loan will be valid.

The provision giving Sunnyveg a first refusal on any asparagus crop produced by Quentin for 25 years may be regarded as a collateral advantage obtained from the transaction by Sunnyveg. Such an advantage continuing after the redemption of the mortgage would undoubtedly be void as repugnant to the equity of redemption, as the mortgagor is entitled to have back his property in an unencumbered state (*Noakes* v *Rice* [1902] AC 24). However, this principle would not apply here as the agreement is to subsist for 25 years only. In *Biggs* v *Hodinott* [1898] 2 Ch 307, a mortgagor who agreed to buy only the mortgagee's beer for five years, and thereafter for as long as the loan was outstanding, and where the mortgagee agreed not to call in the loan for five years, was held to be bound by the agreement.

Collateral advantages were discussed by the House of Lords in *Kreglinger* v *New Patagonia Meat & Cold Storage Co. Ltd* [1914] AC 25. In that case, part of the consideration for a loan by wool brokers to a meat-preserving company was a right of pre-emption on any sheepskins for five years. As in *Biggs* v *Hodinott*, there was a reciprocal agreement not to call in the loan for five years. The House of Lords felt that the rigid application of the doctrine of 'no clogs on the equity of redemption' was inappropriate to what was essentially a commercial contract between two business parties, and Lord Mersey referred to the doctrine as 'an unruly dog, which, if not securely chained to its own kennel, is prone to wander into places where it ought not to be'.

It is difficult to see that the asparagus agreement is in any way unconscionable or unfair to Quentin as it is merely a right of first refusal at market value. However, the arrangement does not appear to give any reciprocal rights to Quentin as in *Biggs* and *Kreglinger*, and so may be voidable.

In *Esso Petroleum* v *Harper's Garage* [1968] AC 269 the House of Lords held that any restrictions on trade contained in a mortgage deed are also subject to the general common law rules as to restraint of trade, so that an alternative way in which Quentin might be able to avoid this agreement is to show that it is excessive under the common law rules. As at common law, it is possible to sever the part of the mortgage agreement which is bad as an excessive restraint on trade (*Alec Lobb (Garages) Ltd* v *Total Oil Great Britain Ltd* [1985] 1 WLR 173).

QUESTION 3

Some years ago, when the property market was buoyant, Robin and Anne purchased the freehold of a desirable residence, Orchard Cottage, for £250,000 with the assistance of a mortgage for £175,000 from the Quickslip Bank. Robin unfortunately became redundant a year ago and they began to experience problems in keeping up the mortgage repayments. They therefore obtained planning permission for two bungalows on plots which are part of the orchard, being part of the cottage grounds, hoping to ease their financial problems by selling off these.

They are now six months in arrears with the mortgage repayments and the bank is seeking immediate possession of the property in order to sell it. The agents instructed by the bank have prepared particulars of sale which do not mention the planning permission, although the bank has been told of it.

(a)   Advise Robin and Anne on the bank's rights of possession and sale of the property.

(b)   How would your answer differ, if at all, in the following circumstances:

(i)   The bank have already contracted to sell the property to Cuthbert but Robin and Anne have since received a higher offer for the property;

(ii)   Robin and Anne want to sell to avoid mounting debt on the interest payable on the loan, but the bank refuse as the depreciation in property prices means that the likely sale price will not cover the amount of the loan?

Commentary

This question concerns the remedies of a mortgagee where the mortgagor defaults. It is an area of the law where, for the first time since the 1925 property legislation, the courts have had to consider entirely new social circumstances.

Until the late 1980s property prices had only ever risen, so that it was extremely unusual for the sale price of the property not to cover the mortgage debt. Unfortunately, many people who purchased during the property 'boom' in 1987 subsequently found they had a 'negative equity'. The recession exacerbated this position, resulting in large numbers of repossessions by mortgagees. The remedies of a mortgagee on the default of the mortgagor have always, hitherto, been regarded as available solely for the mortgagee's benefit and he might choose how and when to exercise the chosen remedies. His only duty was to act in good faith. There are cases now suggesting that the mortgagee owes a duty in negligence to the mortgagor and any subsequent encumbrancer on the exercise of his powers. There are recent cases, too, in which the courts have interpreted the applicable legislation on sale more generously towards a mortgagor, recognising that even though a mortgagor has defaulted, his interest should not be entirely disregarded in granting a remedy to the mortgagee.

Lastly, *Cheltenham & Gloucester Building Society* v *Norgan* [1996] 1 WLR 343 gives an entirely new interpretation of what may be regarded as a 'reasonable time' (in s. 36, Administration of Justice Act 1970) to postpone a possession order and allow the mortgagor to pay off arrears.

Suggested Answer

(a)   Unless there is a provision in the mortgage deed to the contrary, a legal mortgagee has a right to possession of the mortgaged property 'before the ink is dry on the mortgage deed' (*per* Harman J in *Four-Maids Ltd* v *Dudley Marshall (Properties) Ltd* [1957] Ch 317). This is because the mortgagee has a legal lease of the property, or, if he has a legal charge, he has all the same rights as if he had a legal lease (Law of Property Act 1925, s. 87(1)).

In practice, a mortgage deed will often provide that the mortgagee's right of possession shall arise only on the mortgagor's default. The courts may be reluctant to limit this to a default on the mortgage repayments, however, and in *Western Bank Ltd* v *Schindler* [1977] Ch 1, it was held that the mortgagee still had a right to possession where he had no other rights. In that case, the mortgagor had not defaulted at all on the mortgage repayments as none at all was due until a life policy matured, thereby providing the capital and interest to repay the loan. The mortgagor had defaulted on the payments due under the life policy. Although the power of sale was not exercisable, it was held that the mortgagee had a right of possession. Buckley LJ said 'It is a common law right which is an incident of his estate in the land. It should not, in my opinion, be lightly treated as abrogated or restricted'. It was held (Goff LJ dissenting) that the Administration of Justice Act 1970, s. 36, still applied to allow the court to postpone possession for a limited period.

If the mortgaged property is a dwelling-house, as in this question, then the mortgagee's right to possession will be restricted by the Administration of Justice Act 1970, s. 36, and by the Administration of Justice Act 1973, s. 8. Section 36(2) of the 1970 Act gives the court a discretion to suspend an order for possession if it appears to the court that the mortgagor is likely to be able to pay off any sums due within a reasonable period. Section 8(1) of the 1973 Act provides that the court may treat as sums due such instalments of the mortgage as the mortgagor would have been expected to pay by the date of the hearing, and may effectively ignore any provision in the mortgage deed making the whole of the mortgage debt due on default on any one instalment.

Section 36, however, gives the court power only to suspend an order for possession for 'such period or periods as the court thinks reasonable'. Such suspension must be for a specified time and cannot be an indefinite adjournment (*Royal Trust of Canada* v *Markham* [1975] 1 WLR 1411). The ground for the suspension is that the mortgagor is likely to make good any defaults, or remedy any other breach of obligation in the mortgage deed, within a reasonable time.

The courts had always regarded a 'reasonable time' as anything between two and four years, and the guidance on s. 36(2) in the *Supreme Court Practice* referred to 'at least two years'. However, in *Cheltenham & Gloucester Building Society* v *Norgan* [1996] 1 WLR 343, Waite LJ said 'the court should take as its starting point the full term of the mortgage' and ask 'would it be possible for the mortgagor to maintain payment-off of the arrears by instalments over that period?' This effectively puts lenders in a position of having to show why a lesser period should be adopted, instead of the borrower having to convince the court that he could catch up on payments within a set period of between two and four years. Evans LJ, who gave a concurring judgment, suggested eight questions which the county court judges should ask in deciding whether or not to exercise this discretion. These include such matters as how the arrears accumulated, whether the borrower's difficulties are temporary, the type and terms of the mortgage, how much remains owing, and any factors affecting the security which should influence the period of repayment.

In *Norgan* the security was valued at a sum of £100,000 in excess of the debt and so was a very adequate security. In this question, the amount of security is not as great proportionately as in *Norgan*, which may justify a lesser period than the whole of the mortgage term.

Even if Robin and Anne are not able to persuade the court to reschedule their repayments over a very much longer period, they may be able to persuade the court that they have every possibility of paying off the arrears by selling the plots with planning permissions, and the court might then be prepared to exercise its discretion in their favour.

In *Target Home Loans Ltd* v *Clothier & Clothier* (1992) 25 HLR 48 the Court of Appeal used the power to suspend a possession order under the 1970 and 1973 Acts for four months to enable the mortgagor to sell the property while in possession. It was accepted that this would be likely to realise a higher sale price than if the mortgagee repossessed and then sold a vacant property. It is possible therefore that Robin and Anne may be able to achieve a stay of any possession order on the ground that they themselves are trying to sell the property and have a realistic chance of doing so.

The case of *Clothier* was considered, however, in *National & Provincial Building Society* v *Lloyd* [1996] 1 All ER 630, where Neill LJ (referring to the judgment of Waite LJ in *Norgan*) said that the court must be even-handed between the mortgagor and the mortgagee. In *Lloyd* the court refused to suspend a possession order on the mortgagor's claim to be able to sell parts of the property (two barns) to pay off only part of the debt. It was said that there was no reason why the mortgagee should have to accept piecemeal sales of parts of the property from time to time.

In practice, a mortgagee will usually seek possession only in order to sell the mortgaged property with vacant possession. A mortgagee who seeks to occupy the property is strictly accountable to the mortgagor for profits which *might* have been made as well as for those which were *actually* made, and therefore is not in a very happy position (*White* v *City of London Brewery Co.* (1889) 42 ChD 237), where the mortgagee of a public house was liable to the mortgagor for the difference in rent which he might have received if he had let it as a free house and not as a 'tied' house).

The mortgagee's statutory power of sale is contained in the Law of Property Act, s. 101, and applies to all mortgages made by deed, unless there is a contrary intention stated. It only *arises* however when the mortgage moneys have become due, that is, when the legal date for redemption has passed. It only becomes *exercisable* under one of the three circumstances set out in the Law of Property Act 1925, s. 103. These are that the mortgagee has demanded repayment of the capital outstanding and the mortgagor has defaulted for three months, that the mortgagor is two months in arrear with interest payments under the mortgage, or is in breach of some other covenant in the mortgage deed, such as a covenant against letting the property. The legal date for redemption is usually inserted, quite unrealistically, into a mortgage deed as six months after the date of the mortgage. This is not because anyone imagines for a moment that the mortgagor will be able to repay the whole of the loan and interest at that time, but so that the remedy of sale is available to a mortgagee fairly early on. Assuming that the legal date for redemption in their mortgage deed has passed, as Robin and Anne are six months in arrears with the interest payments, the power of sale has become exercisable.

In exercising a power of sale, a mortgagee must take reasonable care to obtain a proper market price for the property. In *Cuckmere Brick Co.* v *Mutual Finance Ltd* [1971] Ch 949, the mortgagee instructed estate agents to sell. The estate agents were told that planning permission had been obtained for 35 houses, but not informed that planning permission had also been obtained for 100 flats. The auction advertisements therefore mentioned only the houses. The mortgagor drew the mortgagee's attention to this and requested a postponement of sale to allow the property to be correctly advertised. Evidence was given that house developments are very different from flat developments, the latter involving a larger initial outlay but yielding higher profits. Developers involved in flat developments would not bother to attend an auction of land for housing development. The estate agents received a surveyor's letter indicating that the valuation of the land with planning permission for flats might be approximately double (£70,000) the valuation with planning permission for houses only (£35,000). The mortgagor wrote to the mortgagee on the question of valuation. The auction nevertheless went ahead. It was held that the mortgagee had not taken reasonable care to obtain the market value of the property and was liable to the mortgagor in damages for the difference between this and the price actually obtained.

The more recent case of *Standard Chartered Bank Ltd* v *Walker* [1982] 1 WLR 1410, indicated that mortgagees and receivers would be liable for any negligence in exercising their powers of sale, and the liability could extend not only to the mortgagor but to any subsequent mortgagee who suffered loss as a result of a bad sale. Some doubt has been cast upon this, however, by the Privy Council decision in *Downsview Nominees Ltd* v *First City Corporation Ltd* [1993] AC 295, where the more traditional approach was taken that the mortgage is security for a debt, and that the mortgagee owes no general duty in negligence to the mortgagor or subsequent encumbrancers, but only a duty imposed by equity to act in good faith.

Nevertheless, if Robin and Anne remind both the Bank and the agents of the planning permissions, which will obviously increase the market price of the property, it might be questionable whether the Bank will have acted in good faith if the sale then goes ahead without mention of this. They would have an action for damages against the Bank, which must also be liable for any negligence of the agents instructed by it.

   (b)(i)   In *Duke* v *Robson* [1973] 1 WLR 267 the mortgagor contracted to sell the mortgaged property and the contract was registered as a Class C(iv) land charge. The mortgagee's power of sale had become exercisable however due to the mortgagor's default, and the mortgagee contracted to sell to another person. It was said that the power of sale is to protect the mortgagee on default by the mortgagor, and the mortgagor's proposed sale of the equity of redemption cannot interfere with this. The person to whom the mortgagor had contracted to sell could not be in a better position *vis-à-vis* the mortgagee than the mortgagor himself.

Assuming, therefore, that the price for which the bank has contracted to sell to Cuthbert covers the mortgage debt and interest, then that contract would have priority over any contract which Robin and Anne might enter into.

(b)(ii) In *Palk* v *Mortgage Services Funding plc* [1993] Ch 330 the mortgagors wanted to sell the mortgaged property for approximately £80,000 less than the mortgage debt. Not unsurprisingly, the mortgagee objected to this and applied for possession of the property, intending to let it and sell at a later date when the property market had improved.

The Law of Property Act 1925, s. 91(2), provides that the court may make an order for sale on the request of the mortgagee or 'any person interested in ... the right of redemption'. Notwithstanding that the section had only ever been used in its long history (at least as far back as the Conveyancing Act 1881) to order a sale rather than foreclosure, and that this had only been done where the sale proceeds would cover the mortgage debt, the Court of Appeal held that it had a wide and unfettered discretion under s. 91(2), to order a sale.

In exercising this discretion, the court could take into account not only the interests of the mortgagee (considered by Lord Templeman in *China & South Sea Bank Ltd* v *Tan Soon Gin* [1990] 1 AC 536 to be paramount), but also the interests of the mortgagor. In *China & South Sea Bank Ltd*, Lord Templeman said that it was a matter for a mortgagee as to which of his possible remedies he chose to pursue on default and it was accepted that the mortgagee could only be made to accede to a sale by the mortgagor or his surety if the proposed sale price covered the whole of the mortgage debt. But in *Palk* it was pointed out that a mortgagee still has the right to sue a mortgagor on a personal covenant to pay for any moneys still outstanding after sale.

There were circumstances in *Palk* however which would have made refusing the mortgagor's application for sale particularly harsh on her whilst only giving the mortgagee a possibility of future benefit. The rental income from the property would not have covered the mounting interest debt, so that the mortgagors would be steadily increasing her indebtedness by some £43,000 per annum. Kerr LJ conceded that generally a mortgagee's wishes should be given preference, and if there had been a 'real possibility' even of an increase in price (due, for example, to the possibility of obtaining planning permission for some development) then it might have been more reasonable to postpone the sale. There was no immediate realistic certainty that a postponement of sale would produce a better sale price however — it was merely speculative optimism on the part of the mortgagee. It was said that it would be unfair to the mortgagors for the mortgagee to speculate on the property market at her expense, and that if it wished to do so, it could do so by purchasing the property from the mortgagors themselves (the proposed sale being by the *mortgagors* and not therefore being a sale by the *mortgagee* to itself). The mortgagors were therefore allowed to sell the property.

It is clear, then, that the court regards itself as having an unfettered discretion under the Law of Property Act 1925, s. 91(2), as to whether to order a sale or not, and this will depend upon the circumstances of each particular case. The factors to be taken into account as to whether Robin and Anne are likely to obtain an order for sale are the likely shortfall between the sale price and the mortgage debt, whether any rental income from the property would cover the interest payments on the mortgage, and whether there are any other factors, such as the sale of further plots of the orchard with planning permissions, which might realistically offer an increase in the sale price.

QUESTION 4

What rights and remedies are available to an equitable mortgagee?

Commentary

This appears to be a simple type of bookwork question, but its appearance belies it! The academics argue, and the judges disagree, about an equitable mortgagee's power of sale and right of possession. Moreover, there are different *types* of equitable mortgages, and the remedies vary according to the type. It is an area into which the Law of Property (Miscellaneous Provisions) Act 1989, s. 2, introduced some considerable doubt, as it was not clear whether an equitable mortgage created by the deposit of title deeds was a creature in its own right (*sui generis*), or whether it was merely a contract which was supported by part performance and so void. A decision of the Court of Appeal suggests the latter, although the general academic view favours the former.

To avoid some of the problems about an equitable mortgagee's power of sale, two conveyancing devices are used, and these should be referred to.

Lastly, as the question does not refer to an equitable mortgage of the legal estate, you should mention briefly the equitable mortgage of an equitable interest.

Suggested Answer

The rights of an equitable mortgagee depend very much on the type of equitable mortgage which is created.

The usual type of equitable mortgage is one which arises from a valid contract to create a legal mortgage under the principle of *Walsh* v *Lonsdale* (1882) 21 ChD 9. This type of mortgage must now satisfy the Law of Property (Miscellaneous Provisions) Act 1989, s. 2, and be in writing and signed by both parties. It is doubtful whether the deposit of title deeds of a property, which, before 27 September 1989, would have been a sufficient act of part performance to create an enforceable contract for a mortgage, will still do so. It is argued in *Cheshire & Burn's Modern Law of Real Property*, 15th edn, London: Butterworths, 1994, that such a mortgage exists *sui generis*, but in the decision of *United Bank of Kuwait plc* v *Sahib* [1996] 3 WLR 372 in the Court of Appeal, it was said that the essential nature of such an equitable mortgage is contract-based, and that it cannot stand *sui generis* independently of contract. Such a mortgage should therefore comply with s. 2 if it is to be valid.

The equitable mortgagee's rights are necessarily more limited than those of a legal mortgagee's as he does not have a legal estate vested in him. The legal mortgagee has a right of possession of the mortgaged property as soon as the mortgage is made as a result of the legal term of years vested in him, and s. 87 of the Law of Property Act 1925 gives a mortgagee by way of legal charge the same rights as one by way of demise. It is a subject of academic argument as to whether an equitable mortgagee by way of contract has a right of possession of the mortgaged property, although it is accepted that he would have such a right if he obtains a court order for this, or if the mortgage specifically reserves the right (*Barclays Bank Ltd* v *Bird* [1954] Ch 274).

The main remedy however of such an equitable mortgagee is to obtain an order from the court for foreclosure, requiring the mortgagor to convey the legal estate in the land to him freed from the mortgagor's equity of redemption.

In practice, however, where an equitable mortgage was accompanied by an informal deposit of the title deeds, such a deposit would frequently be recorded by a memorandum of deposit by deed. The reason for this is to give the equitable mortgagee certain remedies which are available under the Law of Property Act 1925, s. 101, to a mortgagee whose mortgage is created by deed. Provided any such memorandum by deed satisfies the Law of Property (Miscellaneous Provisions) Act 1989, s. 2, and is signed by both parties, then it will create a valid equitable mortgage. As there is a deed the equitable mortgagee will have the rights in the Law of Property Act 1925, s. 101, including (*inter alia*) the right to sell and appoint a receiver.

Because of questions raised in *Re Hodson & Howes' Contract* (1887) 35 ChD 668 as to exactly *what* estate an equitable mortgagee has vested in him to sell, it is customary to use one of two conveyancing devices to ensure that he may in fact sell the *legal* estate in the mortgaged property. Either the equitable mortgagee will be appointed attorney of the mortgagor, or the memorandum of deposit will include a declaration that the mortgagor is a trustee of the legal estate for the mortgagee and that the mortgagee has power to appoint someone else (including himself) as trustee of the mortgtagor defaults.

An equitable mortgage may also take the form of an equitable charge, which will be by deed. This merely designates certain property as security for a loan, with no transfer to the mortgagee of any legal or equitable estate. The remedies available to an equitable chargee will be an order by the court for sale, or for appointment of a receiver if the property is producing an income. He has no rights of possession or foreclosure, as these are incidents of the mortgagee's equitable estate in the land.

In the case of both types of equitable mortgage, the mortgagee will of course have the right to sue the mortgagor for repayment of the mortgage debt on the mortgagor's personal agreement to pay.

An equitable mortgage may also arise by the mortgage of an equitable interest. There were interests under a trust for sale or a settlement but after 1996 these will be interests of beneficiaries under a trust of land. These types of mortgages usually take the form of an assignment of the equitable interest, which is required by the Law of Property Act 1925, s. 53(1)(c), to be in writing and signed by the mortgagor or his authorised agent. The mortgagee should give notice of this to the trustees of the trust or settlement to preserve his priority, and he will be entitled to receive any income from the mortgagor's interest.

Where one beneficiary under a trust for sale purported to mortgage the whole property by forging the signature of another beneficiary, it was held that the forgery was ineffective to mortgage the legal estate. The purported mortgage of the legal estate is effective to mortgage the equitable interest in the property of the forger, thereby creating an equitable mortgage of his share (*First National Securities Ltd* v *Hegarty* [1985] QB 850). This will presumably effect a severance of any equitable joint tenancy in the same way as an assignment of a joint tenant's equitable interest. There would seem to be no reason why this decision should not be followed, with the same result, if a beneficiary under a trust of land were to forge his co-owners signature to a mortgage deed.

QUESTION 5

Five years ago, Peter and Wendy decided to live together and bought a house for £100,000. They each put £10,000 towards the deposit of £20,000 and took a mortgage from the Pan Bank plc for the balance of the purchase price of £80,000.

Peter has a double glazing business, but about a year ago began to experience financial difficulties. He approached the Pan Bank plc for a second mortgage, indicating that he would like to borrow a further £25,000 on the security of the house to pay some business debts and to expand his business. The manager of the local branch of the Pan Bank plc agreed to this.

Peter knew that Wendy would not feel happy about the loan, and so told her that he was borrowing only £10,000. He asked her if she would call in with him one lunchtime at the Pan Bank plc to sign the necessary form to enable him to borrow the money. As Wendy did not wish to quarrel with Peter, she went along and signed the form, which was given to them by a temporary typist as the manager was at lunch. Wendy did not read the form, and assumed it was a mortgage for £10,000 and not £25,000.

Peter and Wendy are now in arrears with the repayments on the second mortgage and the Pan Bank plc are seeking possession of the house. Wendy says that she did not understand the true implications of the form which she signed, which were never explained to her.

(a) Advise Wendy.

(b) Would your advice differ if Wendy had seen the manager with Peter, but the manager had been told that the money was to build an extension to their house?

(c)   How would your advice differ if the Pan Bank plc had instructed solicitors to act for them in connection with the second mortgage, and Wendy had called at the solicitors' offices on her own, unaccompanied by Peter, to sign the charge?

Commentary

This question requires knowledge of an area of the law which has recently been the subject of two authoritative decisions in the House of Lords: the extent to which one co-owner, A, who has mortgaged property jointly-owned with another, B, can set aside the mortgage on the basis that A entered into the transaction by reason of undue influence or misrepresentation. The undue influence could be that of the mortgagee itself (as was alleged in *National Westminster Bank plc* v *Morgan* [1985] AC 686), or of the co-owner, B. In the latter instance, the mortgage can be set aside *vis-à-vis* A either if it is shown that B acted as the agent of the mortgagee, or if the mortgagee had actual or constructive notice of the facts giving rise to possible undue influence. The principles of these two cases have also been applied to guarantors who offer security for the indebtedness of someone exercising undue influence over them.

The two leading cases which develop and refine the doctrine of notice in this area are (*Barclays Bank plc* v *O'Brien* [1994] 1 AC 180, and *CIBC Mortgages plc* v *Pitt* [1993] 3 WLR 802). If your course deals with this area, you should read both cases thoroughly.

Since these House of Lords cases, there have been a number of Court of Appeal cases where co-mortgagors and sureties have met with differing degrees of success in seeking to apply *O'Brien* to set aside a transaction which they did not like. For the reasons mentioned in the introduction to this chapter, this is hardly surprising, and each case will turn on its own peculiar circumstances. In so far as it is possible to extract any general principles from these cases (and they are all slightly different), the following guidelines are suggested:

A transaction which is manifestly disadvantageous to a co-mortgagor or surety will raise a presumption of undue influence, and may also serve to put the lender on notice of this. (*Goode Durrant Administration* v *Biddulph* [1994] 2 FLR 551; *Bank of Baroda* v *Rayarel* [1995] 2 FLR 376; *Credit Lyonnais Bank Nederland NV* v *Burch* [1997] 1 All ER 144.)

A lender which instructs a solicitor to explain the transaction to a co-mortgagor or surety, so discharging the undue influence, is entitled to rely upon that solicitor's professional skill and may assume that he has

properly explained the transaction, even if it is the same solicitor who is acting for them and for the mortgagor. (*Massey* v *Midland Bank plc* [1995] 1 All ER 929; *Banco Exterior Internacional* v *Mann* [1995] 1 All ER 936; *Bank of Baroda* v *Rayarel* (supra); *Barclays Bank plc* v *Thomson* [1997] 1 FLR 156.)

A solicitor's knowledge of circumstances giving rise to undue influence will not necessarily be imputed to the lender. (*Midland Bank plc* v *Serter* (1995) EGCS 38; *Halifax Mortgage Services Ltd* v *Stepsky* [1996] Ch 207.)

There are conflicting decisions on whether advising a person who may be under undue influence to seek independent advice will protect a lender dealing with such a person. (*Coldunell Ltd* v *Gallon* [1986] 1 QB 1184) (was sufficient); *Banco Exterior Internacional* v *Thomas* [1997] 1 WLR 221 (actually receiving independent advice enough); *Credit Lyonnais Bank Nederland NV* v *Burch* (*supra* — advising a person to take independent advice not enough: must ensure they actually receive it.)

Where the size or circumstances of the loan are misrepresented to the co-mortgagor or surety, then it will be void against them *in toto*. (*Barclays Bank plc* v *O'Brien* [1994] 1 AC 180; *TSB Bank plc* v *Camfield* [1995] 1 All ER 951.)

There is a statement by Mummery LJ in *Barclays Bank plc* v *Boulter* [1997] 2 All ER 1002 to the effect that the burden of proof is on the lender to show that it did not have constructive notice of undue influence affecting the transaction and was not subject to the equity raised thereby, or that it took any necessary steps to discharge the undue influence.

There is a criticism by Staughton LJ in a recent case of *UCB Bank* v *Sharif* [1997] 16 April (unreported), to the effect that the doctrine of undue influence applied in this area is capable of giving rise to injustice. There is a presumption that it arises in family relationships, and the lender has no means of contesting it and is unlikely to be able to obtain the necessary evidence to do so. Lenders are therefore very much at the mercy of the presumption.

A final complication was mentioned, and was the deciding factor, in *Woolwich Building Society* v *Dickman and Todd* (1996) 72 P & CR 470, where the equity arising from a similar type of transaction was held to be an overriding interest under s. 70(1)(g), Land Registration Act 1925. It may be, therefore, that Mummery's observation in *Boulter* that it is irrelevant whether the title to the land is registered or unregistered is dubious!

Suggested Answer

(a)   Although Wendy has joined with Peter in granting a second mortgage on the house, she may be able to resist the bank's action for possession if she can show that the mortgage is not binding upon her. She may be able to do this if she can show that she executed the legal charge by reason of Peter's undue influence which would enable her to set the mortgage aside *vis-à-vis* the Bank. In *Barclays Bank plc* v *O'Brien* [1994] 1 AC 180, the House of Lords considered the extent to which a wife was bound by a mortgage which she signed jointly with her husband. The mortgage had been misrepresented to her by her husband as being to secure an overdraft facility of £60,000; whereas, in reality, it was to secure a facility of more than twice that amount.

The Court of Appeal had decided that the wife, being in a special position *vis-à-vis* her husband, was under his undue influence, and the mortgage was only binding to the extent of the £60,000 of which she knew.

The speech of Lord Browne-Wilkinson in the House of Lords was also in favour of Mrs O'Brien, but on a different ground. He said that the ground for avoiding such a transaction is not so much the undue influence itself, but the notice which the lender had, or ought to have had, of it. The fact that a loan is for the benefit of one only of the two borrowers should be sufficient to put a lender on notice of possible undue influence by that party, particularly if the relationship between the two borrowers is a close one.

A right which a debtor would have to avoid a transaction for undue influence will bind a creditor if he knows, or ought to know, about it. He can have no better right than the deceived debtor, and cannot take free from it.

Lord Browne-Wilkinson expressed the opinion that a creditor's notice (actual or constructive) of undue influence should be relevant in any relationship where undue influence might arise, and he expressly mentioned the situation where two parties are cohabiting. The only way in which a creditor can avoid the effect of the undue influence is to ensure that it is dispelled by requiring the influenced party to take separate and independent legal advice. He observed that this was the recommendation given to bankers in the Code of Banking Practice adopted by banks and building societies in 1992. It should apply wherever a private individual gives a guarantee or other security for another's liabilities.

Mrs O'Brien therefore fared better in the House of Lords than she had done in the Court of Appeal, as it was held that she had been acting under undue influence, of which the bank should have had notice, with regard to the whole of its loan. She was not even bound therefore to the extent of the £60,000 of which she was aware.

It may be that the Pan Bank plc should have had notice of possible undue influence as the loan was for Peter's benefit alone. As Wendy does not appear to have received any independent advice separately from Peter, she will not be bound by it (not even to the extent of £10,000), and the bank cannot enforce possession against her in respect of a default on it.

(**b**) If the manager had been told that the loan was to build an extension to the house, it is possible that there are no circumstances which would put the bank on notice of any undue influence, as the loan appears to be for the benefit of both the borrowers. This was the situation in *CIBC Mortgages plc v Pitt* [1993] 3 WLR 802, which was heard by the House of Lords, and judgment given, at the same time as the appeal in *O'Brien*.

As Professor Mark Thompson has pointed out, there is a curious result in applying the doctrine of notice to this situation. The more dishonest the party instigating the loan is in explaining its purpose to the bank as being of benefit to both parties, the more likely it is to be binding upon the innocent party (Thompson, [1994] *Conv* 145).

(**c**) If the Pan Bank plc had instructed their solicitors to explain fully the circumstances of the loan to Wendy, and to suggest to her that she should obtain independent legal advice before signing the charge, they may be able to rely on the professional judgment and expertise of the solicitors in being satisfied that Wendy was not acting under the undue influence of Peter (*Massey* v *Midland Bank plc, Banco Exterior Internacional* v *Mann, Bank of Baroda* v *Rayarel* and *Barclays Bank plc* v *Thomson*). This must be a matter of fact for the court to decide in each case and may not be sufficient in every instance.

QUESTION 6

(**a**) Zena is the owner in fee simple of Red House, the title to which is unregistered. She entered into the following mortgages of the property:

On 1 April 1990, a legal charge to Abel for £10,000 protected by the deposit of the title deeds;

On 1 May 1994, an equitable mortgage to Barrie for £15,000;

On 1 June 1994, a legal charge to Celia for £5,000.

Barrie registered his equitable mortgage on 2 June 1994 and Celia registered her legal mortgage on 3 June 1994.

How would these mortgages rank for priority?

(**b**)   How would your answer differ in the following circumstances?

Abel had handed over the title deeds to Zena in 1991, at her request, to deal with a boundary dispute. Abel never requested their return and Zena used the title deeds to obtain a mortgage for £5,000 from Celia in August 1994, with whom Zena deposited the deeds.

(**c**)   How would your answer to (**a**) differ if the title to Red House were registered?

Commentary

The law relating to the priority of mortgages was radically changed by the 1925 legislation. Before 1926, it was only possible to have one legal mortgage by the conveyance of the fee simple, but mortgages by demise or by legal charge allow for the creation of two or more legal mortgages. It is still possible to have two or more equitable mortgages.

Whereas priority before 1926 depended upon the time-honoured maxim *qui prior est tempore potior est jure* (whoever is first in time is favoured in law) and the precedence of a legal mortgage over an equitable one, priority after 1925 depends upon possession of the title deeds and a system of registration. It is no longer of prime importance after 1925 whether a mortgage is legal or equitable. A legal or an equitable mortgage may be protected by the deposit of the title deeds, in which case it will not be registrable under the Land Charges Act 1972. Either type may also be created without the deposit of the title deeds, in which case it will be registrable — a legal mortgage as a puisne mortgage, Class C(i) land charge, and an equitable mortgage as a general equitable charge, Class C(iii) land charge.

There are conflicting provisions in the 1925 legislation which the courts have never been called upon to resolve. This is no doubt because, for most of the time since 1925, property prices have been rising, so that the increasing value of a property will more than cover substantial borrowing on its security. For those academics who have pondered the type of insoluble problem which could arise (as in part **(b)** of this question), and who would dearly love to have their proposed solutions judicially considered, time is running out . . .!

In part **(b)**, a detailed working of a solution by subrogation can be found in most of the larger books on land law (but it is not something which we would suggest you read carefully unless your lecturer has drawn attention to it and regards it as important).

Registered title is increasingly prevalent and there appear to be similar conundrums in the Land Registration Act 1925. It is for this reason that we have included part **(c)** in this question, thereby making it unrealistically long for a genuine examination question. Priority of charges in registered land is, however, becoming increasingly important, and it is envisaged that many land law courses will reflect this fact. Given a comparatively recent Court of Appeal case in this area of the law, we decided that it ought to be included.

Suggested Answer

(a) After 1925, a mortgage protected by the deposit of the title deeds, whether legal or equitable, is not registrable under the Land Charges Act 1972. The mortgagor's inability to produce the title deeds, because they are held by the mortgagee, is deemed to operate as notice to any subsequent mortgagee or purchaser that there is a subsisting mortgage on the property.

Such a mortgage ranks for priority as at the date of its creation. Abel's mortgage ranks as at 1 April 1990 and therefore has priority over both Barrie's and Celia's.

A mortgage which is not protected by the deposit of the title deeds is registrable, whether it is legal or equitable. If legal, it is registrable as a puisne mortgage Class C(i) land charge, and if equitable, as a general equitable charge Class C(iii) land charge. In both cases, the purpose of registration is to give notice of it to any subsequent mortgagee or purchaser, who should of course search the register before completion.

The two provisions relating to priority of mortgages are the Law of Property Act 1925, s. 97, and the Land Charges Act 1972, s. 4(5) (formerly the Land Charges Act 1925, s. 13(2)). Section 97 of the 1925 Act provides that a legal or equitable mortgage of the legal estate in land shall rank for priority according to the date of its registration under the Land Charges Act 1972. Section 4(5) of the 1972 Act provides that a Class C land charge (*inter alia*) shall be void against a purchaser of the land it affects unless it is registered before the completion of the purchase. ('Purchase' in this section includes of course a subsequent mortgage, as a mortgagee is within the definition of a purchaser in the Law of Property Act 1925, s. 205.)

Applying s. 97, Barrie's mortgage has priority over Celia's as it was registered before hers. Applying s. 4(5), however, Barrie's mortgage is 'void' against Celia's as it was not registered under the Land Charges Act 1972 when hers was completed.

There is no judicial decision as to which of these two sections should prevail, although academic opinion has favoured the Land Charges Act 1972, as its predecessor, the Land Charges Act 1925, was enacted after the Law of Property Act 1925 (Megarry & Wade, *Law of Real Property*, 6th edn, London: Sweet & Maxwell, 1994). Presumably there is an even stronger argument now that the provision has been re-enacted in the Land Charges Act 1972. Also, s. 97 refers specifically to the Land Charges Act 1972 (formerly 1925), suggesting that it might defer to the provisions of that Act. If this were so, then Barrie's mortgage would lose priority to Celia's.

(b) The position as to priority between Abel's and Barrie's mortgages is probably unchanged, as Abel's mortgage ranks as at the date of its creation and Barrie's mortgage is created subsequently.

Barrie's mortgage is registered at the date when Celia's mortgage was created, and therefore ranks before Celia's according to both the Law of Property Act 1925, s. 97, and the Land Charges Act 1972, s. 4(5).

There seems little doubt that Abel has been negligent in releasing the title deeds to Zena for such a long period of time, and in failing to recover them. Before 1926, a mortgagee who was 'grossly negligent' in failing to obtain the title deeds was postponed to a subsequent mortgagee (*Walker* v *Linom* [1907] 2 Ch 104). It was said in *Northern Counties of England Fire Insurance Co.* v *Whipp* (1884) 26 ChD 482 that a mortgagee whose gross negligence in *releasing* the title deeds to the mortgagor was so serious as to implicate him in a fraud on a subsequent mortgagee (to whom the deeds were presented as security) was postponed to that mortgagee. This was disapproved by Parker LJ in *Walker* v *Linom*, who opined that Fry LJ in *Whipp* was in any event referring to equitable fraud, which includes gross negligence. As there was no gross negligence in *Whipp* (a company which had taken a mortgage from their manager could hardly have expected him to steal the deeds from their safe), it is possible to regard what Fry LJ said as obiter anyway; so that gross negligence, rather than fraud, is probably sufficient to postpone an earlier mortgagee.

There is nothing in the 1925 legislation to alter this earlier law with regard to lost priority by a mortgagee who fails to obtain, or who releases the deeds. It is more likely, in the modern age of technology and easy access to photocopiers, that it would be grossly negligent for a mortgagee to part with the deeds at all for the purpose of dealing with a boundary dispute. It is probable therefore that Celia's mortgage ranks for priority before Abel's.

Another point on the 1925 provisions for the protection of mortgages, which has never been litigated, is whether Abel's mortgage, although originally one protected by the deposit of the title deeds and therefore not registrable, becomes registrable if Abel parts with the title deeds. If so, for how long does he have to be deprived of the title deeds to make it registrable? And if the title deeds are returned, does his mortgage become unregistrable again, so that the mortgage has 'a kind of Cheshire Cat existence, entering and leaving the Land Charges Registry as often as the mortgagor "borrows" back his deeds and returns them'? (*per* P. B. Fairest, *Mortgages*, Modern Legal Studies, 1980, Sweet & Maxwell). Perhaps the better view is that such a mortgage, having originally been created by the deposit of the title deeds, remains so. In any event, as Abel has not registered it, it is a purely academic point which does not affect the priorities in this question.

The priorities are then as follows:

Abel's mortgage ranks before Barrie's;
Barrie's mortgage ranks before Celia's;
Celia's mortgage ranks before Abel's.

This produces a circle with no clear priority. It is suggested by E.H. Burn in *Cheshire & Burn's Modern Law of Real Property* (15th edn, London: Butterworths, 1994) that the mortgagees might receive payment *pari passu* in the event of the security being insufficient to cover all three mortgages. A further solution proposed is that of subrogation, whereby one debtor is paid to the extent that the one whose priority he assumes has priority over the third. This solution, however, is necessarily arbitrary as to the point at which one enters the circle.

(c)   In land with registered title, a legal mortgage can be made only by registered charge. Until it is registered, however, a charge by deed can take effect only as an equitable mortgage. Since Abel's mortgage was not registered at the time Barrie's equitable mortgage was created, priority between them is determined on the basis that they are both equitable mortgages. The Land Registration Act 1925 does not expressly resolve priority in these circumstances; and it has been left to the courts to apply the equitable principle that, where the equities are equal, the mortgages rank for priority according to the order in which they were created (*Barclays Bank Ltd* v *Taylor* [1974] Ch 137, CA). Barrie cannot obtain priority over Abel by registering his equitable mortgage as a minor interest (*Mortgage Corp Ltd* v *Nationwide Credit Corp Ltd* [1994] Ch 49, CA). Therefore, as there is nothing in the facts of part (a) to indicate that the equities are not equal, as between Abel and Barrie, Abel has priority.

Celia's registered charge takes priority over earlier equitable mortgages, unless they were either protected by registration as a minor interest or as an overriding interest under the Land Registration Act 1925, s. 70(1)(g). As there is no evidence that Abel was in actual occupation when Celia's legal charge was registered, Celia will have priority over Abel. Celia will, however, take subject to Barrie, as Barrie's equitable mortgage was registered before Celia obtained registration of her legal charge.

There would therefore appear to be a circle of priorities in these circumstances, just as there is in unregistered land, i.e., Abel has priority over Barrie, Barrie has priority over Celia, but Celia has priority over Abel. The possible solutions to this dilemma have not been considered by the courts, and have been discussed in part (b) above.

15   Perpetuities and Accumulations

INTRODUCTION

On undergraduate courses, the law of perpetuities and accumulations seems to be a topic in general decline. This may be partly because the reasoning underlying it is somewhat different from that of other topics in land law or trusts. Nevertheless, it is an important area of law, and it still appears in many land law or property syllabuses. Most students find perpetuities difficult at first; and the complexities are, indeed, Byzantine. The principal features are clear though, and when the penny has dropped the student should not have too much difficulty. Indeed, the well-prepared student can here score highly. Perpetuities also has the advantage of being an area in which case law plays a less important role — so there are relatively few decisions which the student needs to know in depth.

The first important matter in dealing with a problem question on perpetuities is to note when the disposition was made. There are three important periods for this: the period before 1926 (i.e., before the Law of Property Act 1925), which is purely common law; the period after 1925 and before 16 July 1964, which is common law with modification (age-reduction under the Law of Property Act 1925, s. 163); and the period after 15 July 1964, which is one to which the new regime of 'wait and see' and other refinements apply.

Even if the disposition was made after 15 July 1964, however, it is necessary to look to the common law first, as 'wait and see' applies only if the disposition is void at common law.

If copies of the relevant legislation may be brought into (or are provided in) the examination room, you will probably be expected to specify the particular sections, subsections and paragraphs on which your answer relies. Do not simply copy out whole chunks of the legislation from the statute book: this wastes time and effort. Summarise the effects of the relevant provisions in your own words, and ensure that the examiner can see how you apply them.

Where legislation is susceptible to more than one interpretation, the examiner will be more impressed by the candidate who considers various reasonable interpretations than by the candidate who assumes that there is only one correct answer. This is particularly the case with the Perpetuities and Accumulations Act 1964. Since 'wait and see' applies to post 15 July 1964 dispositions only, there has been very little case law as yet on its provisions. In a number of instances, this piece of legislation remains, more than 30 years after its enactment, somewhat enigmatic.

To this end, useful articles on perpetuities include the following: Morris and Wade, 'Perpetuities Reform at Last', (1964) 80 *LQR* 486; Pritchard, 'Two Petty Perpetuity Puzzles', [1969] *CLJ* 284. For those deeply interested, there are several articles dealing with the problem of 'lives in being' at common law and under the Act: the following notable pieces have appeared in the *Law Quarterly Review*: Allen, (1965) 81 *LQR* 106; Maudsley, (1970) 86 *LQR* 357; Deech, (1981) 97 *LQR* 593; and Dukeminier, (1986) 102 *LQR* 250. A helpful modern work on the subject is Maudsley, *The Modern Law of Perpetuities*, London: Butterworths (1979), which also contains a useful analysis of the law relating to accumulations — including an interesting account of the activities of Peter Thellusson, a testator whose will was largely responsible for the passing of the first legislation relating to accumulations of income. A summary of the present law is contained in the Law Commission's Consultation Paper, No. 133 'The Law of Trusts: The rules against perpetuities and excessive accumulations' (1993), which provisionally favours either abolition or reform in both areas.

Because a cool head is needed in tackling a perpetuities or accumulations problem, it is probably best not to attempt such a question as your first answer.

QUESTION 1

(a) By her will, Tess, who died in 1963, devised Greenacre to the first child of Algy who should attain the age of 25. Algy (who was an orphaned bachelor at Tess's death) had three children: Belinda, Charles and Damian, who were born in 1966, 1971 and 1972 respectively. Algy died on 31 December 1973. Belinda died in 1990 aged 24.

Discuss who is entitled to Greenacre.

(b) How, if at all, would your answer to (a) differ if Tess had died in December 1964?

Commentary

This is a classic type of question on perpetuities. The alternative dates of Tess's death are important, and the student should spot this straight away. Thus, in part (a), her death in 1963 means that the relevant rules are those of common law as modified by the Law of Property Act 1925, s. 163. In part (b), by contrast, her death in December 1994 means that, even if the disposition is void at common law, it may nevertheless be saved by the Perpetuities and Accumulations Act 1964.

The fact that the gift is contingent upon attaining 25 should make the candidate suspicious that the question might involve (as indeed it does) age-reducing. Age-reducing operates differently after the 1964 Act, so this is a further difference between the answers to parts (a) and (b). Under the 1964 Act, 'wait and see' applies before age-reducing. How exactly it applies, however, remains an unsolved mystery, though legal sleuths have suggested various possibilities. The problem is designed to test your ability to spot the difficulty of applying age-reducing on these particular facts. A good answer will not flinch from tackling these issues. A vintage question in every way.

Suggested Answer

(a) At common law, a gift is void for perpetuity unless, at the time the gift is made, it is certain that, if it is going to vest at all, it will do so within the perpetuity period. The basic perpetuity period at common law is 21 years after the death of a 'life in being', i.e., the life of a person alive or *en ventre sa mère* (i.e., conceived but not yet born) at the date the gift is made. A gift is vested for the purposes of perpetuity only when the person entitled to it is in existence and ascertained, when the size of his interest is ascertained, and when any conditions attached to the gift are satisfied. A gift by will is made at the death of the testator.

The devise by Tess is therefore void at common law because, as Algy is alive at Tess's death, there is a possibility, looking at matters from the point of Tess's death, that the first child of Algy to satisfy the condition of attaining 25 will do so more than 21 years after the death of Algy.

However, in the case of a gift (such as that made by Tess) which is made after 1925 but before 16 July 1964, special provision is made by the Law of Property Act 1925, s. 163. This states that where a gift is void for remoteness because the age specified for vesting exceeds 21 years, the age of 21 years is to be substituted. This means that, from the death of Tess, the age of 21 was substituted as the age for vesting. Thus Belinda attained a vested interest on her 21st birthday. Therefore, unless Belinda disposed of Greenacre *inter vivos*, it will, on her death, have passed under her will or intestacy.

(b) In the case of a gift made after 15 July 1964, a gift which is void for perpetuity at common law may be saved by the Perpetuities and Accumulations Act 1964. As Tess dies a few months after this date, the Act applies to her devise. The Law of Property Act 1925, s. 163 does not apply, and is repealed in respect of post-1964 Act dispositions. Instead a gift (such as Tess's) which is void at common law is subject to the regime of 'wait and see' under s. 3, and to age-reducing under s. 4.

Section 3 is applied first. This provides that, where a disposition would apart from the provisions of that section and ss. 4 and 5, be void for remoteness of vesting, the disposition is treated, until such time as it becomes established that the vesting must occur (if at all) after the end of the perpetuity period, as if it were not subject to the rule against perpetuities. For the purposes of 'wait and see', the perpetuity period is determined by reference to the statutory lives specified in s. 3(5). Algy is a statutory life because he was an individual in being and ascertainable at the commencement of the perpetuity period (s. 3(4)(a)) who falls within s. 3(5)(c), i.e., he was a person, any of whose children, if subsequently born, would fall within para. (b)(ii). Thus, since Belinda is capable of attaining 25 within 21 years of the death of Algy, there would have been a period of waiting to see if Belinda did in fact attain 25. Since neither Charles nor Damian can attain 25 within 21 years of Algy's death, the death of Belinda at the age of 24 was the moment at which it became clear that 'wait and see' could not save the gift.

Section 4(1) is applied on the death of Belinda, because the devise of Greenacre would not have been void for perpetuity at common law had the specified age been 21 instead of 25 (s. 4(1)(b)). The reason is that, whenever Algy dies, his children must always attain 21 years by the end of a period of 21 years (plus a period *en ventre sa mère*) after his death. Section 4(1) provides, in effect, that the age should be reduced only so far as is necessary to save the gift from being void for remoteness. This is somewhat ambiguous: as discussed by Pritchard, [1969] *CLJ* 284, there are several possible interpretations.

First, s. 4(1) may mean that the age of 23 is substituted at this point, since this is sufficient to save the gift for Charles. 'Wait and see' is thereupon applied again under s. 3. Thus if Charles attains 23, Greenacre vests in him. Were Charles to die under the age of 23, it becomes clear upon his death that 'wait and see' cannot save the disposition. Section 4(1) is therefore applied once more to reduce the age to 22, which is sufficient to prevent the gift from being void for remoteness in relation to Damian. If Damian attained 22, his interest will have vested. In the event of Damian's death under the age of 22, Greenacre will have fallen into Tess's residuary estate, or (failing a residuary gift) will have passed to her next-of-kin. This construction, which leads to age-reduction by stages, might be supported by the words of s. 4(1)(a), which state only 'apart from this section', not 'apart from this section and section 3'.

Secondly, s. 4(1) may mean that the age substituted is such as is necessary to save it from remoteness in all eventualities: age-reduction is therefore once-for-all . On this basis, age-reduction is applied on one occasion only (upon the death of Belinda) to reduce the age to 22. If this is the case, then Charles acquired a vested interest upon his birthday in 1992. This construction derives support from the opening words of s. 4(1), which refer to 'a subsequent time' not to 'a subsequent time or times'.

A curious consequence of 'wait and see' in combination with either of these interpretations of age-reducing is that Belinda died without having attained a vested interest, even though she had attained an age higher than either Charles or Damian is required to reach under s. 4(1). A third possibility therefore arises, namely that when s. 4(1) reduces the age of vesting (whether to 23 or to 22), it does so retrospectively. This would mean that Belinda, who died after attaining either of those ages, is now to be treated as having died with a vested interest in Greenacre, which passes under her will or intestacy.

There are merits in each approach: but which construction is the correct one can be resolved only by the courts.

QUESTION 2

The following gifts were contained in the will of a testator who died last year:

(a) 'I devise Blueacre to my trustees to hold in trust for Louis for life, then to any widow of Louis for life, remainder to the children of Louis living at the death of the survivor of Louis and his widow.'

(b) 'I give Yellowacre and the accumulated income of Yellowacre to the first of my grandchildren to attain 21.'

At the time of the testator's death, Louis was a bachelor and without children.

Consider the validity of these gifts.

Commentary

The issues raised by the devise lettered **(a)** are not difficult for those who have previously worked through and understood one of the obscurer areas of perpetuity — the unborn widow trap. If ever there were an old chestnut in the law of perpetuities, this is it. Where students sometimes go wrong in this sort of question, however, is in assuming that a devise such as this contains only a single gift. This is not the case: there are separate limitations here, for Louis, for his widow, and for the children, and each of these limitations needs to be tested separately for compliance or contravention of the rule against remoteness of vesting.

The structure of the answers is:

(a)
    (i)   Validity at common law of limitations to Louis, his widow, and the children.
    (ii) Impact of 'wait and see' and s. 5 of the 1964 Act:
        saves gift if widow dies before end of perpetuity period;
        if widow then still alive, invoke s. 5.

(b)
    (i)   Validity of perpetuity period.
    (ii) Validity of expressed accumulation period:
        invalidity *pro tanto*;
        court's choice of lawful accumulation periods;
        application of income after the end of the selected accumulation period.

Suggested Answer

(a)   The limitations to Louis and to his widow are valid. The woman who may become Louis's widow will not be identifiable until Louis's death; but her interest will vest on his death. For this purpose, Louis is therefore a 'life in being'.

The limitation to the children is, however, void for perpetuity at common law. The reason is that at common law it must be certain at the time that a gift is made that, if it will vest at all, it will vest within the perpetuity period. At common law, this is the period of a life or lives in being plus a further period of 21 years, and including where necessary a period *en ventre sa mère*. At common law, any possibility, however remote, that the gift may vest too late, is sufficient to render it void for perpetuity.

In this problem, the gift to Louis's children is subject to a contingency: it will vest only if the children are living at the death of the survivor of Louis and his widow. Looking at matters from the time of the testator's death, it is possible that Louis may die leaving a widow who was not herself alive (or *en ventre sa mère*) at the testator's death, and who is not therefore a 'life in being' at common law. It is also possible that such a widow may survive Louis by more than 21 years; in which event the interests of the children must vest too late. Although such a possibility is somewhat remote, it is sufficient to render the gift void at common law (*Re Frost* (1889) 43 ChD 246). The last limitation falls into what is known as the unborn widow trap. At common law, therefore, the remainder would be held on a resulting trust for the testator's estate.

Since the testator died last year, however, the limitation in favour of the children is saved by the application of the Perpetuities and Accumulations Act 1964. 'Wait and see' under s. 3(1) applies where the disposition is void at common law. It does not therefore apply to the first two limitations in favour of Louis and his widow; but it does apply to the remainder. We wait and see if Louis dies leaving a widow who outlives him by more than 21 years. The period of 'wait and see' for this purpose is measured by the statutory lives specified in s. 3(5): Louis is a statutory life under s. 3(5)(c). However, even if Louis marries a woman who was born at the testator's death, she will not rank as a statutory life for 'wait and see' since to rank as such a life, the individual must be ascertainable at the commencement of the perpetuity period (s. 3(4)(a)) — which such a widow is not.

If the widow dies within the perpetuity period, the gift vests in those children of Louis then living. If, however, the widow is still alive at the end of that period (i.e., 21 years after Louis' death), s. 5 provides that the disposition is treated as if it had been limited by reference to the time immediately before the end of the perpetuity period. This means that the interests of the children vest immediately before the end of 21 years after Louis' death. Their interests will not vest in possession, of course, until the death of the widow. For the purposes of the rule against perpetuities, however, this is immaterial, since it is sufficient that the gift is vested in interest.

(b) The gift of Yellowacre is valid at common law since the testator's children are 'lives in being' at common law, and the gift is bound to vest within 21 years of their deaths. In other words, the first grandchild of the testator to attain 21 must do so within 21 years (plus if necessary a period *en ventre sa mère*) of the death of their parent.

If all the testator's children have died at the time of his death, the accumulation is valid, since an accumulation for 21 years from the date of the death of the testator is a permitted period of accumulation (Law of Property Act 1925, s. 164(1)(b)).

If, however, at least one child of the testator survives him, the position is different. The accumulation of income of Yellowacre does not exceed the perpetuity period, and it is not therefore void *in toto*. However, an accumulation starting at the testator's death does exceed the six periods of accumulation permitted by statute and specified in the Law of Property Act 1925, s. 164(1), and in the Perpetuities and Accumulations Act 1964, s. 13(1). The period specified in s. 164(1)(c) is exceeded since the expressed period of accumulation includes the minorities of children born after the testators' death (cf. *Re Watt's Will Trust* [1936] 2 All ER 1555). The accumulation is therefore void *pro tanto*. In such instance, an accumulation is permitted for a lawful period of accumulation which best conforms with the intention of the testator according to a proper construction of the will (*Re Ransome* [1957] Ch 348). Thus what is chosen is the period which is most appropriate, not necessarily the longest (see Maudsley, *The Modern Law of Perpetuities*, p. 208).

This being a testamentary disposition, the effective choice of accumulation period is either:

(a) 21 years from the death of the testator; or

(b) the minorities of any grandchildren of the testator who are living or *en ventre sa mère* at the death of the testator (Law of Property Act 1925, s. 164(1)(b) and (c)).

In the present case, the expressed accumulation until the *first* grandchild attains 21 might be difficult to construe as close to an intention to accumulate during the minorities of *any* grandchildren living at the testator's death (cf. *Re Ransome*). The court might therefore select an accumulation period of 21 years from the testator's death. If this were so, the accumulations made during that period would be held for the first grandchild to attain 21.

The issue which then arises is how to deal with any income arising after the end of the selected period of accumulation. The gift is a contingent specific devise, which therefore carries the intermediate income except so far as it is otherwise expressly disposed of (Law of Property Act 1925, s. 175(1)). The income arising from the end of the accumulation period is not otherwise expressly disposed of: therefore, every grandchild of the testator alive at that date is thereafter entitled to receive a proportionate share of the income arising from Yellowacre until the contingency is satisfied.

If any grandchild is under the age of 18 at the end of the accumulation period, their share of the intermediate income will be subject to an accumulation trust under the Law of Property Act 1925, s. 31. Statutory accumulation under this provision is in addition to any period of accumulation specified in the instrument (or, as in this case, selected by the court) (Law of Property Act 1925, s. 165). Thus a combination of this section and s. 31 of the Trustee Act 1925 might produce a period of accumulation far exceeding any of those specified in either the Law of Property Act 1925, s. 164(1), or the Perpetuities and Accumulations Act 1964, s. 13(1) (*Re Maber* [1928] Ch 88).

QUESTION 3

By her will, a testatrix who died in 1972 devised Orangeacre 'to such of my grandchildren as shall be admitted as a solicitor, but if none of my grandchildren shall be so admitted then to my cousin, Ruth'.

The testatrix had two children, Alan and Beth, both of whom were living at her death. Alan (a widower) had two children then alive: Clare (then aged 4) and Darren (then aged 2). Beth was unmarried at her mother's death. In 1991, Beth gave birth to a child, Ellen.

Consider the validity and effect of the gift in the light of each of the following *alternative* sets of circumstances:

(a)   In 1992, Clare was admitted as a solicitor. In 1994, Beth gave birth to a second child, Fiona.

(b)   Clare died in a road accident in 1992 before being admitted as a solicitor. Alan, Beth and Darren died in the same accident. Ellen is therefore the only surviving grandchild of the testatrix.

Commentary

This is yet another classic question on perpetuities, this time involving contingent class gifts, the class-closing rule, class-splitting, and expectant and dependent interests. Class-closing has nothing itself to do with perpetuities, but its effect (which ensures early vesting) can sometimes save a gift that would otherwise be void at common law.

Suggested Answer

(a)   The gift to the testatrix's grandchildren is a class gift, because the share to which each member becomes entitled depends upon the number of members who take. The gift is also contingent because it does not vest until the requirement of being admitted as a solicitor is fulfilled. At common law the gift to the testatrix's grandchildren is void for perpetuity. This is because, looking at matters from the moment of the testatrix's death, there is the possibility that more grandchildren will be born subsequently, who will not therefore rank as lives in being, and any of whom may be admitted more than 21 years after the death of any person now living. The interests of some members of the class might therefore vest outside the perpetuity period of a life or lives in being plus 21 years. The fact that the interests of some members of the class who are alive at the testatrix's death, namely Clare and Darren, must vest, if at all, within their own lives, does not save the gift; at common law a class gift cannot be good in part.

Although the testatrix's gift is void at common law, since it was made after 15 July 1964 it may be saved by the application of the principle of 'wait and see' under the Perpetuities and Accumulations Act 1964, s. 3(1). It is necessary to wait and see if any grandchildren of the testatrix are admitted as solicitors within 21 years of the dropping of the last statutory life under the Act (s. 3(4)). The statutory lives for this purpose are the lives of Clare and Darren (both within s. 3(5)(b)(i)), and Alan and Beth (both within s. 3(5)(c)).

Applying 'wait and see', Clare in 1992 satisfied the contingency attached to the gift. The size of her share was not then calculable, however. When she was admitted, Clare was one of three grandchildren; but the birth of a further grandchild (such as Fiona) who satisfies the contingency within the perpetuity period would diminish Clare's share, which would be highly inconvenient for her. This problem is avoided if the rule known as the rule in *Andrews* v *Partington* (1791) 3 Bro CC 401 applies. This states that, where there is a class gift, the class closes as soon as the first member of the class attains a vested interest and is entitled to demand his share. If the rule were to apply here, the class would close when Clare is admitted as a solicitor. This would mean that future born grandchildren (such as Fiona) would be excluded from the class, and therefore from the gift.

The application of the rule would make it possible to calculate the minimum size of Clare's share, i.e., one-third. Its maximum size would still remain uncertain until the other two members of the class (Darren and Ellen) are either admitted or die, or, in the case of Ellen, until it is clear that her interest, if it is to vest at all, must vest outside the perpetuity period (s. 3(1)). Thus if, for instance, Darren were to die without being admitted as a solicitor, Clare's vested share would increase from one-third to one-half. If Ellen were similarly to die during the perpetuity period without being admitted, Clare's vested interest would increase to the whole of Orangeacre. Clare's share, upon her being admitted as a solicitor in 1992, would thus be vested subject to open, i.e., vested as to one-third, with the possibility that it might become vested in respect of a further proportion at some time in the future.

Although convenient for those within the class, the class-closing rule operates harshly against those, like Fiona, whom it excludes. For this reason, the courts are, in modern times, more willing to oust the application of the rule (which is merely one of construction) by finding that the testator had a contrary intention (*Re Henderson's Trusts* [1969] 1 WLR 651). This is particularly the case in circumstances where (as in the problem) there is a likelihood of future members of the class being born. It is, therefore, necessary to construe the testatrix's gift in the context of the will as a whole to ascertain if there is a contrary intention.

If the rule is held not to apply, the class remains open, and it is necessary to continue to 'wait and see' until the end of the statutory perpetuity period if the interests of Fiona and any other future born grandchildren of the testatrix vest in time. If, at the end of such perpetuity period, Fiona has not been admitted as a solicitor, she is excluded from the class (s. 4(4)). Any other future-born grandchildren who have not been admitted by that date are similarly excluded.

Under the 1964 Act, therefore, a class gift, can (in contrast to the rule at common law) be good in part.

(b)   In these circumstances, it is necessary to 'wait and see' under s. 3(1) if Ellen, who is now the only person who can satisfy the contingency, attains a vested interest within the perpetuity period under the 1964 Act. Since the accident caused the dropping of all the statutory lives, this means a further period of 21 years of 'wait and see'. Ellen will be only 22 at the end of the perpetuity period and is therefore very unlikely to be admitted as a solicitor in time. 'Wait and see' applies however since it is not yet established that the vesting 'must' occur, if at all, until too remote a time: s. 3(1).

If Ellen is not admitted in time, the class gift becomes void for perpetuity. It is then necessary to consider the validity of the second limitation, which is also contingent, in favour of Ruth. This gift is also void for perpetuity at common law because, at the time of the testatrix's death, there is a possibility that the class of grandchildren could include future born grandchildren who may be admitted as solicitors more than 21 years after the death of Ruth. There is therefore the possibility that Ruth's interest may vest too late (*Proctor* v *Bishop of Bath and Wells* (1794) 2 Hy Bl 358).

Since the gift to Ruth is void at common law, it is necessary first to 'wait and see' if Ruth's interest does in fact vest in time. For this purpose, the relevant statutory lives are Ruth herself (s. 3(5)(b)(ii)), her parents and grandparents (s. 3(5)(c)). If Ellen dies within this period without having been admitted, the gift to Ruth vests either in her or (if she is dead) in her estate. The latter outcome is possible because the contingency attached to the gift is not personal to Ruth. Her interest is therefore transmissible on her death, and will vest in her estate on the contingency being satisfied (Ryder, *Hawkins and Ryder on the Construction of Wills*, 3rd edn, 1965). In such circumstances, Orangeacre would pass under Ruth's will or intestacy.

What, however, is to happen if, at the end of the perpetuity period relevant to the limitation for Ruth, Ellen, whilst not having been admitted, is nevertheless still alive? Had the gift to Ruth been expressed merely to be 'subject to' the disposition to the grandchildren, s. 6 of the 1964 Act would have applied, and Ruth's interest would have been accelerated, i.e., it would have vested in her estate at the end of the perpetuity period because the prior gift is void for remoteness. As it is worded in the problem, however, the gift to Ruth cannot be saved by s. 6. That section says that the vesting of an interest shall not be prevented from being accelerated on the failure of a prior interest 'by reason only' that the failure arises because of remoteness. Since, however, the gift to Ruth is expressed to be contingent upon none of the testatrix's grandchildren being admitted, this contingency is not met where Ellen could be admitted outside the perpetuity period. Acceleration is not, therefore, possible. In these circumstances, the gift to Ruth also becomes void for remoteness, and Orangeacre reverts to the testatrix's estate.

Index